Religious Dialectics
of Pain and Imagination

ॐ

SUNY Series in Rhetoric and Theology

Stephen H. Webb, Editor

Religious Dialectics of Pain and Imagination

❦

Bradford T. Stull

State University of New York Press

Grateful acknowledgment is made to the following publisher for permission to quote
from this work:
Thomas Merton, *The Geography of Lograire*. Copyright © 1968,
1969 by the Trustees of the Merton Legacy Trust.
Reprinted by permission of New Directions Publishing Corporation.

Published by
State University of New York Press, Albany

© 1994 State University of New York

For information, address State University of New York Press,
State University Plaza, Albany, N.Y. 12246

Production by M. R. Mulholland
Marketing by Theresa A. Swierzowski

Library of Congress Cataloging-in-Publication Data
Stull, Bradford T., 1961–
    Religious dialectics of pain and imagination / Bradford T. Stull.
        p. cm. — (SUNY series in rhetoric and theology)
    Includes bibliographical references and index.
    ISBN 0-7914-2081-7 (alk. paper). — ISBN 0-7914-2082-5 (pbk. :
    alk. paper)
    1. Pain—Religious aspects—Christianity. 2. Imagination-
-Religious aspects—Christianity. 3. Rhetoric. 4. Liberation
theology. 5. Postmodernism. 6. Burke, Kenneth, 1897–1993.
7. Merton, Thomas, 1915–1968. 8. Freire, Paulo, 1921– .
9. Romero, Oscar A. (Oscar Arnulfo), 1917–1980. I. Title.
II. Series.
BT732.7.S76   1994
233—dc20   93-39435
                                                   CIP

10 9 8 7 6 5 4 3 2 1

⌘

*To Maggie
For the fragrance
of what
has been, will be*

⌘

Contents

Acknowledgments

Writing *Religious Dialectics of Pain and Imagination* has only reinforced my belief that we do, as Dr. King declared, live in a "network of mutuality" (King 290). I hope that this book both returns and extends the gifts that I have received from many compassionate people.

This book began as a doctoral thesis within the English Department at the University of Illinois at Chicago. I am grateful for William A. Covino's dedication to wondering and wandering rhetoric, Donald G. Marshall's commitment to tight writing and ethical vision, Michael Anania's extraordinary knowledge of modern and contemporary poetry, Marc Zimmerman's passion for Latin America, and Anne E. Carr's dedication to the texts of Thomas Merton and her willingness to travel beyond the bounds of her own university in order to help a former student.

Many others also helped this book come to be, more than I explicitly mention here. I thank my parents, Thomas A. and Marilyn J. Stull, for their utopic belief that education is a way to transform self and society; Susan M. Simonaitis, Susan M. St. Ville, and Rebekah Miles for the intense conversation of young scholars in process and on trial; Stephen H. Webb for an old friendship and delight in this book even as it was only partially complete; and C. W. Maggie Kim for the detailed reading, pointed comments, electric dialogue, and unswerving commitment that only a spouse who is an intellectual compatriot can provide.

1

The Way to Proceed

High mountains, deep waters, and a dense jungle of high grass—

—Kusan Sunim, *The Way of Korean Zen*

Pain. This word powerfully names a specific something, a thing most humans (and all other creatures for that matter) would rather avoid. The sight and/or sound of the word itself often evokes a visceral response that appears to need no further explanation. Yet, finally, pain names nothing in particular. It is far too generic to have any real meaning; it is far too abstract to speak to the specificity of the often intense experience it attempts to represent.

What, after all, does it mean to say something like "that wound must be painful"? One can, as an attempted answer, rearrange the words: "pain fills the wound." But what, precisely, is that which fills the wound? Is it the resonance of the sounded letters? Is it the typography of the read word? If it is these graphic and phonic traces only, how can it fill the wound that weeps on the soldier's leg? Obviously, it can't. Or, it can only if one works wholly in the dimension of language and brackets the somatic world. Thus the traces of the "pain" syntactically fill the traces of the "wound." But, if one wants to link the linguistic and somatic worlds, if one wants to speak from and about the weeping wound, if one wants "pain" to serve semantically as well as syntactically, what can one do?

One possible tact is to qualify "pain" syntactically so that it has semantic specificity: "the soldier's searing cut moans; it moans minutely." Still, despite the use of adjectives, nouns, pronouns, verbs, adverbs, and other syntactical devices, can this "pain" now qualified ever be more than words to another? Can one ever feel the profound suffering of another's shrapnel-invaded foot, his electrocuted testicles, her vagina torn open by gang rapists, his kneecap broken by a hammer blow?

Paradoxically, pain both defies linguistic representation and generates it. Pain defies it because language can never fully speak/write what the psychosomatic entities that we call human beings experience when they experience what we call pain. Too, as Elaine Scarry has masterfully argued, pain does not simply defy linguistic representation; it destroys language itself. At its most extreme, pain reduces the pained to preverbal moans and grunts. It reduces the unpained other, who views the one in pain, to visceral horror or, even worse, incomprehension or disbelief.[1]

Yet pain also generates language. Again, as Scarry maintains, pain is a site of "invention" (22) and thus leads to the production of "things" that attempt to represent the pain and forestall its future occurrence. These things can be anything. Winter coats, for instance, are products of a painful impulse: they are constructed, finally, to protect wearers from the searing effects of cold. So too the book of Job was, in part, generated by pain. It is structured by Job's afflictions and the narrative attempts to write the origins and ramifications of suffering.

As a site of destruction and invention, pain is the province of many disciplines. Garment makers, Biblical writers, doctors, theologians, poets, politicians, and others often find themselves challenged and guided by the power of pain.[2] Like any experience, however, pain is always open to interpretation. The perverse, for instance, are guided and challenged by pain to inflict pain in order to gain power and pleasure.[3] Soldiers may fulfill their duty not out of a sense of patriotism but out of a desire to make people suffer: they bayonet not for democracy but for the charge of power and pleasure they receive when people bleed at their hands. So too a parent may spank his child not out of love for the child and with the hope that spanking will stop the child from touching, say, a hot stove, but because he enjoys inflicting pain upon a helpless human and the delightful power that accompanies this. As David Morris argues, sex, pain, and pleasure are indelibly linked. The Marquis de Sade represents the human impulse to find pleasure in painful sexual activity (224–43).

Fortunately, many find themselves at pain's inventive site and respond compassionately: they are guided and challenged by pain to prevent and alleviate suffering. Thus, in response to her encounter with

Central American political refugees in Chicago, a young pastor may dedicate herself to work in El Salvador in order to help Salvadorans recover from a devastating civil war. So too a young college student, searching for a career, may decide to become a pediatrician after having worked on a pediatric cancer unit. Certainly, pain guides and challenges people to alleviate pain in less all-encompassing ways. A middle-aged, middle-class suburban woman may see pictures of starving Somalian children on television and decide to contribute monthly to a relief organization working in Somalia.

All of these people, from the soldier to the suburban woman, produce 'things' in response to the inventive impulse provided by pain: the soldier, a bayonet thrust; the parent, a spank; the pastor, administrative and counseling work; the doctor, medical treatment; the woman, money and thus food, clothing, medicine and other goods. Scarry argues well that most, if not all, cultural artifacts find at least part of their origins at the inventive site of pain.

This is as true for rhetoric as it is for any other human activity. Scarry's book alludes to rhetoric, but only alludes to it, thus missing what is perhaps at the heart of her work: the relationship between pain and rhetoric. Her use of the word *invention*, one of the classic categories of rhetorical theory, coupled with her attention to language (such as the documents of Amnesty International), opens up an area of exploration that she herself ignores: the dynamics that exist between pain and rhetoric.

Rhetoric can respond to pain negatively, neutrally, or positively. By negatively I mean destructively. Rhetoric can arise from pain and attempt to inflict more pain. Certainly, rhetoric has been, and is, used in this way, as I will discuss more fully in ensuing chapters. Rhetoric can also respond neutrally. That is, it can recognize pain as a site of invention but not attend to it. This option, given the omnipresence of pain in the world, is simply irresponsible. If rhetoric ignores pain, it will lose whatever cultural value it may still have. Rhetoric can also respond to pain positively, that is, constructively. Rhetoric can accept pain's reality, pain's destructive and inventive power, and begin to discern how it should respond to pain in order to help prevent and alleviate suffering.[4]

One path for such a task lies in this direction: rhetoric can be reconceived as what I call a "religious' dialectic and it can make paramount the dialectic that exists, as Scarry argues, between pain and imagination. Rhetoric must explicitly highlight, explore, and respond to pain because it must boldly confront the bruises, the burns, the cuts, the breaks, the physical damage that people inflict upon one another in an attempt to destroy both soma and psyche. Rhetoric must fully and explicitly embrace imagination because imagination allows rhetoricians to speak of pain and the possibilities for a less painful world.

In order to begin to open this path, this book will attend, in particular, to the dialectic of pain and imagination as it appears in the efforts of certain representatives of postmodern and liberation rhetorics: Kenneth Burke and Thomas Merton, Paulo Freire and Archbishop Oscar Romero. The nexus of postmodern and liberation rhetorics is an important trailhead, perhaps the most important in the contemporary world. Read badly, it leads only to a debilitating morass of sloganeering. Read well, it can serve the larger purpose of a rhetoric of pain and imagination. It can provide the inventive force for the construction of a new dialectic aimed toward the prevention and alleviation of the 'sociopolitical' pain that humans heap upon each other with stunning frequency and ferocity.[5] As I will argue later in this chapter, this dialectic is finally religious because it is guided by visions of the excessive, of what is, finally, the religious.

Rhetoricians of all types—students, critics, teachers, practitioners, and theorists[6]—are diligently working to reinvent rhetoric. Once central to education and civic life, rhetoric in education was reduced to stylistic concerns and relegated to composition and speech classrooms. In civic life it was labeled a tool of liars. These pages, while affirming the importance of speech and composition classrooms, and basic language education in general, have the grandest view in mind: rhetoric as crucial to the functioning of the painful body politic, in all of its manifestations, from the rarefied circles of high academic theory to the cultural critics attempting to speak to the world, from practitioners laboring with rhetoric to teachers who see themselves as rhetoricians regardless of their discipline, teachers reinventing, strengthening, and propagating a rhetoric invented at sites of pain and suffering.

As an approach to this end, the remainder of this chapter tentatively defines the extremely ambiguous and troubled, yet key, concepts in play: rhetoric, postmodern, liberation, pain, imagination, religious. I heed well Clifford Geertz's reminder that "definitions establish nothing." I grant that the trail I am building is tentative. Yet Geertz also reminds one that if definitions "are carefully enough constructed, [they] provide a useful orientation, or reorientation, of thought, such that an extended unpacking of them can be an effective way of developing and controlling a novel line of inquiry" (*Interpretation* 90).

Rhetoric

Anyone familiar with the history of the word *rhetoric* knows that its meanings are many. Rhetoric was in various ways considered to be a 'good' discipline from the late Classical period through the Renaissance, part of essential education, a praxis to be mastered by any who would be educated (Valesio 5; Perelman 1–8). Beginning with Ramus' attacks, rhetoric has suffered since early modernity: it is no longer understood to be essential to literate education. By all but a few academics, it is at best thought to be concerned with ornamentation; at worst it is associated with glib, deceitful talk. It is 'mere' rhetoric. However, among certain academic fields, such as English, anthropology, theology, and the history of science, rhetoric has been undergoing a period of 'reevaluation' with the likes of Peirce, Richards, Perelman, Tyteca, and Burke attempting to rewrite its meaning (Valesio 5, 260).

While helpful and hopeful, this twentieth-century rewriting of rhetoric is problematic. The plethora of theories has led to an almost chaotic abundance of definitions. For every two theorists, there are three meanings of this ancient word. As I will discuss below, relative to the postmodern recognition of the plurality of language, this is not a wholly undesirable state: language is indeed ambiguous; words are fillable forms. Yet one must finally claim a meaning, however tenuous, in order to proceed. It is most helpful, as Paolo Valesio argues, to return to Aristotle, but with a twist: rhetoric is not simply a branch of dialectic, as Aristotle argues; it *is* dialectic.[7]

In a potentially meaningless fashion, Valesio states boldly that all language, organized into discourse, is rhetoric (7). Lest this seem too vague, dangerously close to the chaos of complete ambiguity, he later specifies that "rhetoric is dialectic" (66). For Valesio, and for me as well, discourse is functionally organized primarily by dialectic (115), by "an alternation or antithesis" of "inverse . . . contrary . . . contradictory" statements, or "intellectual or psychological movements" (108).[8] Insofar as rhetoric is discourse, discourse is dialectic. Discourse, as dialectic, as rhetoric, is marked by internal and external struggle. Internally, that is, internal to the linguistic formation of discourse, rhetoric "is that of managing a continuous battle among its components" (23). Externally, that is, in the relationship between the discourse and the surrounding semiotic frame, dialectic manages "a struggle among ghosts: the images of actions, things, and events" (24). For my purposes, the components and ghosts are pain and imagination as they are discerned and constructed as rhetoric by these representatives of postmodern and liberation rhetoric, respectively: Burke and Merton, Freire and Romero.

Dialectic is not to be understood always as leading to synthesis because a wish for synthesis often leads to forced, invalid melding and, finally, ideology (117). Ideology is *"decayed rhetoric—rhetoric that is no longer the detailed expression of strategies at work in specific discourses"* (66). In other words, ideology is anti-dialectic: it is the prevention of the dialectical movement (98). As such, ideology forbids "access to politics" because rhetoric is *"the political dimension that every discourse possesses"* (99). As dialectic, as rhetoric, politics is the continual "alternation or antithesis" of opposites in discourse. Ideology, then, is a threat to human community because it is a threat to the discourse that makes a community human. It stops discourse as it prevents dialectic. By contrast, rhetoric supports the community because it is human discourse itself. It is the alternation and antithesis of opposites that comprise human language and being. Ideology threatens the "fluidity" of rhetoric; rhetoric as dialectic "is perhaps the most powerful weapon we can use against the continuous, subtle, pervasive assaults of ideology" (66). It is the copenetration of opposites with which this study is concerned: liberation and postmodern, pain and imagination.

To theorize rhetoric as dialectic is to place oneself, as a rhetorician, squarely into politics. As Valesio argues, rhetoric as dialectic is politics (44, 99). This is a critically important step for a rhetorical theory that would both be practiced outside the classroom and transform that classroom. To understand rhetoric as politics is to place rhetoric back into public life, the location of potential and actual pain. Rhetoricians can understand themselves, and teach others to understand themselves, as important members of the body politic. Perhaps, as well, budding public figures (which would ideally include all citizens) should again explicitly study the theory and practice of rhetoric. Also, to understand rhetoric as dialectic as politics is to revolutionize the teaching of writing and speech: it demands a classroom where teachers and students must engage themselves and each other in a rigorous exchange and exploration of competing ideas. Of course, this pedagogical practice need not limit itself to writing and speech classes. Any teachers who understand rhetoric to be fundamental to their work may benefit.[9]

In defining rhetoric as dialectic as politics, I consciously link myself to the efforts of Herbert Marcuse and the Frankfort School. About dialectic Marcuse writes this: "Interpretation of that-which-is in terms of that-which-is-not . . . has been the concern of philosophy wherever philosophy was more than a matter of ideological justification or mental exercise" (447). Rhetoric, as dialectic, is neither the servant of ideology nor a cerebral gymnast. It is, rather, both a historical actor and that which works with those forces that oppose reification of any form of human being. As Marcuse argues, dialectic deals with "*historical* factors and forces" and proposes "ultimately a *political* negation" (449).

This point is critically important for all types of rhetoricians: dialectic deals with *historical* factors. Rhetoric is neither theorized nor practiced well if it is not practiced with conscious attention to history. The rhetorician who practices cultural criticism, for instance, stands to benefit from this reminder. If one studies the rhetoric of a popular film like *Rambo*, it is not enough to study the internal dialectics, that is, the dialectics at play within the text of the film itself. The rhetorician must also look beyond the bounds of the screen in order to study the dialectics between the film as film and the societies out of which it emerged (say America during the Vietnam War era and America during the filming of the movie) and the societies into which it is has been received (the various cultures that comprise the United States and other countries). This historical task, certainly, is a return to the demands of classic rhetoric. The rhetorician must study both the invention and the audience.

The import of Marcuse's insight concerning history is twofold. First, it highlights the political facet of the dialectic of pain and imagination with which Burke, Merton, Freire, and Romero deal. By placing this dialectic at the center of their rhetorics, these four challenge any linguistic/social system that would attempt to reify any sociopolitical order based on a single understanding of pain and imagination. Burke, for instance, castigates any Marxism that would uphold a single utopia as globally valid. The second import of Marcuse's insight is this: postmodern and liberation rhetoricians, even as they share the dialectic of pain and imagination, challenge each other as dialectical partners. Necessarily their systems are involved in the oppositional movement that is rhetoric. As such, neither is wholly adequate, neither can be seen as the ultimate rhetoric for the twenty-first century. Rather, their tension provides a site of departure: in their dialectic one can begin the invention of a painful, imaginative rhetoric.

Postmoderns versus Liberationists

One could justifiably argue that postmoderns and liberationists can only shout at one another. Both attend to the dialectic of pain and imagination, but they do so in such ways that any conversation between the two may appear to devolve into hopeless opposition. Postmodern work, or at least the best variants of it, attempts to alleviate oppressive pain and to construct a less painful world by speaking pain and imagination within a worldview that conceives of language as plural, history as ambiguous. In fact, postmoderns hold that much, if not all, oppressive pain is the result of worldviews that don't recognize the plurality of language and the ambiguity of history. Liberationist thought also attempts to alleviate oppressive pain and to construct a less painful world by speaking pain and imagination. It does so, however, with reference either to nonplural language and/or unambiguous history. Liberation thinkers would be befuddled, if not angered, by the postmodern reticence to commit to a specific language, a particular history. The postmodern tendency is to claim that all histories and languages are relatively equal. Liberationist thinking holds that, finally, the language and history of a particular group are superior for both interpretation and political programs. Thus the conflict between postmodern thought and liberation thought is perhaps set, precluding fruitful conversation. Yet, if read well, it is precisely this antithesis that can help invent a new rhetoric.

The meaning of 'postmodern' is as ambiguous and troubled as is that of 'rhetoric.' David Tracy, a Roman Catholic theologian, has thus far provided the most succinct and encompassing definition. Typical of the Western academy, 'secular' theorists have largely ignored Tracy. One imagines that his status as a priest is not considered kindly by secular academics still afraid of the religious. Nonetheless, Tracy's understanding of the postmodern worldview is invaluable. Simply put, to be postmodern is to take seriously both the plurality of language and the ambiguity of history. Like any definition, this belies plurality: it attempts to anchor firmly a word that floats. Definitions of postmodern are rightly many and varied; yet Tracy's both encompasses and helpfully delineates what is implied in the definitions provided by others.[10]

Against positivism, which holds that language can transparently "articulate and communicate scientific results as facts rather than interpretations" (Tracy 49), and romanticism, which maintains that language can transparently "express or represent some deep, nonlinguistic truth inside the self" (49), I, with Tracy, maintain that language is doubly plural. First, there is an "ineradicable plurality of languages and forms of life"; language communities are many and varied (51). Second, there is "plurality within language as an object of differential relations" (60). That is to say, the relationship between the signifier (language) and the signified (the extralinguistic) is one of convention and guided by a rhetoric of tropes, such as metaphor and analogy (58–59).

This delineation of the plurality of language as a key component of postmodern praxis is important for a number of reasons. Among these, Tracy seems to focus primarily upon what one might call its inescapability (one must attend to the plurality of language because language *is* plural). However, this delineation is especially important for rhetoric for another reason. As Tracy himself suggests (49), modernity has been dominated by a positivist understanding of language that has been the cause of cultural impression, if not oppression.[11]

This is a particularly important point for rhetoricians who are concerned about pedagogy. Speaking, reading, and writing, of whatever forms, always imply worldviews and impose worldviews on students.[12] Education and literacy theorist David Olson details this phenomenon in his work on the emergence of the positivist understandings of language. Olson argues that as western European culture shifted from a

predominantly oral to a predominantly literate mode of linguistic inter-
action (evidenced, by the way, in Plato's *Phaedrus*), there was "a transition from utterance to text both culturally and developmentally and . .
. this transition can be described as one of increasing explicitness, with
language increasingly able to stand as an unambiguous or autonomous
representation of meaning" (258). Heralded by John Locke and the
Royal Society of London, this "Essayist Technique" (Olson 268–270)
gave rise to the possibility of "objective" knowledge, Olson argues:
essayist language stands on its own; it is an autonomous, clear marker of
the writer's meaning. To make this specific, generations of students in
America have been taught not to use the first person, I, in their writing.
The rhetorical position of such a stance is clear: the one who speaks is
not a historical person imbedded in her own text but a voice above the
flux of human affairs.

At the very least, this understanding of language is impressed upon
students in the course of schooling. In many cases, it may be a positive
impression. However, as postmodern ethnographers Ron and Suzanne
Scollon argue, such an understanding of language can also oppress. They
duly note Olson's work (43), but claim further that it is this essayist
understanding of literacy that leads to cross-cultural conflict and oppression.[13] Working among the Athabaskan peoples in Alaska, Scollon and
Scollon have come to realize that Euro-Americans (and this includes
Canadian and U.S. citizens) have "taken a particular model of prose style
as the central, organizing model of our view of language" (41), that this
to a large extent defines "modern" consciousness, and that this prose
model is that of the essayist tradition (49–51). As a result, Scollon and
Scollon have discovered ethnographically what Tracy has discovered
through the reading of philosophy: language is doubly plural.[14]

As Euro-Americans have come into contact with the Athabaskan
peoples, and with more contact inevitably to come with the expiration
of treaties that protect Athabaskan land from Euro-American develop-
ers (6), essayist literacy/modern consciousness has caused at least two
problems for Athabaskans, according to Scollon and Scollon. First,
Athabaskan children have difficulty in the Euro-American school system because their own consciousness has not been formed by the essayist
tradition. However, teachers expect them to perform as moderns, expect
them to ignore what Scollon and Scollon have identified as their own

"bush consciousness" (100). As a result, Scollon and Scollon have found that these teachers are biased against students whose "reality set" (41) is bush consciousness (5, 17). Second, Scollon and Scollon argue that the difference between Euro-American essayist literacy/modern consciousness and Athabaskan bush consciousness has led to an underservicing of the Athabaskan people by the Euro-American government (6). Euro-Americans tend to dominate and control communicative situations between Athabaskans and themselves, due to the differing linguistic styles that are formed by their respective reality sets (22). Euro-Americans furthermore expect Athabaskans likewise to attempt to dominate. Hence, when Athabaskans don't attempt such discourse strategies, Euro-Americans treat the Athabaskans unfavorably in such encounters as job interviews (18–19). Furthermore, Scollon and Scollon well demonstrate the social ramifications when a dominant group of people doesn't account for the plurality of languages and expects others to speak its language, which is, of course, the "natural one."

As one is led to understand that one lives among plural languages, one is also led to understand that these languages are both the products and producers of history. As Tracy writes: "to acquire a native language is to acquire the means to articulate thought and feeling in a manner native to a particular history" (66), and to be in a particular history "is to be born, live, and die bounded by a particular sex, race, class and education" (66). I would amend Tracy's point. "Bounded" is too restrictive. Consider the metaphor 'founded' instead. It indicates that one belongs in a certain place, that one does not, cannot, float endlessly among the peoples of the world. But founded also allows for movement beyond one's location. Such movement is not only necessary but inevitable. Also, to Tracy's list of particularities I would add religion, writing systems, and a host of other foundations that work to construct human beings. Still, Tracy's point is useful. Humans don't simply learn language as if it were separate from a historical location. Languages are historically particular: English, French, Christian, Muslim, Marxist, capitalist, southern, northern, urban, rural, and the like. Given the plurality of languages, the postmodern also realizes that no history is paramount. Upper-class, white, U.S. males, for instance, must realize that they live within a history that differs from that of Latinas and vice versa. Each group has a set of experiences and traditions that the other does not share and that are not necessarily inferior or superior, relative to the other.

The ambiguity of history, furthermore, adds a much more ominous dimension. "To be an American, for example, is to live with pride by participating in a noble experiment of freedom and plurality" (68). Yet to be an "American" is to be a member of a historical community that has nearly destroyed the indigenous population of the United States and enslaved, within our country, parts of the primal population of another continent (68). At once we celebrate democracy and realize that, historically, we have violated the democracy we cherish. We live "a montage of classics and newspeak, of startling beauty and revolting cruelty, of partial emancipation and ever-subtler forms of entrapment" (70).

However, the postmodern recognition of the violation of democracy need not lead to debilitating guilt. Out of the ambiguity, the violent interruptions that shatter our sense of a pure and pristine history, postmoderns can claim responsibility. Tracy holds that "responsible here means capable of discarding any scenarios of innocent triumph written, as always, by the victors; capable of not forgetting the subversive memories of individuals and whole peoples whose names we do not even know" (69). In rooting the plurality of language in an ambiguous history, postmoderns announce themselves as embodied creatures who must act to live. A postmodern rhetorician, thus, will face suffering and speak out of its inventive site, rather than retreat to a safer, less ambiguous space. This announcement is an attempt to answer a question common to many postmodern theories: How can a postmodern, who has given up claims to the transparency of language, and the surety of history, act responsibly in the world?

Certainly, as Edith Wyschogrod attests, the postmodern claim to historical responsibility is not commonly held to be part of postmodernism by its critics or even some of its adherents. Postmodernism is generally understood to be a "system" that defends nihilism (xiii) and as a result is thought to look toward a world that must "go under in an orgy of conflicting and self-destructive struggles for power" (xxi). Wyschogrod, with candor, admits that this is one possibility of a way of thinking that has given up all claims to sure moorings. Yet she also urges her readers to consider another possibility: a postmodern ethic of alterity (xxi). Wyschogrod's project is not far from my own. Like her, and Tracy, I seek to demonstrate that historical responsibility is a postmodern potential. Unlike her fascinating and fruitful turn to hagiography, I seek within rhetoric a place from which postmodern rhetoricians can, in Wyschogrod's terms, find a "sensible alternative to apocalypse" (xxi).

Liberation rhetoric, however, proclaims that this would be a very difficult, if not impossible, task for the postmodern. Finally, liberation rhetoricians claim, one concerned to act responsibly must side with a particular language and a specific history, because both form the matrix in which those most in need of liberation live. To forfeit language and history to plurality and ambiguity is to forfeit those most in pain. From the liberation rhetoric perspective, for instance, Tracy's claim concerning the responsibility one finds in one's history is still marked by a debilitating ambiguity. He calls upon postmoderns to face the interruptions in history, to discard any triumphalism, to remember "peoples whose names we do not even know." In so doing, Tracy says, postmoderns make a beginning. But even this beginning is not marked by a call to liberate oppressed people. It is not marked by the powerfully resonating line spoken by Moses, which Martin Luther King, Jr. so well used: "Set my people free!" It is marked, instead, by a call to listen to the oppressed's voices. Postmoderns belong to a group of celebrated oppressors but they also want to belong to the oppressed group(s). Yet this is impossible because they don't even know these groups' names; they are not the postmoderns' neighbors, their friends, their family.

Postmoderns, from the liberationist perspective, are privileged theorists who can criticize, teach, and learn in the comfort of a protected zone. Typical postmodern theorists in America, for example, teach at a university, enjoy extended periods when they don't have to teach or hold office hours, and have the leisure to dabble in the fluctuations of language and history. In contrast, liberation rhetoricians are always concerned about practice in the 'streets.' How, they ask, can theory, pedagogy, and criticism serve practice, a practice that engages in the struggles of oppressed, pained people?

Unlike Tracy, liberation rhetoricians know their histories, their languages, and make calls for liberation based on this knowledge. Philosopher of education and literacy theorist Henry Giroux is one such liberation rhetorician. Arguing for an emancipatory literacy that helps readers comprehend how critical individual perceptions are marginalized (*Schooling* 152), Giroux looks to the "Dangerous Memory" of oppressed and suffering peoples both living and dead. One of Giroux's central themes is that "America is becoming a land without memory" and that the dominant ideology operates so as to extinguish discordant and suffering voices that would necessarily disrupt the status quo (80). In order to counter this selective amnesia, Giroux suggests that radical educators should turn to liberation theology, which would have educators reclaim the dangerous memory of the oppressed and thereby rupture the monological voice that attempts to silence the memory (91). He argues that once educators recall the narrative memories of suffering people, truth will come from struggles that cannot be abstracted from networks of power and control.

Giroux borrows heavily from the work of Rebecca Chopp, especially *The Praxis of Suffering*, which details the relationships between political and liberation theologies.[15] Chopp argues that liberation theology turns to the history of the oppression of the poor in order to "reveal a new identity and vision of the human subject in history" (8–9). In so doing liberation theology declares a preferential option for the poor (22) and reads history through the eyes of those who suffer in it. Political theology, through the voice of the European academic bourgeoisie, makes a similar claim (42), and together, Chopp argues, liberation and political theologies point to the suffering human as the subject who ruptures modernity's "plastic mask," its "freeway of progress" (2).

As Chopp notes, liberation theology locates God, Christ, and the Church in the history of those who suffer (3). So too, Chopp claims, political theology continues the anthropocentric turn of modernity (43). Despite their challenge to the claims of modernity, liberation and political theologies, as examples of liberation rhetorics, are not postmodern: language is not completely plural, history not completely ambiguous. The poor are privileged: their voice and history judge. God and God's Word are not forever slipping and sliding in plurality and ambiguity; they are located, beyond the claims of postmodernity, in the lives of the oppressed.

At least one postmodern rhetoric theorist, Jean-François Lyotard, is aware of the differences between postmodern sensibility and liberation sensibility. As a postmodern, Lyotard in *The Differend* identifies and criticizes both Marxist and nationalist rhetorics for making group claims that are finally oppressive. Marx's mistake, Lyotard argues, is that he interpreted the enthusiasm shared by the Paris Commune and other workers as enthusiasm for an unambiguous, homogeneous historical and cross-linguistic group (sections 237–39). The problem is that the Communist Party had to supply proof that such a proletariat existed, but it couldn't do so. Hence, the Party mistook as a singular proletariat what are the real, and plural, working classes. In so doing, the Party made itself into the arbiter of truth; it claimed the power to define the 'worker.' Similarly, Lyotard notes, nationalism, which makes claims to liberation based on nationalist grouping (a homogeneous historic and linguistic entity), is problematic because it tends toward hegemony (section 261) and, as a narrative, conceals the heterogeneity that is part of any linguistic/historical group (section 219).

While I generally agree with Lyotard, I do not dismiss liberation rhetorics. Given my station in life, it is easy to be postmodern. Also, my acceptance of the plurality of language and the ambiguity of history is perhaps only therapeutic: as Tracy suggests, I can call to consciousness the demons of the history my fathers made and claim responsibility for them. Lyotard himself recognizes the potential problem with his own postmodernism when, at the end of *The Differend*, he tells his readers that the heterogeneous "doesn't make a story, does it?—Indeed it's not a sign. But it is to be judged, all the way to its incomprehensibility. You can't make a political 'program' with it, but you can bear witness to it." (No. 1). I applaud Lyotard's courage to want to speak the differend, the heterogeneity, the space between phrases, which calls into question any homogeneous claims about language and/or history. Like a prophet, he bears witness to the silence between languages and histories. Yet in some situations, political programs are necessary, life-saving; hence a liberation rhetoric based on and propagating homogeneous claims, one that founds political programs, is perhaps also necessary. Bearing witness to the differend is not what the peasants to whom Archbishop Oscar Romero spoke needed most. The situation in which they found themselves demanded a rhetoric of sure claims to language and history, namely, their language and their history.

If postmoderns too easily dismiss liberation rhetoric, they may miss the opportunity for fruitful dialogue that can focus rhetoric's attention on pain, imagination, and the religious. In their treatment of language and history, both postmodern and liberation rhetorics share a concern with these three crucial dimensions of human being. Postmoderns would be hasty, and foolhardy, not to engage liberationists in conversation about pain, imagination, and the religious because, despite their differences, their shared concerns would emerge. Such emergence may have revolutionary impact on the direction of rhetoric at the end of the millennium.

Pain

Pain, at its most destructive, disintegrates the human life-world as it disintegrates language: one's physicality is made so overwhelmingly present that one cannot speak it; one can neither point to nor construct objects in which the pain can be placed. Pain, Scarry writes, is "an intentional state without an intentional object" (164).[16] Simultaneously, however, pain demands a language that would speak it. Pain's paradox is that it is not simply destructive; it can also generate language.

For rhetoric, the problem of destructive pain is one of public verbalization: How can people adequately write/speak their own pain? How can people adequately write/speak the pain of others? The former is a problem because "physical pain does not simply resist language but actively destroys it, bringing about an immediate reversion to a state anterior to language, to the sounds and cries a human being makes before language is learned" (4).[17] Hence, any attempt to speak publicly one's own pain is done after the pain has lessened or ceased, thereby distancing the rhetoric from the situation it attempts to speak.[18]

The attempt to rhetoricize the pain of others is a particularly acute problem because another's pain is experienced only indirectly (4). While one may empathize with someone who is in pain, one cannot feel another's pain. One cannot even be sure, outside of the claim of the other, how the pain feels or even if the pain is real. Language seems woefully inadequate to the task. If one cannot know whether or not another's pain is real, then how can one speak it? If one speaks what one does not know, then isn't one engaging in deceit?

Yet as Stanley Cavell argues in his essay concerning *King Lear*, humans search suffering for meaning (47). And nothing means without language. Thus, as humans approach pain they are caught in a bind.

Sufferers know that their own suffering is essentially inexpressible. The observers of suffering know that their distance from another's pain precludes expression. At the same time, however, sufferers and observers of suffering alike seek to express the inexpressible: they wish to put pain into language. Elie Wiesel provides an outstanding example of this dilemma. After surviving Auschwitz, Wiesel traveled to France where he studied and worked as a journalist. For years he said nothing about the Shoah. This period of silence, when pain seemed to have destroyed Wiesel's capabilities for expressing his suffering, was a period of germination that bore fruit in the justly famous and eloquent *Night*.

The theologian Dorothee Soelle also recognizes the character of pain relative to language. As Soelle argues, pain makes humans mute. The human challenge is both to use language to lament the reality of pain and to change the painful situations in which humans are found (73). As I will argue throughout the ensuing chapters, the work of each of the four rhetoricians who form the core of this book recognizes both the destructive and generative power of pain. Romero, for instance, speaks of the pained and voiceless campesinos but refuses to allow their suffering to silence rhetoric. Rather, their pain, coupled with the pain of Christ on the cross, serves as a fundamental generative point for Romero. It serves to create language intended to bond those who suffer with one another and with those who do not suffer.

It is important to consider the rhetoric of pain because pain, and pain on a massive scale, is *the* fact of the twentieth century. The litany is obvious: the World Wars, the Shoah, Nagasaki and Hiroshima, Korea, Vietnam, Afghanistan, Chernobyl, famine in Africa and elsewhere, the Kurds, the targets of gun violence in America's inner cities, the victims of rape around the world, to name only the most well-known instances of mass pain. Any twentieth-century rhetoric that does not understand pain as one of its origins is antiquated at best, perhaps dishonest and manipulative at worst. Insofar as pain is a fact of human community, and insofar as rhetoric is community language, rhetoric must concern itself with pain.

The attempt to rhetoricize pain is central to liberation rhetorics. European political theologies and Latin American liberation theologies, representative of liberation rhetorics at large, share suffering as their fundamental generative point (Chopp, *Praxis* 1–7). Yet pain is also a concern of postmodern rhetoricians. Scollon and Scollon are deeply concerned about the plight of the Athabaskan people, and offer a conception of postmodern rhetoric to aid interethnic communication. Tracy writes postmodern rhetoric in the face of his own language and history that has repressed and oppressed those who have been identified as other. Lyotard's project in *The Differend* centers on the question of the Holocaust and how it can be spoken, how it is that postmoderns can respond to it. So too Wyschogrod locates her postmodern project within the frame of pain. As she writes,

> Why a postmodern ethic now? The twentieth century is witness to the deaths of millions within ever more compressed time frames: death through nuclear, chemical, and biological warfare, through death camps, through concentration and slave labor camps, and by means of conventional weapons. Newly emerging biological and chemical instruments for mass destruction are in the process of development. (xii–xiv)

It is important, in addition, to attend to the relationship between rhetoric and pain because pain can serve as a source of criticism. The pain-aware rhetorical critic or practitioner might ask the following questions: Have I accounted for the pain in this situation? Is the situation's rhetoric contributing to another's pain? If so, is the rhetoric wrong? This, I take it, is implicit in Tracy's argument. Once one recognizes that one participates in oppression and that one must act responsibly in oppressive situations, one is concerned about the ways in which one's rhetoric may be causing pain.

Pain can also provide a cross-cultural link. One of the most stultifying aspects of some postmodern rhetoric is the claim that it is extremely difficult, if not impossible, for people living in different linguistic communities to speak to one another in a way that can either connect them or adjudicate differences between them. As I indicated above, this is certainly the position Lyotard takes: at the end of *The Differend* he can speak only the space between languages and history; he can only bear witness to the heterogeneity that constitutes human being.

Other postmodern rhetoricians, such as Richard Rorty in his *Contingency, irony, and solidarity*, see the possibility of cross-historical and cross-linguistic solidarity in the rhetoric of pain. One dimension of this new rhetoric is the recognition that, despite the heterogeneity that characterizes our languages and histories, humans are bound together, cross-culturally, by pain and humiliation (177). One of the tasks of Rorty's new rhetoric is to expand the sense of 'we' that is based on the similarities that humans have with respect to pain and humiliation (192). Rorty firmly believes that this is not possible through the work of metaphysical rhetoric and its search for universal human rights, a core self, or a God because such a search is impossible: truth is the property of sentences, sentences depend on vocabularies, vocabularies are made by humans, and truth, then, is made by humans (17, 173, 177, 192). Rorty suggests instead that journalism, ethnography, and novels best extend the sense of 'we' because they best speak, in detail, pain (94, 145, 169, 192).[19] I find Rorty's work limited, though helpful. His claim that the suffering have no voice and hence need others to speak for them is simply not tenable (94). I would argue that humans can also be bound to each other across cultures by more than pain: hope, love, and respect come to mind. However, his attempt to begin to sketch a cross-cultural rhetoric of pain is helpful, especially since it is the attempt of a postmodern rhetorician to move beyond what Tracy has recognized as a tendency in postmodern rhetoric toward complacency (69). Rhetoric, involving pain, may help one to bridge cross-cultural impasses. This is, no doubt, ironic. Pain is the most divisive of human experiences because when one is pained, one cannot share this precise experience. One suffers uniquely (Scarry 4). Yet when rhetoricized, pain can provide a basis for solidarity. If people from vastly different, even opposing, cultures can share their languages of pain, perhaps these people will be less likely to seek to make each other suffer. If, for instance, the U.S. public heard the pain of burning Iraqi children, it would have less vehemently supported the 1991 Gulf War. If a mother and father from the Midwest came to understand that the children of those others screamed and hurt as their own child does, solidarity and not animosity may have been the tie that binds.

Imagination

As it works toward solidarity among divergent peoples, pain's dialectical partner is imagination. Defined by Scarry as "an intentional object without an experienceable intentional state" (164), 'imagination' can be tentatively understood as linguistic manipulation of the facets of human experience, including the elements of sense reality and whatever realities there may be beyond or within the sensible world. My understanding of imagination is akin to Coleridge's.[20] He argues that there are three levels: memory, fancy, imagination. Memory and fancy provide "to all faculties their objects and to all thought the elements of its material" (54). Memory, for instance, may recall to the person the elements of a book, or a building, which the person can then use in imaginative activity. Fancy is memory "emancipated from the order of time and space" (160). In short, fancy recalls the materials of existence but is able to rearrange them creatively. Imagination, for Coleridge, has two levels: primary and secondary; they differ only in degree. They are the prime agents of human perception, creators and synthesizers, repeaters and echoers of the "eternal act of creation" (159–60). Thus, imagination works with the elements and activities provided by memory and fancy but also introduces the intangible element of what Coleridge calls "the infinite I am" (159–60).

Consider the creation of a novel city. Simply put, one takes from memory and fancy other cities that exist in physical and textual form—that is, cities in which people live and cities planned but never accomplished. However, one is not content to act as photocopier, simply reproducing or even rearranging what has already been produced. Rather, one works with these elements and, if one is to create the new, one adds what Coleridge calls the power of the "eternal act of creation."

This process is that with which all rhetoricians—theorists, practitioners, teachers, students, critics—struggle. The task, always, is not simply to reproduce the already produced. Teachers, for instance, constantly struggle with the dilemma of student writing and speaking, in whatever discipline. How is it that a teacher guides a student away from regurgitation to creativity? The effective practitioner similarly seeks creativity. The political preacher might ask, for instance, these vexing questions: How can I learn from Dr. King and yet not simply repeat him? How can I speak to my own people in my own time?

Unaccounted for, however, in Coleridge's work on the imagination, is an imaginative dimension Scarry finds first in the Hebrew Bible. While she claims that "the only evidence that one is 'imagining' is that imaginary objects appear in the mind" (162) and that "imagination is only experienced in the image it produces" (164), she notes that there is another tradition: "Almost never is the imagination 'imagined' without an object, though the Hebraic scriptures come very close to requiring that believers do just that, that they apprehend the capacity for creation devoid of representable content: attributing to God a representable form is explicitly forbidden" (164). While Scarry wants to modulate this insight and back away from a theory of nonrepresentational imagination (164), I suggest that imagination is both object-oriented and process-oriented: that it is both a process that produces things and a process that reveals a process. In the former, the produced object is primary; in the latter, the produced object serves to point to the process itself.

My studies of Burke, Merton, and Romero will specifically address this point. Each, in his own way, proposes that imagination is not simply limited to the representable objects it produces. Rather, the imagination is also a process and these three rhetoricians press themselves and their audiences into it. This dimension of their work makes them truly revolutionary rhetoricians. For each, there is no codifiable image, no end dream toward which human histories and languages move inexorably. Instead, the imaginative process constantly disrupts its own products. Significantly, this separates them from the more doctrinnaire Freire, a Marxist who codifies a specific image of a classless utopia. For Freire, the process has an ending. The making of images is not an endless movement, each image replaced by subsequent images. There is a final image and all imaginative activity must work toward that end.

As with pain, the problem of imagination for rhetoric is one of public verbalization. Freire, for instance, may have an image of a classless utopia, but he must also decide how best he can communicate this image. Borrowing from and amending an example first proposed by Scarry (170–71), one can see the problem clearly if one considers the dynamics of rhetoricizing one's image of a city. One may have created, privately in one's mind, or in notes that would be incomprehensible to a public, a vision of a city that encompasses all that one believes a city should be. But how is it possible to express the complexity of the city, the joys and sorrows one receives from its imagined textures, sights, sounds, and smells to another who is both outside of one's body and outside of the textual world of one's private notes? Moreover, if one has experienced the dimension of the process-oriented imagination, how can one speak no-object? Such a dimension, like pain, destroys the verbal, hence causing a problem for one who would rhetoricize it.

Imagination is central to postmodern rhetorics. William A. Covino, for instance, seeks to re-read the history of rhetorical theory in light of what he sees as the dominant characteristic of postmodernism: the play of language. He seeks, he claims, "a student writing whose model is Montaigne or Byron or DeQuincey or Kenneth Burke or Tom Wolfe," writing that "is informed by associational thinking, a repertory of harlequin changes, by the resolution that resolution itself is anathema" (*Art of Wondering* 130).[21] Similarly, Rorty proposes that society support both liberals who imagine a larger sense of 'we' than that which currently exists in society and ironists who attempt to create themselves as humans never before known or to be known (96, 101).

Just as postmodern rhetorics are concerned about pain, liberation rhetorics attempt to rhetoricize imagination. No better example is extant in the United States than Martin Luther King, Jr.'s "I Have a Dream" speech (*Testament* 217–20). Speaking for the "negro," King's rhetoric is a paramount demonstration of imaginative technique. His line "Let freedom ring" echoes the anthem "America the Beautiful" to great effect, linking this song to the liberative efforts of the American "negro." King's speech also speaks an imaginative realm: a land of equality and justice presented in the form of a litany of dreams.

Imagination is a fact of human being. Humans, both individually and communally, constantly imagine and attempt to put the imagination into practice. If rhetoric deals with the human being, it must deal with imagination. Any study of rhetoric must look for the ways in which both theory and practice concern themselves with the imaginative capacities of human being. As language-users, humans have a life beyond the matter from which being arises: with the help of language humans create human culture.

Attention to the imaginative dimensions of rhetoric is also important because it reveals liberative possibilities for pedagogy, and pedagogy, historically, has been a consistent concern of rhetorical theory. If students were taught that one part of being human is to think/write/speak imaginatively, they would perhaps learn that life contains few certainties and that it is possible to begin to understand the 'other.' The word American, for instance, would yield to its user an ambiguity not now taught: Does 'American' mean simply U.S. citizens or citizens of Canada, and Central and South America as well? If the United States, why? If the others, why? Or, if one can teach wealthy Caucasian students to imagine what it is to be poor and Latino, perhaps one is on the way to solving grave social problems. This, I take it, is one of Rorty's points. He turns to novelists, for instance, to help people achieve solidarity based on the cross-cultural similarity of pain because imagination, and the imaginative act of language use in novels, can bridge seemingly unbridgeable gaps. Rorty claims, and perhaps rightly, that it is only imaginative acts, and not appeal to presumed universal claims that arose rather late in human history and remain localized (93), which provide a way for one person to find solidarity with another.

Finally, it is imagination that allows rhetoricians to delve into another's pain, speak it, and imagine its alleviation. As I argue above, one cannot feel another's pain. One cannot, for instance, know the burning foot of another as one's own. One can, however, imagine it as one's own, and once this imaginative empathy has transpired, one can then begin to speak this burning and work to imagine and produce its alleviation. Burke, Merton, Freire, and Romero all engage in this process: they show how rhetoric can explore the pains of various others, speak these pains, and imagine and create healing.

The Religious

In so doing, they demonstrate that rhetoric can, and does, operate religiously. For certain readers of this book, this claim will perhaps be obvious because three of the four rhetoricians I have chosen as representative are well identified with what is a commonplace understanding of the religious: they are professed members of an institutional religion. Two, in fact, were clerics: Merton, a Trappist priest, and Romero, a diocesan priest and archbishop. Freire's Marxist Roman Catholicism is well known. But the obvious is too obvious and borders on the trite. Membership in an institutional religion is only one form that the religious impulse takes, and not necessarily the 'highest' or most 'primal' form at that.

When rhetoric takes seriously the claims of both pain and imagination, it operates religiously because, as Stephen Webb argues, "religion is nothing less than that which is excessive, that which is, by definition, more than what can be known or felt, described or contained" (xiv). To operate religiously, then, is to operate in worlds beyond the realm easily accessible by languages, worlds that demand recognition but defy easy representation. These are the worlds of pain and imagination.

Webb, himself, is much more concerned about the relationship between rhetoric and the imagination. Tropes, in particular, figure large in his work. He has set about exploring, in his most recent book, the hyperbolic and how it is, perhaps, the zenith of imaginative strategies employed by rhetoricians. As he asks: "can we again find the connection between religion and hyperbole—a hyperbolic imagination?" (xiii).

Yet Webb, though he does not make it explicit, is aware of the painful dimension of rhetoric, the dimension that contributes and makes more complex its religiousness. For instance, he deals with the work of Georges Bataille, who "equates excess with sacrifice" and thereby turns religion "against itself to liberate from worn moral codes the power of liberation itself" (60). While Webb finally diverges from Bataille over the question of God (86), Webb nonetheless has begun to find, through Bataille, the link between imagination and pain and its implications for rhetoric as a fundamentally religious activity.

It is not surprising that pain and imagination inform the fundamental metaphors offered by the world's religions.[22] Central to Christianity, of course, is the imaginative vision of Christ dying on the cross. While the various representations of the crucifixion may well be rooted in a historical event, this historical event survives only in the imaginative texts of Paul, the Gospels, various paintings, sculpture, reliefs, and the like. Significantly, each representation is different: human imagination works, as Coleridge suggested, with the stuff of memory and fancy but changes it in accord with the impulse of creativity. Human imagination has turned again and again to the pain of Christ on the cross and explored and presented it anew. These imaginers offer metaphors (Christ is your Lord), analogies (take up your cross), and other rhetorical strategies meant to move people, finally, to 'ultimate reality.'

'Ultimate reality' is an outlandish, if not dangerous, term for the secular academy in the postmodern era. If, as Wyschogrod argues, postmodernism gives up claims to assured truth, how can it work within the frame of something ultimate? But 'ultimate reality' is a deceptively crucial phrase. It reminds people to be honest: everyone operates with ultimate principles in mind. Some scholars, for instance, are guided finally, and thus completely, by career concerns. They base decisions upon this career principle: Will this article help me win tenure, a better job, more office space? While career concerns pale next to King David's desire to please God, they are ultimate reality for these scholars: they live to fulfill them.

Yet 'ultimate reality' is always open to revision because, finally, it is a phrase composed of two words that, as words do, change with time and space. For Christians, Jesus Christ may define ultimate reality but, the cynic may ask, which Christ? The Catholic Christ? The Protestant Christ? The Biblical Christ? The Quaker Christ? A child's Christ? An old woman's Christ? There is no one Christ: there are Christs that may or may not connect analogically. Ultimate reality is changeable because the things humans experience change and because words, finally, are fillable forms. Merton, as I will discuss in chapter 3, makes this eminently clear. The Trappist priest, son of the mother church, delights in word-play: he knows that words change and are changeable, thus making tenuous any human endeavor.

This, not incidentally, must be one of the most exciting and greatest challenges that teachers and students in introductory religion classes face. What a shock it is for a moderately devout Christian youth to encounter the fact that the Gospels present different, and at times contrasting, images of Christ. What a shock it is for this same youth to encounter two different creation narratives, one right after the other, each of which presents a different cosmology. Religion professors are in the position to be able to help students open up the imaginative play of the rhetoric of religion and in so doing help students become more imaginatively daring. This, certainly, is a frightful task for all concerned. Professors ask students to become different people: they ask them to imagine their religions, and thus themselves, anew. Students, for their part, enter the hard work of reimagining their own worlds and risk the possibility of losing themselves.

'Ultimate reality' is concerned more with practice than with belief, more with the ways to reality than this reality itself. These ways include, but are not limited to, formal theology, the use of scripture, and contemplation (Tracy 84, 89, 91–92, 95). I would include rhetoric on this list. It deals with the excesses of pain and imagination, those excesses that take people into realms beyond the ordinary. These ends of human being—pain and imagination—speak of the ultimate realities that concern human beings: extreme suffering and death and the possibility of pain-free existence and life eternal.

Burke, Merton, Freire, Romero

In order to discover this religious rhetoric of pain and imagination, I offer readings of four examples of postmodern and liberation rhetorics. Chapter 2 fathoms the postmodern rhetorical theory of Kenneth Burke, a prolific American academic rhetorician who never graduated from college. The rhetorical practice of Thomas Merton, found in his poem *The Geography of Lograire*, is probed in chapter 3. Merton, who was a Ph.D. candidate at Columbia and a professor at St. Bonaventure University in western New York, left the academy in 1941 in order to take vows as a Trappist monk at Gethsemane, Kentucky. Chapter 4 delves into the work of Paulo Freire, a Brazilian university professor and rhetorical theorist who was jailed and exiled by a Brazilian junta in the 1960s for his work in adult literacy. The Pastoral Letters of the martyred Oscar Romero, who practiced rhetoric as the Roman Catholic archbishop of San Salvador, El Salvador, are measured in chapter 5. Based on the discussions of the work of these four rhetoricians, the Afterword proposes a direction for rhetoricians in all of our guises: theorists, practitioners, critics, teachers, and students.

I have chosen to focus on the work of these four, as representative of postmodern and liberation rhetorics, for two reasons. The first is that it is their work that has led me to my thesis. I did not come to the rhetorical theories of Burke and Freire and the rhetorical practices of Merton and Romero with a template. I approached them with some vague ideas that both shaped my reading of the four and were shaped by it. As much as this study is a reading of the four, it is an avenue by which the four speak through me. They are my teachers; I am their student. This point suggests my second reason: if one can really *decide* to give voice to one's teachers, I give voice to these four in juxtaposition because such juxtaposition is particularly evocative of a number of important questions and answers.

One question concerns the nature of the Americas. Can the Americas become a just community? It is more than coincidental that all four of my rhetoricians are 'American.' By studying them together, I hope to begin to conceive a truly American rhetoric that can speak across the north/south gap that has marked the relationship between 'America' (the United States) and its neighbors to the south. Rhetoric may well be the child who leads the Americas to a new community.

Another question concerns the relationship between theory and practice. In what way can one engage in both theory and practice? Clearly, this study is theoretical, but I hope it will mark a new way to practice rhetoric. I have chosen theorists and practitioners in order to demonstrate the necessity of attending, always, to theory and practice. One without the other is incomplete.

A third question concerns the textual heritage of rhetoric. Who should be a part of this? While Merton and Freire have been the subject of numerous studies, they have yet to be placed within the tradition of rhetoric. Burke, while recognized as a rhetorician, has not been recognized as an important and potentially germinal postmodern thinker. I hope this study will help establish Burke as an important postmodern: his work is as fine as any of the more current and stylish figures such as Derrida and Foucault. Romero, at least within the North American academy, has no place. His work has given rise to little English language scholarship and little, if any, scholarship beyond the work of clerics. I hope chapter 5, which discusses his Pastoral Letters, will build on the efforts of scholars like the American Jesuit James Brockman and the translations of the Salvadoran Jesuit Jon Sobrino.

A final question concerns the use of the four figures. How should they be read? While I don't claim that my reading is definitive, these four must be read as postmodern and liberation rhetoricians who offer trailheads into the religious dialectic of pain and imagination. Surely, there is no more important task for rhetoric in the age of the Holocaust.

2

Burke's Beloved Cynosure and Sinecure

Peggy and Malcolm, Kenneth and Lily—these were the friends I visited when I was in New York. . . . At that time Kenneth was translating, editing *The Dial* and writing the first of his strange books.[1]

—Dorothy Day, *The Long Loneliness*

It isn't surprising that Dorothy Day, in her Greenwich Village days, days before Peter Maurin and the Catholic Worker Movement, knew Kenneth Burke. They shared devotion to socialist ideas and politics; they shared devotion to language. Both were in love with reading and writing; both were committed to revolution; both used the written word to further it.

It is also not surprising that Day found Burke's work to be strange. At that time, after all, she was a socialist journalist and activist dedicated to the concrete use of realistic narrative to help improve the lives of workers, women, and other oppressed peoples. Burke, while certainly dedicated to the oppressed, was following a different path. He was beginning to write what would become the first parts of a body of rhetorical theory dedicated to nothing short of changing the world by changing human beings' understanding of language.[2]

This corpus is composed of Burke's erudite ranging through theology, political theory, trope theory, history, philosophy, literary criticism, and more. Burke simply ignores traditional walls between the academic disciplines; his home is all discourse. This, certainly, makes Burke somewhat strange: What is it that he does? Is he a theologian? A political scientist? A trope theorist? A historian? A philosopher? A literary critic?[3]

In spite of, or perhaps because of, his range, Burke is best understood as a rhetorical theorist.[4] The evidence that Burke understood
himself as such is plentiful. His final two full-length books are titled as
rhetorics, thus indicating a conscious shift in this period toward an
explicit formulation of his rhetorical theory. He is constantly concerned
with tropes, which are crucial parts of rhetoric. Also, in one place where
he tried, he is unable, and finally unwilling, to distinguish between
"rhetoric" and "poetics" (*Language* 307). Everything for Burke, it could
be said, is poetry, is rhetoric, is both.[5] More significantly though, Burke
is a master theorist of the dialectic of language and, importantly, the
dialectic at the heart of his work is that of pain and imagination.

As an academic theorist, Burke brought the full weight of his
erudition to bear upon the problem of pain in the twentieth century.
Like Day, he attempted to help ease sufferng; he tried to fulfill his desire,
first announced in *Permanence and Change*, for a rhetoric that can heal
a world painfully divided (163). Unlike Day, however, who founded her
revolutionary practice on a belief in the primacy of the historical voice
of the downtrodden and on orthodox Roman Catholicism, Burke roots
his rhetorical theory, if the metaphor 'to root' can be used here, in the
plurality and ambiguity of postmodernity and a language mysticism
whose end is found in the dimension of imagination beyond and within
all images: the process of imagination itself.

Although Burke's main works were written prior to the advent of
postmodernism, they anticipate and incorporate it.[6] However, one of
the most prominent theorists currently at work, Frank Lentricchia,
vehemently denies this: he argues that Burke's *A Rhetoric of Motives*
profoundly embarrasses postmodernism. Postmodernism, according to
Lentricchia, aestheticizes rhetoric, thus separating it from politics (93,
159–60). His own reading of *A Rhetoric of Motives* shows to him that
Burke does not adhere to postmodernism thus defined (88). Lentricchia
maintains a variant of Marxist criticism and while he does not claim that
Burke is a Marxist, he argues that Burke is amenable to his Marxist
vision.[7] Clearly, Lentricchia and I disagree over the definition of
postmodernism. I won't quibble over definition. Rather, I will elucidate
a much more interesting point: Lentricchia's reading, despite its own
intention, begins to reveal Burke as a postmodern as I have defined the
term. Lentricchia's reading of Burke shows that the plurality of language

and the ambiguity of history are fundamental to Burke's attempt to rhetoricize the dialectic of pain and imagination.

The Ambiguity of History

Lentricchia's own fine elucidation of Burke's notion of the synecdochal fallacy well reveals Burke to have recognized and accepted that all histories are particular, that to live historically is to participate in oppression, and that to live historically is to act responsibly.[8] Lentricchia claims that the synecdochal fallacy entails a two-part cover-up. First, synecdoche—the trope of part/whole relationships—works fallaciously when it masks the fact that it represents only one strata of the social order. Synecdoche is false when it attempts to pass itself off as above the movement of politics, when in fact it is engendered by politics: the whole's claim to represent the part is always open to question. Synecdoche is part of the social order, of the movement of history. So too, then, are humans who use it.

Second, Lentricchia claims that misused synecdoche does not simply mask its own political origins; it also denies history's ambiguity. Consider, again, Lyotard's criticism of the nineteenth-century European Communist Party, discussed in chapter 1. The Party, according to Lyotard, claimed that one understanding of 'worker,' its own, completely defined the term. In so doing, the Party denied the heterogeneity of the 'workers': it homogenized what was not homogenizable. As Lentricchia argues, Burke, in his 1935 speech to the American Writers' Congress, decried the import of the word *worker*. It simply could not represent the American situation because America is not Europe. The class relationships that define, or defined, European life are not as strictly and obviously set in America. Rather than borrowing European language, America needs, and needed, revolutionary rhetoric rooted in its own history (31). As Lentricchia claims, Burke sought a symbol, which he found in 'the people,' that recognized both the whole and the heterogeneity of the whole (34). Lentricchia finds in Burke, then, a recognition of the first sense of the ambiguity of history: humans must recognize that their particular histories are not necessarily universal. Lentricchia's Burke is well aware of the ambiguity of historical formations.

Moreover, Lentricchia's Burke recognizes as well that people participate in the oppression of the other as they homogenize the heterogeneous. This is the second dimension of the ambiguity of history. Focusing still on Lentricchia's discussion of Burke's 1935 speech, I find Lentricchia claiming that Burke urged the change from 'the worker' to 'the people' because the phrase 'the worker,' in the United States, perpetuates the oppressive plight of workers. It does so, as Lentricchia reads Burke, in two ways. First, 'the worker,' which well details the oppressive conditions perpetuated by capitalism (27), actually works to repulse the people to whom it is directed (27). The 'worker' becomes the other and rhetoricians who continue to use the word actually perpetuate the 'workers' 'conditions: if the non-'workers' who hold power don't identify themselves with the 'workers,' they will not work on behalf of the 'workers.'

Second, Lentricchia claims, the Marxist 'worker,' which ideally marks oppressive class relationships, becomes perverted by capitalist society. Rather than engendering revolution, it is used as the conceptual bulwark for a rhetoric of commodity gratification. Workers are educated to believe that their oppression is best relieved through consumption (29). Capitalist society takes the workers' desire for freedom and channels it into 'freedom' found through the purchasing of consumer goods. Yet this freedom is never realized because the capitalist system continues to produce new commodities that it educates the 'workers' to desire (30). This, Lentricchia claims, simply isolates and quarantines the oppressed's pain (32). The Marxist use of 'the worker' as synecdoche, according to Lentricchia's Burke, leads the Marxist both to deny the heterogeneity of the U.S. situation and also to participate in the oppression of those the Marxist hopes to liberate: the Marxist is caught in the double bind of historical ambiguity.

However, Lentricchia's Burke is not debilitated by this ambiguity; rather, the ambiguity generates the possibility of responsible action. Lentricchia's Burke, in his 1935 speech, calls on Marxists to delve into the American locale, to speak out of and into the American experience (33). To do so is to discover 'the people,' a figure that allows for the heterogeneity that is America (33–4). For Lentricchia's Burke, this term's ambiguity is its strength. At once it names unity and diversity and is thus flexibly resilient (34). Later in his book, Lentricchia identifies this part of Burke as the ability to join synchronous and diachronous understandings of history (70). Though Lentricchia himself doesn't do so, I will join together, in what follows, his discussion of synchrony and diachrony in Burke to Burke's advocacy of 'the people' and add some observations of my own.

Synchrony perpetuates the history of a whole: the people. It names what American citizens feel to be true: Americans have been a people, are a people, should be a people. 'People' plays on the words of one of our founding and unifying documents, capturing the utopian hope that is part of the U.S. experience: "We the people in order to form a more perfect union." Yet simultaneously, 'the people' allows Burke to name the diachrony of the whole, that is the whole's heterogeneity (Lentricchia 70) that is 'the people;' it makes "heterogeneous historical textures that tradition and system would homogenize" (70). While it unifies Americans, reminding them of the totality that they think was, is, and should be true, it also allows the heterogeneous to speak. Part of 'the people' are divergent peoples who haven't always been included: slaves, indigenous peoples, women, and Catholics, to name a few. 'The people' both allows for the heterogeneity that is part of the U.S. experience and captures the country's historic utopian yearning. In so doing, it can effectively lead to radical social change (34–5).[9]

Burke's recognition of the ambiguity of history spans his career. Just as it was present in his 1935 speech to the American Writers' Congress, so is it throughout thirty years of books.[10] Consider, for instance, his treatment of Shakespeare's Shylock in A Rhetoric of Motives (193–94). This discussion emerges from a larger consideration of how competing rhetorics move beyond dialectical eternity, where the participating poles remain equal, to a moment of "transcendence" where the poles, at least momentarily, move beyond their dialectical opposition.[11] Burke's study of Shylock, by the way, points to his interdisciplinary erudition, which I would argue is a mark of the rhetorical theorist par excellence. Just as Burke did not sacrifice Marxist political theory to political scientists, he did not imprison Shylock within the camp of literary criticism. Burke ranged through all texts: no discipline was closed to him as a rhetorician. Burke's Rhetoric of Religion, for instance, dares to discuss both Genesis and Augustine; A Grammar of Motives treats Darwin, among others. Burke's daring is a lesson to be learned by all rhetoricians—theorists, practitioners, critics, students, teachers. The stuff of rhetoric is discourse in general, not a particular kind of discourse. Rhetorical critics, for instance, should range widely: popular media and elitist art are both within their range. Teachers should dare to have their students study theology as well as biology, psychology as well as Shakespeare's Shylock.

Shylock, Burke argues, adjudicates the dialectic that structures *The Merchant of Venice* by taking on the guise of the Christian: the one partner of the dialectic, who has suffered at the hands of the other, simply argues that he, in fact, is a Christian. Like Christians, Shylock argues, Jews have hands, senses, organs. Jews, like Christians, eat and bleed. Hence, since Jews are like Christians in all these ways, since Jews are human in the way Christians are, then Jews shall be Christian. This includes, not incidentally, the avenue of revenge. When Jews hurt Christians, Shylock notes, "Christian humility" leads them to exact revenge upon the Jews. Hence, since Jews are Christians, Jews shall act likewise: when hurt by other Christians, they shall exact revenge.

Ambiguity reveals itself at two levels, at least. The text demonstrates that Burke sees ambiguity in Christian/Jewish relationships: while preaching humility, Christians, for the most part, treated Jews with something less than humility. Burke writes that Shylock's speech perhaps accurately gauges Christianity's perversion of its basic tenets in order to defend its material property (194). Burke's qualification of Shylock's argument with the word *might* indicates the other level of ambiguity. Some interpreters might claim that Shylock does not justly characterize Christianity when he plays with the connection between vengeance and humility (193–94). Others might interpret Shylock's understanding of Christian practice as extremely accurate (194).

Burke is content with neither level of ambiguity: the competing interpretations lead only to a chaotic morass. Shylock's solution simply reifies the existing order. He condones both violence and his people's status as an oppressed minority (194). So too, Burke claims, the character Bigger in Richard Wright's *Native Son* responds as a criminal Negro and thus mimics Shylock's reponse as a Jew. Both are oppressed minorities who accept their status and reify it by acting in a prescribed manner (*Rhetoric of Motives* 194). Bigger has accepted the restrictions of the larger society and seeks vengeance within the imposed, and accepted, code. Burke is unhappy with Shylock's solution; so too he is unhappy with Bigger's.

Importantly, this is an instance of Burke demonstrating that he is unhappy with liberation rhetoric. In *Attitudes Toward History* Burke makes public his awareness of liberation rhetoric, with only a descriptive eye, it seems. He maintains that oppressed peoples create a history of themselves and others in order to reclaim that which they understand to be rightly theirs (315). The myth for Shylock is the myth of Jewish/Christian humility; for Bigger the myth of the negro. In *A Rhetoric of Motives*, however, Burke rejects what I am descriptively calling "liberation rhetoric." Burke himself, certainly, never used the phrase. He rejects this kind of rhetoric because it accepts the rules of and wreaks vengeance (a bloody and painful vengeance, as Shylock argues) within the imposed system. This is not a healthy option, Burke contends, because it continues the spiral of pain he wishes to halt. So too Merton, as I will discuss in chapter 3, reveals this tendency of liberation rhetoric. As Merton sees it, the 'liberation' of one group seems inevitably to lead to the oppression of another.

Burke maintains that rhetorics of " 'racialist' or 'nationalist' doctrines of emancipation" at first seem to be the way to liberation. However, inevitably they fissure: the heterogeneous forces they attempt to unify always break the whole (*Rhetoric of Motives* 194). In addition to the fact that they may seek vengeance under the guise of humility, Burke finds liberation rhetorics limited because finally they lead to only more ambiguity: what seemed like an ultimate solution is revealed within ambiguous history to be one more instance of ambiguity. A 'one' always comprises the 'many' and the many inevitably break the one apart. Nothing is purely homogeneous; there is always heterogeneity within homogeneity. Burke's principle would tell us that even Europe, that most lambasted unity in this multicultural era, is not a homogeneous culture. There is no Europe any more than there is an Africa: it is composed of heterogeneous forces that cooperate and compete. Burke is not content with relativism, it must be emphasized: he does want a language that will resolve violent dialectics, that will avoid equations such as vengeance = humility. He doesn't find it, however, in liberation rhetoric.

The Plurality of Language

Burke's concentration on the fluidity of the word *humility* in his discussion of Shakespeare reveals not only the ambiguity of history; it reveals the fluidity, the plurality of language itself.[12] Shylock's speech, if nothing else, complicates humility so that one is left unsure as to its meaning: Does one define it by the vengeful practice of the Christians who use it to name themselves? Does one define it by doctrine? Does one define it, following Shylock, as simply a word that takes on meaning as people give it meaning?

Without doubt, Burke would answer yes to the last question. Various language communities may understand the same words differently. Lentricchia, too, recognizes this in Burke. Social structure is made unstable not only by competing historical formations within a single society. Lentricchia reminds his readers that language is eminently appropriatable: no single group owns a word or groups of words (79). Shylock seizes the Christian symbol of authority, humility, in order to turn it against the Christians. The word can shift contexts; it is open to appropriation; it is not permanently bound to any one people and the meanings with which they invest it.

Lentricchia maintains that it is Burke's awareness of this dimension of the plurality of language (though Lentricchia, certainly, doesn't identify it as plurality) that accounts for Burke's treatment of the historical formations of the word *rights* (80). Burke argues in *Attitudes Toward History* in a section called "Stealing Back and Forth of Symbols" that Marx stole "freedom" from bourgeois "rights," which in turn stole "rights" from a church that had stolen it from secular authorities that had used it to claim that kings had "divine" right (328). The term *rights* has meaning only as communities give it meaning and the meanings vary with the communities: the word, like the communities, is plural.

Burke, moreover, is also aware of the second dimension of the plurality of language. Language is plural not only because it belongs to varying communities that invest words with contextual meaning. It is plural, as well, in that language, as language, isn't what it claims to be: there is always a gap between words and that to which words refer.[13] Consider, for instance, Burke's treatment of metaphor and analogy in *Permanence and Change*. Burke claims that the ability to abstract is fundamental to human beings (103–6) and is what distinguishes humans from other creatures (5–6). A trout, Burke notes, may have some power of abstraction. If it can safely escape the "jaw-ripping" hook that tricked it, it may be able to abstract from that situation into others in order to avoid another jaw-ripping. But, Burke claims, "a different kind of bait may outwit" the trout if it doesn't look like the original jaw-ripper. Trout simply do not have the abstracting capabilities of humans.

Senses, Burke argues, are abstractors because they make a sign out of an event. Humans use this sign (a smell, a sound, a taste, a touch, a sight) to find their way through life. As a child, one might smell and taste in one's father's kitchen a delightful cookie and spend much of one's life after that judging cookies based upon this sense experience: "This one? No, it doesn't quite *smell* like *that one* I once smelled. This one? No, I'm afraid that it doesn't quite *taste* like *that one* I once tasted. Sorry. I'll keep looking." Or one might see the twisted metal and broken bodies of a car crash at a curve and always keep that sight in mind as one drives in other situations, attempting to avoid the same accident. One may even avoid that particular curve in the road or all kinds of curves in all kinds of roads. One uses the remembered sight abstractly when one carries it over to other actual or potential situations in order to judge them.

Interestingly, despite the different conclusions he draws from his understanding of this process, Freire shares with Burke a deep concern about abstraction. Freire, as I will discuss in chapter 4, makes abstraction central to literacy education. The first stages of his program require the students to objectify and make abstract social, natural, and linguistic structures so that they, the students, can begin to separate themselves from their immediate surroundings and make global connections between their own lives and the lives of others. Finally, however, Burke champions the process of abstraction; Freire champions the end. For Burke, most important is the act of abstraction: it is key to human being. For Freire, abstraction serves to create an end: one learns to read and write in order to build the final utopia, not to revel in the continuous making of liberating metaphors.

All abstraction, Burke holds, is a metaphorical process (95). One takes a fact and links it analogously (a variant of metaphor) to all other facts of the same class. One says, for example, that one's father's cookie is the cookie by which all others are to be judged: that cookie defines the class of cookies. This process of metaphorical analogization is as true for science as it is for poetry, though science and poetry differ slightly. Whereas poets tend to use metaphor in order to illuminate experience briefly, scientists use metaphors systematically to organize extensive inquiries into experience (96). This, by the way, again points to Burke's belief that rhetoric is an interdisciplinary activity. Scientific and poetic discourses are open to rhetorical analysis because both, finally, share structures and strategies that all discourses share.

That such a process of metaphorical analogization reveals and engenders the plurality of language for Burke is seen in his discussion of the metaphorization of 'man' (*Permanence and Change* 95). He writes that "we have, at different eras in history, considered man as the son of God, as an animal, as a political or economic brick, as a machine, each such metaphor, and a hundred others, serving as the cue for an unending line of data and generalizations." 'Man' has no fixed referent to which it eternally refers; all the other terms that are used to metaphorize man are likewise plural: they refer to numbers of referents, none of which better informs the terms than the others do. 'Brick' refers to that material object out of which walls are made and to that material object out of which the economy is made, and finally, 'men' are the 'bricks' of the economy. Does this mean, then, that 'men' are the material objects out of which brick walls are made? They are, perhaps, if 'wall' refers to racial divisions in a neighborhood. One may argue against the integration of one's neighborhood because one doesn't want one's children to be influenced by bad elements. One's children, in this instance, become a wall between one and another.[14]

The danger of metaphorical analogization, Burke warns, is that one forgets that the new oneness is never a oneness in any sense other than that it was made so by an act of language. As he writes, the danger is that "*similarity* is taken as evidence of an *identity*" (97). This, without doubt, is the potential problem with synecdoche outlined above: one takes a part of the whole for the whole and forgets that one has simply defined the whole by a linguistic act alone. Lentricchia focuses on the way in which synecdoche masks the ambiguity of history; it can also mask the second dimension of the plurality of language. One might, Burke notes, say that "some part of the social body . . . is held to be 'representative' of the society as a whole" or that the color of a tree represents a tree (*Grammar of Motives* 508). The fallacy would arise when one stops the synecdochal exploration of the thing by claiming that one synecdoche is the whole. For a synecdoche, like all other tropes, is necessarily a linguistic reduction of that to which it refers (507). To forget that synecdoche necessarily reduces in order to name is to deny the plurality of language: there are other synecdochal relations that are repressed, for the moment, when one chooses a particular synecdoche. One may say that the color of a tree is the tree, but in so doing one represses the other possibilities: that the tree is its sound, is its smell, is its taste, is its sight, or that it is none of these exclusively and is something else.

Furthermore, as Burke argues in *The Rhetoric of Religion*, if one is to use language properly, one must discount it. Though there is correspondence between the thing to which the word refers and the word itself, the word isn't that to which it refers. This, he claims, is the paradox of the negative, linking language theory to negative theology and marking a place in which religion and the religious pervade Burke's work: "Quite as the *word* 'tree' is verbal and the thing tree is non-verbal, so all words for the non-verbal must, by the very nature of the case, discuss the realm of the non-verbal in terms of *what it is not*" (17). Burke claims that metaphor, which is fundamental to human being, reveals this well. Metaphor presumes the negative: to say that a dog is a garbage disposal is to explore, in a new way, the dog. It doesn't, however, make the nonverbal dog into a nonverbal garbage disposal (*Grammar of Motives* 503).

Imagination

The play of metaphor and analogy is, of course, a manifestation of human beings' imaginative capacities. Thus, to understand Burke's argument about the play of these tropes, and the effect that they have on history and language, it is imperative to study Burke's understanding of imagination. This takes one into the heart of Burke's work, into the realms of object-oriented and process-oriented imagination and the relationship that they have with their dialectical partner, pain.

Throughout Burke's work, two dimensions of imagination are elucidated, another simply marked. The dimension simply marked is this: imagination as that which records sensory perception. Coleridge, as I discussed in chapter 1, would call this "memory." The two elucidated are these: imagination as object-oriented and imagination as process-oriented. Briefly, imagination as that which records sensory perception is like a template. It accepts the imprint of the sense world but it does not alter it. Object-oriented imagination is more creative: it works with these imprints and recombines them into both recognizable and un-recognizable shapes. Process-oriented imagination, like object-oriented, works creatively. But unlike the latter, it does not reach its culmination in the production of new images. Rather, it produces things in order to reveal the process of production itself.[15]

Burke himself never names these three dimensions as such, though he comes close to doing so in *A Rhetoric of Motives* and in "A Dramatistic View of the Origins of Language and a Postscript on the Negative" (*Language* 460). In *A Rhetoric of Motives* Burke argues that the concern with imagination as a "suasive device" is relatively recent, a develop-ment that reached its zenith in modernity (78). Basing his discussion upon such moderns as Kant and Coleridge, Burke cleanly delineates the first two dimensions of the imaginative: that which records sensory perception and the object-oriented (86). He separates the two and thus separates imagination as reproductive from imagination as productive. Burke simply marks the reproductive dimension; he acknowledges its existence but finds it to be relatively unimportant. The productive dimension, the object-oriented, allows one to disintegrate and reinte-grate aspects of experience, thus creating objects that are not necessarily 'real,' that is, not necessarily a part of what we sense in the world (78–79). It is the productive imagination that is poetic, 'creative' in the sense that 'creative' is commonly used.

Burke again notes (in a footnote) his distinction between repro-ductive and productive (or object-oriented) imagination in "A Dramatistic View of the Origins of Language and a Postscript on the Negative." In addition, Burke introduces what he maintains as the third dimension of imagination, which I am calling "process-oriented." The note is intended as a preemptive response to expected criticism. Burke, in the essay, develops his theory that images and ideas are separate because ideas are infused with the negative, with 'No.' Images, on the other hand, are not. Yet Burke does argues that images are infused with idea. Hence the expected criticism. Since ideas are infused with the negative, his imaginary critic proclaims, and ideas infuse images, are not images therefore infused with the negative?

Anticipating this criticism, Burke claims that only images that are "mere physical receivings" are purely positive. As "sheer sensory perception" they are not infused with No. But, Burke claims, this is only one dimension of imagination. Another is imagination as "re-combinations of sensory images that Coleridge called fancy," imagination as that which I am calling "object-oriented." This dimension corresponds to the productive imagination discussed in *A Rhetoric of Motives*. Opposite the dimension of sheer sensory impression, and beyond the object-oriented dimension, is the third dimension of imagination: the process-oriented. Burke writes that it is the dimension of "the ability even to transcend the world of image and sensation entirely" (*Language* 460). As I will argue below when I discuss process-oriented imagination within the context of the religious in Burke, this is what appears in *A Rhetoric of Motives* as language mysticism. What follows in this section is a discussion of the place of the object-oriented imagination in Burke's work. This will lead into a treatment of the place of pain as it challenges the object-oriented imagination. The discussion of pain, in turn, will raise to consideration the third dimension of the imagination, the process-oriented, as it religiously responds to the challenge of pain.

Object-oriented imagination, Burke holds, includes both envisionment and technique. Consider, for instance, Burke's discussion in *A Rhetoric of Motives* (84–85). He argues that while object-oriented imagination may build upon reproductive imagery, it moves beyond it, creating things that have never existed and may never exist. For instance, an imaginative house may be built by linguistic strategies that are finally independent of sense reality. This imaginative act is object-oriented, but the object is not a mere reproduction of other houses that exist outside the image. It is, according to Scarry's definition as provided in chapter 1, "an intentional object without an experienceable intentional state." The image is created when one acts with one's verbal resources: it doesn't exist until the action occurs. Certainly, one may not be in complete control of the verbal manipulation: one's image may not match what one wanted. One may have a vague sense that the image isn't quite right and hence decide to try again. Nonetheless, verbal manipulation must occur for any image to exist.

Object-oriented imagination involves not only vision but technique. In order to envision the imagined object, one must, Burke maintains, *manipulate* one's verbal resources. All three dimensions of the dictionary definition of 'manipulate' are helpful: "1. to handle, manage, or use, esp. with skill, in some process of treatment or performance. 2. to manage or influence by artful skill: *to manipulate a person*. 3. to adapt or change (accounts, figures, etc.) to suit one's purpose or advantage" (*Random House* 813). All the definitions involve agency, action: to handle, to manage, to adapt. As Burke notes in "A Dramatistic View of the Origins of Language and a Postscript on the Negative," insofar as images are infused with idea (and all but the reproductive are: productive imagery, like the house, is infused with idea and the No insofar as it negates other houses that one has encountered) they are bonded "with the realm of *action*" (460). Object-oriented imagination is active, involving manipulation. Definition 2 is particularly useful. It calls attention to the fact that manipulation involves "artful skill": object-oriented imagination, Burke claims, is "poetic." Especially revealing is definition 3. Manipulation involves the changing or adapting of "figures" to one's advantage. It seems the dictionary means by "figures," given that it is coupled with "accounts," the second definition the dictionary itself provides: "2. a numerical symbol, esp. an Arabic numeral" (492). Yet given the plurality of language, "figure" also means, the dictionary reminds us: "11. *Rhet.* a figure of speech." This definition is pointedly telling in relation to Burke's discussion of the technique involved in object-oriented imagination. It is verbal, and figures such as metaphor and analogy are part of the process of verbalization, and their manipulation is crucial to object-oriented imagination.

Another helpful way by which to approach the two dimensions of object-oriented imagination in Burke is through *Attitudes Toward History* and its elucidation of "The Bureaucratization of the Imaginative."[16] In history, the "imaginative," Burke claims, are the "possibilities" that usually begin as utopian visioning (225). The imaginative is bureaucratized when one imaginative possibility is made incarnate in the complexity of human social existence. The imaginative then becomes both the guiding force of history and an unattainable goal. It provides human life with its energy, but human life, in turn, denies its realization because humans are imperfect. (225).[17] In other words, imagination here is understood as object-oriented: it involves utopian envisionment of new possibilities. Also, its bureaucratization involves both language and history, the key components of postmodern rhetoric. Finally, it is never complete because the world is not, and cannot be, perfect. Language and history, plural and ambiguous, never allow for the full presence of the utopian vision: they can't capture it, and it can't be captured.

In Burke's ensuing discussion, he inserts into the imaginative and its bureaucratization the second dimension of object-oriented imagination: technique. The modern West, Burke claims, has worked toward the perfection of inventive strategies, strategies that are, finally, the culmination of imagination. The genius of the West is that if has made imagination routine; it now has a system that reliably produces things (228). The imaginative, then, is marked both by utopian vision and the method of invention from which the vision comes (in A *Rhetoric of Motives* this process is called "verbal manipulation").

Burke, further elucidating this dimension of technique that is involved in object-oriented imagination, suggests that rhetoric use and propagate "planned incongruity," which parallels the laboratory bureaucratization of the process of scientific invention. Burke, seeming to support Lentricchia, does claim that such bureaucratization would lead to "deteriorization," yet he also argues that the deteriorization would be offset by strengthening the minds of more people: imagination and its obects would become the province of all (228–29). As a result, people who aren't scientists or poets would become comfortable with relativism. They too would realize that language and history are manipulatable and changeable, that stasis is illusion (228–29).

Burke accepts bureaucratization as necessary and helpful. It is, he holds, the way to democratize his own postmodern understanding. As he writes later in *Attitudes Toward History*, imagination is the "seed," bureaucratization the "fruit" (246). Clearly, Burke understands that it is crucial to imbed the imaginative in social texture. Burke, unlike the liberationist Freire, or even Romero, expends little effort on pedagogical concerns. Freire's entire career has been pedagogically directed. As a liberation rhetorician, he has committed himself not to the production of academic theory meant to be read only by a highly educated elite, but to the production of theory that could inform pedagogical practice in oppressive situations. His classic *Pedagogy of the Oppressed*, for instance, is as much a handbook for revolutionary teachers as it is anything else. Much of his career has been spent in the practical application of his theory. He has developed literacy education programs in different parts of the world and has influenced the development of such programs. Freire, above all, has wanted to institutionalize his liberation rhetoric. Likewise Romero, before his assassination, planned to write his next Pastoral Letter on popular education in the churches. As a liberation rhetorician, he saw the need to institutionalize what he wrote and preached.

Burke, in contrast, is a quintessential American postmodern theorist. He discusses texts, not institutional programs. However, his discussion of bureaucratization does reveal a postmodern impulse to institutionalize its insights. Burke is unknowingly struggling to articulate an educational program; he is trying to outline how it is that teachers can take his insights to students, how it is that more than a handful of people can become comfortable with imaginative activity and the implications such activity has for people's understandings of their own languages and histories. Burke is not content simply to wander through the texts of rhetoric, developing a fascinating theory about plurality, ambiguity, imagination, pain, and the religious. He also suggests that the readers of his texts should begin to consider to whom his theory can be taught, how it is that his theory can become part of the historical linguistic practices of Americans.

Planned incongruity, for instance, once institutionalized, would make all people masters of metaphor: they would no longer believe in unchangeable truth; they would realize that truth is open to change because language is (228–29). Planned incongruity would teach people to understand the plurality of language. Yet like Tracy and Wyschogrod, as I discussed their positions in chapter 1, Burke is not a relativist: the postmodern turn is the necessary way to move beyond the old society into a new, less painful one.

Planned incongruity, moreover, impinges upon history and the making of history. Due to habit, words come to be understood as unalterably linked to specific categories. Planned incongruity would have people move words around; people would learn to be able to attach words to one category and then another (308).[18] Planned incongruity is, Burke notes, irreverent: it defies all categories. As "metaphorical extension" (230) this technique is a process of conceptual punning (308). One makes links between words through the discernment of conceptual, rather than tonal, similarity, thereby defying given conventions.[19] One may, for instance, take the 'rights' that are claimed by a dominant group and apply them to an oppressed people. The dominant and oppressed groups may not be, for instance, the same color, but they may have other characteristics that one can conceptualize and thus use as a place to attach 'rights.'

Pain

Like Tracy and Wyschogrod, Burke looks to postmodern rhetoric for a way to move beyond the old society into a new one. Though 'planned incongruity' seeks to make people at home in a relative world, it doesn't suggest that people become so comfortable with relativism that directed change becomes impossible because people are educated to become content with everything. Rather, 'planned incongruity,' as one dimension of Burke's rhetoric, teaches people about the relativity so they learn that directed change is possible and that it can occur when language is used well.

Importantly, this reveals one way in which Burke differs from Richard Rorty, who offers what is perhaps currently the most well-known and influential example of American postmodern thought. Even though both Burke and Rorty highlight the place of the imaginative in rhetoric designed to counter pain, Rorty would not bureaucratize techniques such as planned incongruity. He argues, against Burke, that most of the population should not be taught that 'truth' is contingent, that one can create meaning by the reordering of words (87). To do so, argues Rorty, is to risk the destabilization of the entire society. Rorty would have only a few master the intricacies of language. Burke, ever the democrat, wants the populace at large to delve into the plurality of that which marks them as human.

The master of language, Burke argues, has the comic attitude and therefore meditates upon the bureaucratization of imagination (*Attitudes Toward History* 1955 Introduction). In so doing this person contains all:

bureaucracy and imagination, transcendental and material (167). Rather than an aestheticization and reduction of history, the comic attitude attempts to account for the heterogeneity of the social situation while not becoming crippled by it. The comic attitude is not incapacitated by guilt; it moves society toward a new incarnation (173).

The difficulty with this move, Burke notes, is the actuality and threat of war (344). Written in the chaotic years between the two World Wars, it is not insignificant that *Attitudes Toward History* ends with this:

> The important thing is to continue to search for a vocabulary that . . . could provide humility without humiliation. A comic vocabulary should be framed with this as its ideal. But a comic vocabulary of motives, we admit, cannot be attained insofar as people are at war, or living under the threat of war. Militarism makes naturally for the extremes of heroic euphemism, with corresponding dislocations of gauging. Yet even in war itself, much that happens falls within the category of peace. . . . And to the extent that war is not a mere act of physical risk, but draws upon the organization of peace, the area of comedy is kept intact. (344)

Burke hopes that the comic attitude, concerned with the material and transcendental, with bureaucratization and imagination, can subvert war to its own end. Aware of the heterogeneity of language and history (the comic attitude is humble), it nevertheless refuses to cower before war (it refuses humiliation).

As I will discuss in chapter 3, Merton shares Burke's desire to explore the meaning and importance of humility. Perhaps, finally, humility will become the mark of the postmodern. One who holds that language is plural and history is ambiguous has no grounds for arrogance. If one is arrogant, one is not postmodern. One must also wonder, then, what this implies for liberation rhetorics. Can libertion rhetoricians, so sure of particular languages and histories, ever be humble enough to listen seriously to the concerns of the other? Or are liberation rhetoricians bound to ignore the other in order to advance their own histories, their own languages?

With all due humility, the comic attitude looks within the organization of war to find the organization of peace.[20] This, I take it, accounts for Burke's analysis of the French, U.S., and Russian armies (282–84). All, he argues, have utopian visions of what it is to make war; all bureaucratize the utopian vision as they attempt to enact it. Thus, for instance, France's grandiose plans for World War I led to the trenches. Insofar as war-makers participate in this bureaucratizing process, one can find in wars that process that one finds everywhere. War is not a total other, a behemoth to fear, to avoid, to cringe in front of as it rages. Rather, it is to be studied, and through this study, to be subverted. War involves the same kind of object-oriented imagination that pervades all life. As Burke says in the lengthy quotation above, war has its heroic euphemisms (its visions of the soldier) and involves dislocations of gauging, that process of incongruity that conceptually puns words, supporting and creating euphemisms, across categories. For Burke, war can and should be countered by symbol-users at the level of symbols. In "The Rhetoric of Hitler's Battle," written about the same time as *Attitudes Toward History*, Burke studies *Mein Kampf* in order to find within it Hitler's vision and technique so people in the United States can uncover, make public, and challenge all "Hitlerite distortions" practiced by U.S. politicians (*Philosophy* 219). Like the talk of the language of war in *Attitudes Toward History*, Burke finds in Mein Kampf universal language, and he seeks to uncover it in order to make it ineffective.

Similarly, in "War, Response, and Contradiction," also written around the time of *Attitudes Toward History*, Burke proposes that one must understand the language of war in order to create one's own language so that the ends of war can be subverted. Wars, for Burke, are what we make of them (*Philosophy* 238). They, no less than anything else, are subject to the plurality of language and the ambiguity of history. Consider, for instance, his response to Archibald MacLeish's claim that a photodocumentary of World War I was dishonest and incomplete, manifesting "Marxian absolutism"; MacLeish suggests that he himself knows the 'true' war. Burke writes: "does he not himself grow absolute in assuming that the war possesses one definite, absolute character which must remain unchanged throughout history?" (238). Certainly, Burke finds even the horror of war muddied by human culture: it is not an event that transparently delivers sure meaning. Humans refract it through systems of representation, bound in cultures; hence, it is open to constant interpretation and reinterpretation.

Though Burke is critical of MacLeish's tendency toward absolutism, he employs MacLeish to make a point about how one might use representations of war to subvert cultures' tendencies to make war. "War, Response, and Contradiction" is a demonstration of the comic attitude specifically at work. Burke argues that antiwar material often works to the advantage of war. Here, Burke shows that he is clearly aware of the problem pain presents for rhetoric. While antiwar material may present "photographs of mutilated bodies" in order to show the horrors of war, this material may in fact affect young people in an unintended manner. Young men may be led to enlist because they may place the photographs within a web of analogical linkage that connects the horror of war and the imagery of heroism: the bloodier the mess, the more heroic the person who attempts to clean it. Moreover, a constant and tremendous barrage of carnage may lead to a "psychological callus" (240), which prepares men for the battlefield. Instead of this constant and unremitting barrage, Burke suggests that one mix images and visions of hardness and tenderness, carnage and courage, basing his argument upon the work of MacLeish. Tenderness and courage warm one, remind one of the beautiful possibilities of human being (the imaginative vision—the object). Counterpointed by carnage and hardness (the imaginative technique), such work would remind one of what the "way of culture-through-war" really involves (240).

One may wonder whether or not such a response to the possibility and reality of war is adequate, since it risks being an aestheticization of that which causes pain on a massive level. It is adequate, at least for rhetoricians as rhetoricians. Burke is suggesting that rhetoricians subvert the culture of war by using the skill they have, by engaging in one of the strategies that war itself uses: rhetoric. As Lentricchia argues regarding Burke's speech to the American Writers' Congress, Burke thinks that rhetoricians should use rhetoric to engage in social action, since rhetoric is their expertise (26). Without doubt, this concern for how the literary intellectual should act is why Burke ends "War, Response, and Contradiction" with a discussion of writing style. As opposed to what he calls the style of "business Christianity," which is rational and nonconfrontational, Burke endorses the style of "poetic Christianity," which highlights the contradictory, such as salvation through a suffering God. Burke recognizes that Christianity is plural and ambiguous: it offers at least two styles. He finds in one, poetic Christianity, an example of the comic attitude that embodies contradictions (the material and transcendent, the bureaucratic and imaginative, God and suffering) in an attempt to save. Such a style, it seems for Burke, resists the creation of easy and sure foundations upon which one can make decisions. God is wholly royal and wholly slavish, wholly transcendent and wholly immanent, both beyond death and subject to it. The God of poetic Christianity, hence the style of poetic Christianity, is a dialectic that calls into question any resolution. Though one cannot easily label Burke as a Christian rhetorician, Burke does link his own project to that of a counter-Christianity. As will become evident in the following chapters, this links Burke to Merton, Freire, and Romero.

While *Attitudes Toward History* obliquely refers to actual and potential pain, requiring one to look outside the book in order to help elucidate its point, Burke's *A Rhetoric of Motives* begins with and is punctuated by the naming of pain.[21] In this book Burke locates the origin of rhetoric in the lapsarian world of Babel (23). Note the two religious metaphors, the fall and Babel, Burke uses in order to locate the place of rhetoric. No doubt, their dimensions are many; I would like, however, to concentrate on three.

The fall, Genesis reveals, means that humans no longer have the close relationship with God that they once had. For disobeying God, humans are cast out of the garden wherein they walked naked with God. The fall also means strife and pain. Women will be pained by childbirth, men by toil. Humans will hurt each other as Cain does Abel. Babel indicates the shattering of communication between people. For attempting to build a tower to God, humans were scattered into various language groups, beginning, the metaphor tells us, the problem of communication among humans: they can't speak to each other. *A Rhetoric of Motives*, working with pain and imagination, can be read as a response to the fall and to Babel. Burke wants to alleviate pain and strife by moving people to a rhetoric informed by process-oriented imagination.

The world, as Burke understands it, is marked by pain. Accordingly, *A Rhetoric of Motives* is as well. The third sentence of the introduction, which discusses the first part of the book, reads: "Since these texts involve an imagery of killing (as a typical text for today should) we note how, behind the surface, lies a quite different realm that has little to do with such motives" (xiii). This sentence contains three elements that impel elucidation. First, the texts to which the sentence refers, poetry by Milton, Arnold, and Coleridge, are dominated by violence and death imagery; Burke uses the first fifteen pages of the book to discuss the import of the words about pain that fill the poetry. Second, Burke claims that beneath the imagery of killing is another motive that has little to do with killing. While Burke acknowledges that it is important to attend to the language of pain for what it says about pain (17, 19–20), he continues the comic search. Third, he seeks within the language of pain a process common to all language so that he can subvert the language that heroicizes the infliction and suffering of pain. The sentence cryptically, parenthetically, and imperatively notes that "a typical text for today should" include words about pain. Its mystery is perhaps somewhat removed when one remembers what Lentricchia teaches about Burke: one must use the language of the culture if one is to influence it. Hence, as Lentricchia tells us, Burke suggested 'the people' rather than 'the worker' because it better matched the discourse of the United States. Similarly, it seems Burke is suggesting that texts today should involve imagery of killing because one lives among a people who kill, are killed, and talk about both. Burke, moving away from the obliqueness of *Attitudes Toward History* (perhaps as a result of having lived through two World Wars), explicitly sets *A Rhetoric of Motives* within the environment of pain: the environment of the fall.

Following his discussion of Milton, Coleridge, and Arnold, and an explanation why rhetoric is concerned with "identification" and "division" (to which I will turn below in my discussion of Babel), Burke claims that his book deals with people who are at odds with one another. This state, he notes, too often leads to the perversion of cooperative peace: war (22). Ironically, war requires strategies of cooperation in order to destroy communities. War can happen only if people devote their community-making skills to the end of war: the destruction of community (22). War, then, is understood by Burke as central to the concerns of rhetoric: rhetoric studies the dialectical process that often leads to war. As with his work in *Attitudes Toward History*, Burke maintains that war is not something other, a devil from without that usurps the process of culture-making. The possibility of making war, of "destruction," of "disease," of a "culminating blast" (all words that indicate bodies in pain—bodies are destroyed; disease is that which ruins healthy bodies; blasts tear, explode, and implode bodies) is intrinsic to the human condition.

In discussing the conflicts between those concerns that would motivate humans (here God and science), Burke, through a character named "Preen," maintains that science is closely linked with militarism (26). Militarism, not incidentally, links itself onto many things. Preen's friend "Prone" notes that militarism was present even in Biblical times and makes "himself" present everywhere unless he is explicitly ruled out (26). Moving out of the Preen and Prone characters, Burke reintroduces his 'own' voice and claims that rhetoricians (and moralists), insofar as they are concerned with discovering that with which people would identify (26), attempt to rule out the linkages militarism attempts to make (26). Again hinting at his pedagogical concerns, Burke claims that after World War II American science educators have too often identified with militarism because much of scientific budgets are funded by the military. Burke cautions that such identification could warp science education. Rather than promoting science for science's sake, these scientists dangerously promote science as a means to achieve the purposes of war (27).

War would serve as the guiding principle because, as Burke sees it, the scientists have "identified" with the military and have made the concerns of the military their motivation. Burke wants to keep science, but also wants to cut its link with militarism because Burke identifies with another source, another motive that guides him. This marks another dimension of the fall and Babel. People are guided by different 'gods' and different languages that express these gods: they have different pieties. At the point that Burke and the scientists conflict with each other, rhetoric enters. Burke and the scientists share a concern: science and science education. Thus they identify with each other. Yet their identification is not complete. They are divided over the motivating piety of science. If they did not identify with each other, there would be no communication and thus no need for rhetoric. If they completely identified with each other, there would be no conflict and thus no need for rhetoric. Where there is simultaneous identification and division, rhetoric comes into play (25).

As Burke understands it, Eden was a time of complete identification (138). All humans completely identified with the same source: God.

There was no conflict because there was no conflicting source, no conflicting motivations, giving rise to conflicting languages. Yet this is a myth. As soon as humans have a word *identification* they also have its negative *division*; there never was, nor is there, a state of pure identification. Humans simultaneously are identified and divided. As Burke suggests, even what seems to be a whole, the sea, is divided (139). The "sea" refers to another myth Burke tells to explain the myth of Eden (137–40). The point is this: any unifying term with which we would identify necessarily implies division. Insofar as a term unifies, it implies division; there must be a division to unify. Hence, there is no time without strife, without rhetoric, which is that which studies identification and division. For Burke humans are in a state of division and identification. Human life is marked by dialectic.

Humans, Burke claims, have two options when they attempt to deal with the dialectic; intimations of these options can be found throughout *A Rhetoric of Motives*. The first option, Burke tells us, is that the participants in the dialectic, in the divided world following the fall, can choose Babel. They are confronted with their current situation (which is marked in this discussion by property division, 139), and choose either to "liquidate" the status quo by attempting to return to Eden, or to accept the status quo of division. This state of choice and, I take it, the choice to accept the division, is Babel; the fall is marked by communicative strife (139). This, without doubt, is the relativism of postmodernism rejected by Wyschogrod, Tracy, and other postmoderns. Burke, as well, rejects it. He doesn't believe that humans are forever caught in a dialectic that makes war inevitable. At one level, he holds that the dialectic is resolvable without a return to mythic Eden: the source is not necessary to halt the seeming inevitability of war. Yet I will argue below that he also seeks a final return as a way to resolve conflict. His assessment of his own work regarding the inevitability and inevitable justifiability of war based on this inevitability is correct as well.

For instance, in order to deny the inevitability and inevitable justification of war based on myths of this inevitability, Burke rejects scapegoating. He admits its attraction, maintaining that the scapegoat is the perfect model: it is an object of both identification and division (140). It allows the dialectical partners to use each other as "*katharma*" (141). Burke himself has been attracted by the figure of the scapegoat throughout his work.[23] But he finally rejects it in *A Rhetoric of Motives* because it keeps the members of the dialectic apart; they simply pass the dialectic off onto another form and thus never confront it in themselves (141). The scapegoat, as rhetorical practice, simply promotes and justifies division.

Moreover, scapegoating conflicts with Burke's desire, despite his caution, to have humans return to their source. Consider, for instance, his desire to unify Marxists and those whom they criticize as people beholden to ideologies. While they may seem to be at irreconcilable odds, they actually have an organic relationship. They are like the "stomach and liver of a healthy organism" (137). Burke rejects the status quo of division, of Babel; he rejects the ongoing dialectic of the scapegoat. He suggests that these opponents are in fact, whether they know it or not, members of the same organism. This organism, he goes on to say, is guided by "the level of *principles*," which is the level of ideas (137). Despite differences that play themselves out in "the Scramble, the Wrangle of the Market Place, the flurries and flare-ups of the Human Barnyard" (23), one can find that the seemingly endless division "can add up to a transcending of itself. In ways of its own it can move from the factional to the universal" (23). The universal is/are the principle(s)/idea(s) that underlie(s) and guide(s) all languages. It is this universal Burke seeks in *A Rhetoric of Motives* and finds in the process-oriented imagination.[24]

In addition to the levels of reproductive and object-oriented (productive) imagination, Burke posits that there is another realm connected to object-oriented imagination and that if one attends to the object-oriented, one can discern it: all produced objects are guided by "organizational principles" that are translatable into the word *ideas* (*Rhetoric of Motives* 86). What I am calling "process-oriented imagination" seems not to be imagination at all but in fact something beyond imagination. Yet Burke also says that poetic imagination shares this realm of idea with reason. It is not a realm of image, or raw sensation, but a realm that guides the productive formation of raw sensation into poetic images. It is neither visible nor tangible (86): it is process. While it seems to be separate from imagination, imagination shares it as a realm with reason, hence making it part of imagination. Burke chooses the word *titles* (synonymous with "identifications") to indicate this realm (86).

He notes that "titles" and "identifications" correspond to Aristotle's topics, and "shift so easily and imperceptibly between ideas and images that you wonder how the two realms could ever come to be at odds" (86). It is this sense of the imaginative, of the process-oriented imagination, that Burke carefully, albeit in a note, defines in "A Dramatistic View of the Origins of Language and Postscripts on the Negative." He writes that this connection, which is discernible between idea and imagination, brought out by reflection upon the negative that is inherent to language, leads one to realize that there is a dimension of imagination that means "the ability even to transcend the world of image and sensation entirely" (*Language* 460). This dimension of process-oriented imagination is, for Burke, that to which all language points; it is that "master purpose" that unifies heterogeneous rhetoric; it is what can never be fully spoken, hence always defying homogeneous, static, conceptualization. It is, finally, the mark of what could be called "postmodern mystical rhetoric" that seeks to adjudicate the barnyard squabbles that both lead to and support war.

The Religious

Burke's hierarchy of language, which all language exhibits, is an example of mystic ascent as *via negativa* (*Rhetoric of Motives* 183–200).[25] Insofar as the steps of the hierarchy are dialectical, the way to the ultimate is negative: the steps constantly cancel each other. Whatever is produced is necessarily tentative. Thus, the objects of imagination are subordinate to the process itself; one looks beyond their rising and falling to that which makes them rise and fall. What Burke calls the "ultimate order" both encompasses the steps that led to it (positive and dialectical) and surpasses them in such a way that it negates itself (189). Hence, the ultimate is distilled negativity: it is what isn't (311).

Again, Burke refuses Marxist dialectic and the dialectic of the scapegoat because both fail to recognize that all rhetoric is informed by a common hierarchic movement that can ultimately resolve the ongoing dialectics. All language, Burke argues, can be understood to be involved in a process of identification. Such an understanding, he maintains, allows the rhetorician who wants to counter pain to do so. The rhetorician, following *Attitudes Toward History*, can find this process within even movies that glorify war. Through the miracles of movies, by the time a young man is fifteen, Burke holds, "he has 'witnessed' more violence than most soldiers or gunmen experience in a lifetime" (*Rhetoric of Motives* 18). "Nor should we forget," Burke continues, "the possible bad effect of the many devices whereby such brutality is made 'virtuous,' through dramatic pretexts that justify it in terms of retaliation and righteous indignation" (18). Such images provide the youth with a vocabulary of self-description that easily leads him to live a life not averse to causing pain: the youth identifies with the images the movies provide.

Moreover, Burke maintains, certain critical attitudes accept this justified brutality as the primary motive of human existence. Not only does the youth identify with the brutality, describing himself as a son of the men who kill glorifyingly; speculators support such self-identification. Revenge and destruction are upheld as primary impulses (18). While Burke admits that rhetoric is involved in conflict, that it is "*par excellence* the region of the Scramble, of insult and injury, bickering, squabbling, malice and the lie, cloaked malice and the subsidized lie," he holds that one should not commit the synecdochal fallacy and argue that this part of rhetoric defines rhetoric. It also includes persuasion based on sacrifice and love (19). In all its persuasive dimensions, though, rhetoric involves, above and below all, the process of identification. The rhetoric of killing and the rhetoric of love are both about transformation and therefore identification (20). To kill is to transform a thing that has been identified as a particular substance that needs to be killed. The same is true of loving: love transforms a thing that has been named (20).

As I have argued above, Burke is not content merely to name the dialectic of the opposing identities; he rejects the scapegoat paradigm because it leads to endless conflict. Certainly, Burke recognizes that the dialectical opponents—Marxists and capitalists—have no desire to participate with him in the search for the adjudicatory. They refuse to admit that they share traits that could serve as a basis for identification and thus adjudication. Instead, they each claim that the other is the always the other and promote the use of scapegoats (141). Burke, however, remains undaunted by the intransigency of the partners. He refuses to accept their love of war and looks into both to find the common. Those who accept the claims of the dialectical partners engage in "a merely 'dialectical' confronting of parliamentary conflict," which "would leave the competing voices in a jangling relation with one another" (187). Burke, for his part, promotes an " 'ultimate' treatment" of conflict that arranges the competing voices so that one can discern what it is that unifies them. This allows one to promote healing (187).[26]

One potential problem emerges even with an ultimate treatment. The hierarchy can be made static, can be used to unjustly justify the privileges of particular social orders. Burke writes:

> Though *hierarchy* is exclusive, the *principle* of hierarchy is not: all ranks can 'share in it alike.' But: it includes the entelechical tendency, the treatment of the 'top' or 'culminating' stage as the 'image' that best represents the entire 'idea.' This leads to 'mystifications' that cloak the state of division, since the 'universal' principle of the hierarchy also happens to be the principle by which the most distinguished rank enjoys, in the realm of worldly property, its special privileges. (141)

Though some may treat dialectic opposition in an ultimate manner, they use the ultimate vocabulary they have found to make claims concerning the nature of the world, a nature that happens to support their own place at the top of the social order. What they have forgotten is that ultimate terms themselves reveal that they are not ultimate. As Burke argues, the term *identification* implies division. If one claims to identify with another, one can do so only because one and the other are divided. "Identification," Burke writes, "is compensatory to division" (22). Certainly, Lyotard's criticism of the Communist Party's use of the word *worker* could be understood in this regard: as an ultimate term it necessarily reveals the divisions it attempts to unify. The Party mystifies the world of the worker when it claims that its ultimate term is without division.

Furthermore, through its marking of the word *universal*, one finds in the extended quotation above Burke's understanding that there is no universal hierarchy. The marking is a mark of sarcasm, of disdain. Burke argues that while there is hierarchy in language, there is no universal hierarchy. The proper hierarchy that can adjudicate competing claims is situation dependent: it will work only if it is proper to a particular time and space (279). Those who mystify the ultimate order in an attempt to reify their own social position have forgotten, or don't realize, that history is ambiguous: the ultimate terms that justify social structure depend upon conditions peculiar to specific locales, particular times.

However, although Burke is cautious about ultimate treatments of competing rhetorics, well-aware as a postmodern of the plurality of language and ambiguity of history, he nonetheless wants to find an ultimate realm that is universal (276). Consider again Burke's argument concerning the process of identification that underlies even the imagery of killing: "the imagery of slaying is a special case of transformation, and transformation involves the ideas and imagery of *identification*" (20). The three crucial words are "ideas," the second use of "imagery," and "identification." The second use of "imagery" is more crucial than the first because the first is that imagery of object-oriented (or for Burke, reproductive) imagination. The artists—in this case Milton, Coleridge, and Arnold—envision death and make it public through the use of imagery. The second use of "imagery" belongs to the dimension of process-oriented imagination: Burke couples it with "ideas," which, as I have shown above, is in the realm of the No, of negativity. Insofar as "identification" is placed into triadic relationship with "ideas" and the second use of "imagery" it too participates in the negativity, in the dimension of process-oriented imagination. Again consider: Burke argues that the realm of ideas is not at odds with the realm of images and that he uses the words "titles," "topics," and "identifications" to name this realm. Imagery of the object-oriented imagination, be it of killing or love, Burke reveals, points to process-oriented imagination: the dimension of idea, the second use of imagery, the realm of identification, the place of No.

Burke also seems to call this place the realm of "pure persuasion," which is "the essence of language" (252). Pure persuasion is the "Title of Titles" (252), Burke notes near the end of A *Rhetoric of Motives*, which, in line with Burke's postmodern ethos, "in the absolute sense exists nowhere" (269). An understanding of pure persuasion would move humans, Burke hopes, beyond grounding themselves in a desire to best others to grounding themselves "in a *form*, in the persuasiveness of the hierarchic order itself. And considered dialectically, prayer, as pure beseechment, would be addressed not to an *object* . . . but to the *hierarchic principle itself*, where the answer is implicit in the address" (276).

Another way to discern this point in Burke is to consider his elucidation of the 'mythic image.' One moves, Burke claims, from sensory images to ideas, as I argued above. With *"the dialectical critique of ideas"* one can move to the 'mythic image' through ideas. However, the 'mythic image' is not the end of the process; it simply represents the "ultimate universal ground" that defies representation (200–203). This universal ground is the realm of pure persuasion. What Burke seems to say here is that this ground is beyond idea insofar as it is represented by the 'mythic image' that is beyond idea. Yet pure persuasion is best understood as being 'beyond' both mythic image and idea.

Pure persuasion is not *an* identification, but *the* identification, not *a* title, but *the* title, not *an* idea, but *the* idea that can move humans beyond war. Burke prays at the end of *A Rhetoric of Motives*:

> let us observe, all about us, forever goading us, though it be in fragments, the motive that attains its ultimate identification in the thought, not of the universal holocaust, but of the universal order—as with the rhetorical and dialectic symmetry of the Aristotelian metaphysics, whereby all classes of beings are hierarchically arranged in a chain or ladder or pyramid of mounting worth, each kind striving towards the *perfection* of its kind and so towards the kind next above it, while the strivings of the entire series head in God as the beloved cynosure and sinecure, the end of all desire. (333)

In this prayer Burke beseeches humans to understand that the motive that informs all that humans do attains its identification in the hierarchical order, the principle of which is pure persuasion. This leads to the cessation of desire, away from the search for advantage against others.[27] 'God,' clearly, is not the God of traditional Christianity. Rather, God is the principle of persuasion, of hierarchy, of the *process* of identification that informs all language. As Burke writes in *The Rhetoric of Religion*, his God is the "Title of Titles" toward which the process of entitlement proceeds (22–27). Entitlement, in *The Rhetoric of Religion*, is a linguistic process of generalization and abstraction that moves away from sense impressions to a Title of Titles that encompasses all stages that lead to it. It is the same process Burke describes in *A Rhetoric of Motives* as the ultimate treatment. Taken to its full extension, entitlement, as technique, leads to the Title of Titles, which is purely negative: all the positive materiality is left in the particular senses and images from which one moves. God is the Title of Titles is the hierarchical principle is pure persuasion is idea is process-oriented imagination. Burke provides his readers with this process-oriented God who frames rhetoric in a postmodern age so that the Scramble will lead not to the pain of the universal holocaust but to peace. Whether or not this peace is beyond all understanding, a figment of Burke's imagination, remains to be seen. That is, if it can be seen at all.

3

'Poetic Rhetoric and Baffling Illogic': Merton's The Geography of Lograire

There are too many names to know, too many faces, too many stories. And the conclusion is inescapable: If they don't matter to me, these flickering images of mobs and war casualties and starving masses, can I matter to them?

—Michael Dorris and Louise Erdrich,
The Crown of Columbus

To be postmodern is daunting, nearly overwhelming. One can no longer simply recite one's own story, winter night after icy winter night, evoking the names and remembering the faces of one's own lineage in order to rest comfortably, sleep contentedly. One can't because the faces, the names, and the stories of others demand remembrance, evocation, recitation. Once one recognizes and accepts that one's language is not *the* language, that one's history is but one history, and that as a historical being one participates in the oppression of others, one may not sleep at all. One may pace through the night in a painful and imaginative attempt to speak the new epoch. Or, like the voice of my epigraph, a character in Dorris' and Eridrich's novel, one may simply despair, overwhelmed by the dense tangle of languages, histories, and pains that imagistically demand that one enter into postmodernity (*Crown of Columbus* 53).

The early Thomas Merton seems to have been overwhelmed and retreated from it. Unlike his contemporary, Kenneth Burke, Merton turned away from the chaos of a world on the verge of its second global war and entered Gethsemane, a Trappist monastery in Kentucky. While both Burke and Merton acknowledged and analyzed, for instance, the Nazi threat—Burke in his analysis of *Mein Kampf*, Merton in his decidedly bad novel *My Argument with the Gestapo*—Merton retreated from that tumultuous time while Burke embraced it.

Merton's retreat, however, seems to have served a strategic purpose. It seems to have been a retreat in the contemplative and not the military sense. For almost twenty years, the Columbia-educated Merton gathered himself under the rigorous disciplined silence of monastic Catholicism in order to emerge, in the late 1950s, as a postmodern par excellence, a Trappist priest who engaged Marcuse, Camus, Bonhoeffer, Pasternak, Joyce, Dylan, Shakers, Buddhists, Jews, and myriad others in conversation. This was the Merton who spoke out against the Vietnam War and the nuclear arms race. This was the Merton who reached out to gather in the world in all of its beauty and deformity.

This Merton reached his zenith in his posthumously published, booklength poem, *The Geography of Lograire* (hereafter *Geography*).[1] This poem explores the globe of the postmodern epoch, delving synchronically and diachronically into Amerindian, Muslim, African, and European time and space, among others.[2] *Geography* accepts, and revels in, the plurality of language and the ambiguity of history, and in so doing embraces the pained mobs, the war casualties, the starving masses.

In "From Pilgrimage to Crusade," an essay composed before *Geography*, Merton provides a gloss to this wandering poem. He writes: "Man instinctively regards himself as a wanderer and wayfarer, and it is second nature for him to go on pilgrimage in search of a privileged and holy place, a center and source of indefectible life" (*Mystics* 91).[3] Yet Merton writes, contemporary Western humans know that if Eden ever existed, it has been lost. Humans, then, are caught in a bind: they must go on pilgrimage, in search of the holy place, but they realize that this holy place has suffered violence and finally does not exist. The act of pilgrimage itself is an act of hopeful imagination. One seeks what one envisions even though one knows that the envisioned place is not to be found. Merton, like Burke, recognizes the troublesome nature of utopia. Humans have an impulse toward it, even a need for it. Hence, they imagine it and seek it. Yet Merton argues, utopia does not exist. Humans may seek it, may need it, may actively imagine it, but they will never reach it. Still, Merton holds, the search for it must and will continue.

As a way to understand the nature of this search Merton submits 'pilgrimage' to a genealogical analysis much like his fellow postmodern

Burke treated the word *rights*, as I discussed in chapter 2.[4] The analysis reveals that while 'pilgrimage' seems to be an inevitable facet of human being, one can never be certain what 'pilgrimage' is. Its meaning depends on the people who use it, on that to which it refers. At first referring to sacred journeys taken "to the center from which the whole Christian world was charged with the true presence of the resurrection and glory of the Savior" (94), after the fall of Rome the nature and role of 'pilgrimage' changed as the Middle East became inaccessible to European Christians. Irish monks turned it into a special form of spiritual quest (98–99); criminal outcasts were sent on 'pilgrimage,' doomed to wander Europe (100–101); the Inquisition used pilgrimage to punish violators of church order (101); the first crusade was a pilgrimage of violence (102); and the settlers of North America were, it must be remembered, 'pilgrims' (108). Merton's genealogical analysis demonstrates that the word *pilgrimage* is inconstant. Its meaning shifts with changes in motivations, participants, and destinations. To the early Christians, to make pilgrimage was to return to Christ in Jerusalem; to the crusaders it was to recapture Christ by destroying the infidels and retaking the Holy Land; to the pilgrims it was to find Christ in the new world.

Such genealogical analysis is critically important for postmodern rhetoricians in all their guises. It historicizes the postmodern recognition of the plurality of language. Language isn't plural for syntactic/semantic reasons alone. Language is also plural because it is open to historical change and manipulation. One group's understanding of a word will not be the same as another's. The implications of this for the rhetorician who teaches, for instance, cannot be underestimated. The religion scholar/rhetorician may want to organize a study of American religious thought around the changing understandings of the word *Christ*. This teacher could pose a question like this: How have groups used the word similarly? differently? While this strategy may seem commonplace, it isn't if the focus is placed on the dynamic of the word. To the students, Christ as a grouping of letters seems to have stability as a phonic and graphic trace, but it is really unstable; the letters attract and repel meanings constantly.

Liberation rhetoricians like Freire and Romero would agree with Merton to an extent. They too, as I will discuss in the following chapters, use genealogical analysis. Romero, for instance, argues that the Salvadoran oppressors misuse the word *Christ* and that its best meaning is found among the poor. However, while Merton and Burke would claim that words always are open to change and thus subject to constant genealogical analysis, liberation rhetoricians would end the play of words. Freire, for example, understands 'utopia' in a very specific way: it is an egalitarian classless society comprised by workers. For Freire, 'utopia' has conflicting definitions, but he also believes that his own definition ends the conflict.

Even for Merton, that lover of the play of words, 'pilgrimage,' at least since the first crusade, has had one stable facet: it is implicated in the oppression of those considered 'other.' Meant to expiate the violent sins of the pilgrims, the crusades ironically encouraged, and thus made holy, violence against others who were thought to be heathens. This transformation of pilgrimage brought about by the crusades carried itself into the New World where pilgrims and conquistadores alike violently and oppressively sought a holy land (107–10).

The European encounter with the New World, Merton contends, is marked by irony. Europeans simultaneously sought the source of life and ransacked this source. Merton puts it best: "the European white man set foot on the shores of America with the conflicting feelings of an Adam newly restored to paradise and of a Crusader about to scale the walls of Acre" (109). This latter feeling, which led to the pillage of the New World, reveals for Merton both the ambiguity of history and the illusory nature of the source of life. Pilgrimages to the source have led to a desecration of that which is seen to be the source because it is seen to be the other. While "paradise," Merton notes, symbolizes the freedom and creativity of the source of life, the historical encounter with places thought to be paradise has only led to the defilement of the place and the people in the place, thereby destroying the very possibility of a "source."

Though by the end of the essay Merton recognizes the problem with and of pilgrimage, he doesn't alter the position with which he began the essay. "From Pilgrimage to Crusade" ends with a call to a new pilgrimage. He writes: "Our task is to learn that if we can voyage to the ends of the earth and there find *ourselves* in the aborigine who most differs from ourselves, we will have made a fruitful pilgrimage" (112).

The destination is no longer a holy place. but an often despised person. The person is the other who suffered from the swords and guns of the pilgrim crusader and the crusading pilgrim. In this era, which Merton actually once named the "postmodern" (Introduction 1), he calls for a postmodern pilgrimage to the other, to the names, faces, and stories of the other. *Geography* is this pilgrimage.[5]

This idea of a pilgrimage to the other both separates and unifies postmodern and liberation rhetoricians. It unifies them because both encourage encounters with the 'other.' For postmoderns, it is all others. Since no group is privileged, all need to be visited. For some liberation rhetoricians, the same is true. Many Americans, for instance, have concerned themselves with the plight of Salvadorans and Guatemalans; members of *El Norte* reach out to the others of two Central American countries. Yet finally, liberation rhetoricians wish to close the gap between self and other; they wish to identify themselves with the oppressed. Thus Freire, a Brazilian, identifies himself with the oppressed of Guinea-Bissau or of the African-American ghettoes. The true postmodern, however, always keeps the separation between self and other in place simply because there is no call for identification. Postmoderns see no need to join a specific group in order to elevate the group, or themselves, in the face of oppression. Thus *Geography* ends with a continuing pilgrimage. Everything is always other for Merton: he is never home; he is always called to wander.

Missing from Merton's essay on pilgrimage, though wholly consonant with its theme, is Merton's fascination with and study of Zen Buddhism. It was a place of the other to which Merton made a long and deep trip. Zen was integral to the postmodern pilgrim Merton and to *Geography* as the preeminent mark of this man. Without doubt, the best exploration thus far of the place of Zen in Merton's life is Anne Carr's.[6] She argues that Merton sought in Zen a tradition that might "cast light on the psychology and experience of self-emptying which unites the Christian with 'Christ in His kenosis' " (*Search for Wisdom and Spirit* 79). While Carr does not deal with Merton's poetry, her insight into his other work serves his poetry. *Geography* manifests this move Merton made to Zen: it empties itself of sure claims about language and history, but it doesn't stop there."[7] Once emptied, it enfleshes itself with the dialectic of pain and imagination found throughout time and across all space.

Consequently, *Geography* stands as rhetoric. It searches for the suffering other with the aid of another religious tradition that leads the poem through the object-oriented imagination into the realm of the process-oriented.

The Plurality of Language

Understood from a postmodern vantage, language is both particular to varying communities and marked by a split between the signifier and that which is signified. It could be said, then, that language is plural externally and internally, though one shouldn't make too much of this distinction; the external and internal depend upon one another. *Geography* inquires into these dimensions of language, and this inquiry can be understood as influenced by Merton's study of Zen Buddhism.

Merton makes available at least fifty-one different voices in *Geography*, if one counts the appearances by books and advertisements as one voice each. In order, they are: the narrator (a voice that weaves in and out); the Thonga (19); the Hottentots (20); African Missionaries (21); a Zulu (22); Bishop Landa (26); advertisements (e.g., 28); Chilam Balam (31); the Bible (38); police rhetoric (38); a building (44); famous John (48); Sugar Hill (48); Boston (58); Jesus (60); Niggers (60); William Blake (61); Ranters, pamphlets, Puritan lawyers, the English Parliament (63–68); James Law (69); Ibn Battuta (82); a devout Muslim Turk (83); a Muslim heretic and his disciples (84); a governor (84); a Sultan (85); perhaps another Sultan (87); Malinowski (89); a Filipino (89); MacGregor (91); a native (92); a missionary (93); a German Priest (94); the news (99); Kaum (101); John (105); Neloaig (106); Isac (107); a report (108); Joe (110); a sexy ventriloquist (129); American Horse Fast Thunder Spotted Horse (131); Wodziwob (132); Dr. George (134); the "Cornwallis Gazette" (135); a Superintendent (136); John Watchino (136); and Bogus Tom (137).

Significantly, no voice is dominant, including the voice of the narrator. It simply weaves in and out of the other voices, making no preeminent claim for itself. I will return to this assertion when I discuss the dimensions of historical ambiguity recognized by *Geography*. Merton, if the narrator's voice belongs to him, has fully thrown himself into what Burke calls the "scramble of the barnyard," and has done so on a global scale. If Burke is the postmodern theorist of the heterogeneity of human voices in the public realm, then Merton is the postmodern practitioner. The barnyard is huge and Merton wants to let every chicken and rooster speak.

Geography divides the scramble into four spatial sections, in this order: "South," "North," "East," and "West." One might be tempted to surmise that the spatial form of the poem looks suspiciously closed, since it begins with the geography in which Merton lives (Kentucky, in the South), and ends with the West (again Merton's own space; this section is entirely about the United States). It could be argued that Merton, despite his attempt to let the other speak, encloses the other within the boundaries of his own life: "North" and "East" are sandwiched between Merton's Kentucky with which "South" opens and Merton's United States with which "West," and the entire poem, ends.

"West," however, is presented as a geography of failure. Its voices have no claim to dominance; they are simply part of the scramble.[8] "West," and *Geography*, ends with this:

> 31. After a while the dreaming stopped and the Dream
> Dance turned into a Feather Dance. It was just a fun
> dance. It was mostly a white man's show. (137)

The dream dance was, as many critics note, a variant of the ghost dance, which arose among certain native tribes as a messianic movement promising the demise of white people and the ascendancy of the tribes (*Geography* 152, note 130). It eventually lost its revolutionary fervor and transformed itself into an entertainment spectacle (*Geography* 153, note 131). The revolutionary language of a community that stood as other to Merton's own arose and fell, losing its potential to challenge the dominant language and to become dominant itself.

The failure of the geography of "West" is not an aberration; all others fail as well.[9] Consider, for instance, the ending of "East" (116), which concludes Merton's presentation of the cargo cult phenomenon. The cults, Merton reports, involve "symbolic activity" of Melanesian natives who hope to put themselves in touch "with the source of kago, thereby bringing about a situation in which kago would come for [them] and not just for the white man" ("Cargo Cults of the South Pacific" 82).

"Kago" is the cargo of Western goods which European colonizers brought with them when they settled among the Melanesian peoples. The ending of "East" is representative of cargo cult activity; it is a song calling upon "Ghost wind" to bring "Whiteman Times." These "Times" include not only cigarettes and "Whiteman smoke" but "a new white skin." Significant is the fact that the petition goes unanswered: "East" ends and the petition flows into both the silence of the blank space that follows it and into "West," which in turn ends with the failure of a language. All of the cargo activities invented by the Melanesians, variations on a theme within a language community, fail to deliver the desired cargo. Some preach violence (canto IX, 113), others sexual activity (canto VI, 100–101). There are many languages; there is no one language that completely subsumes the others.

One of the most fascinating, and significant, manifestations of this occurs at the end of the first canto in "North" called "Queen's Tunnel." This canto is perhaps the wildest and most impenetrable in the poem; as Merton says with understatement: "This meditation is surrealistic" (*Geography* 2). It ends with Christ going south and thus hints at the poem's linkage of language and pain. The white, northern Christ visits the oppressed, black South, echoing Burke's discussion about race relations in the United States. Whereas Burke analyzed racial dynamics through a discussion of Shakespeare's Shylock from *The Merchant of Venice* and Bigger from Richard Wright's *Native Son*, Merton turns to his imagined scene. He writes:

> 50. So Christ went down to stay with them Niggers and took his place with them at the table. He said to them, 'It is very simple much simpler than you imagine.' They replied, 'You have become a white man and it is not so simple at all.' "
> (60)

From where did Christ come down? Most obviously, he came from the North. If this is so, Christ perhaps then is tinged with the color of the reconstructionist carpetbagger who arrived in the South following the Civil War in order to save the people. Or perhaps Christ wears the color of the northern liberal who went south in the 1960s to help liberate the former slaves. In any case, he is not particularly welcome. What he has to say, his very language, is identified by the "Niggers" as white: Christ, a member of another language community, simply doesn't understand their plight.[10] Christ's language is not as-cendant. His is simply one voice and not a particularly insightful voice at that.

This conflict between Christ and African Americans takes on another dimension if the area from which Christ came down is not north, but heaven. Christ, the incarnate Word of God, is now understood by the "Nigger" linguistic community to be a parochial word, not a univer-sal savior who can deliver them from oppression. Moreover, as a white-man word, Christ attempts to simplify the complexity of the surrealistic situation presented in what precedes his statement. Stanza 48 of the first canto of "North" reveals that "Geography is in trouble all over Lograire. Rape of / maps by military arm" (60). Various clergy and police are involved in urban racial problems, each on different sides. Also alluded to is the power of the military and its incursions into various countries. Finally, all of the sides are commended by institutional religion: "All the fractions are in / jail being complimented by sermons" (60). Rather than recognizing this chaos in which God and God's messengers approve of all parties, even if they oppose each other, Christ preaches a simplicity that the "Niggers" understand to be dishonest.

Significantly, *Geography* offers nothing to dispute their claim: the "Niggers" are given the final word of the first canto of "North." After they deny the universality of the incarnate Word, *Geography* moves on to the second canto of "North," which in no explicit way attempts to answer the charge of the "Niggers": " 'There is a grain of sand in Lambeth which Satan cannot / find' " (61). Jesus is reduced to a simplicity-preaching member of a parochial language community who denies the complexity of the social situation. If there is a balm in Gilead, it doesn't come from Christ.[11]

That *Geography* accords various places to the figure of Jesus Christ also reveals that the meaning of the figure of the savior depends upon context. The figure of Jesus is finally separate from any nonverbal reality; it is not necessarily attached to any one meaning, to any one thing. This is implicit in the "Niggers' " condemnation of Christ who became a white man. Christ, one version of Christian theology argues, emptied himself of heavenly being in order to become human. Christ as salvific figure becomes dissociated from divine content so that Christ as figure can apply to humanity. The "Niggers," however, find that the figure has missed its mark: it applies not to all of human reality but to only a certain segment of it. In Burkean terms, they understand Christ to be a false synecdoche. He is offered by the Church as that figure that represents the whole but the "Niggers" believe that he is only a part that represents a part. Christ is not a universal figure.

Christ as savior again appears in "North," canto III, stanza 7. Canto III deals with the Ranters, a heretical English Christian sect of seventeenth-century England, which preached antinomianism, spiritualism, and pantheism, "believing that God is in every creature" (*Geography* 144, note 63). Stanza 7 recollects the preaching of Jacob Bauthemly who "wrote that / the Devil and Hell were 'the Dark Side of God' "(66). He preached:

> And my heaven is to have my earthly and dark
> Apprehensions of God to cease
> And to live no other life than what Christ
> Spiritually lives in me . . .

> "Sin is the dark side of God but God is not
>   the author of sin
> Nor does he will it. Sin being a nullity, God cannot
>   be the author of it." (67)

In contrast to the Jesus who sat down at the table with the "Niggers," this Christ does not come down to speak, be it from the north or from heaven. This Christ lives in Bauthemly and Bauthemly seeks complete identification with this Christ insofar as he seeks "to live no other life than what Christ / Spiritually lives in me." Bauthemly's Christ is not political, though this Christ did lead to painful political ramifications: Bauthemly's preaching led him to be "burned through the tongue" (66). However, Bauthemly himself, at least as Merton presents him, isn't explicitly political: he is concerned with the discernment of God in himself and the way in which he can live Christ. His sermon has all the marks of theological discourse that is unconcerned with the sociopolitical order. Bauthemly speaks of sin and salvation, inward and outward manifestations of the Spirit of God, immanence and transcendence. This last pairing is especially important when viewed in relation to the Christ at the table with the "Niggers" and the Christ of the cargo cults. Though Bauthemly understands sin to be the dark side of God, and not of the devil, he still wishes to nullify this dark side: "And my heaven is to have my earthly and dark / Apprehensions of God to cease." The opposite apprehension of God, the life that Christ lives in Bauthemly, is presumably unearthly and light. Is this Christ similar to the Christ the "Niggers" have discovered to be a white man? *Geography* certainly doesn't explicitly make this point. The implications, however, are clear. The "Niggers" question the validity of the figure of Christ because he has become white. Bauthemly recognizes that God has a dark side but that Christ (God?) himself seems to point to a way of light.

Geography returns to a dark Christ figure in the cantos concerning the cargo cults. Again, the poem plays with the fact that as a figure of language, Jesus Christ is movable; it has no fixed meaning. In the cargo section, canto III of "East," it first appears in stanza 15. *Geography* reports a sign that appeared among the dark-skinned cultists, who had been missionized by Christians:

> Be ready for big Blackfela Catholic Steamer:
> Most Sacred Heart of Jesus Ltd
> Turns brown man white
> In a quaking boat
> Full of ancestors
> Speaking in tongues. (94)

This fragment is triply significant. First, the cultists, in their want of cargo, identify the steamer that will deliver their goods as "Blackfela Catholic." Unlike the "Niggers," the cultists have no qualms, at this point in the sign, of identifying Christ's church with the color of their skin. The cargo will come courtesy of a black Church. Second, Jesus Ltd, while delivering in a ship identified with dark-skinned people, will also transform the brown men into white men. Rather than rejecting Jesus for having become white, the cultists welcome Jesus precisely because he can make them white. Finally, unlike Bauthemly's Christ, who will help him turn away from earthly things, the Jesus of this cult will help the cultists become more earthly. Jesus is now a merchandiser who delivers what Bauthemly would have undoubtedly found to be mammon. The cargoists are not particularly concerned, at least explicitly, with the 'spiritual' life. They want Western goods, and they transform the figure Jesus into a savior who can deliver what they want. Clearly, Bauthemly also looks to Christ for what he wants. But what he wants is a light and unearthly heaven. The cultists wish for the material goods of earthly existence.

   Geography also indicates that figures of language can be used across space and through time to name nonverbal reality. Consider, for instance, parts of canto IV of "East."

> 1827
> D'Entrecasteaux enters the bay
> Looks it over
> Leaves it with the name of his ship
> "Astrolabe Bay."
>
> 1871–1883
> Baron Nikolai Miklouho-Maclay
> (Tibud Maclay)
> Comes and goes
> Exploring
> Recording the language
> As a reward for hospitality
> Leaves the coast with
> His own name:
> "Maclay Coast"
> To further honor
> The place where he landed
> He called it "Constantine Harbour"
> (Grand Duke Constantine
> President of the Imperial Russian Geographical Society
> Had paid for the trip.) (96–97)

Both stanzas, reporting the exploration of the South Pacific by Europeans, reveal the mutability, some might say versatility, of names. 'Astrolabe,' for instance, refers 'originally,' that is in the poem, to the ship of a European captain. Prior to the naming of the ship, however, 'astrolabe' designated an instrument developed by the Greeks as an aid to navigation (*Random House* 84). The ship itself, through its name, first reveals the inconstancy of the name and naming. Originally a Greek word, the English *astrolabe*, as it refers to the ship, shows that the word's relationship to the nonverbal reality that it signifies is, to a certain extent, arbitrary. The word does refer both to an instrument used for ocean navigation and to a ship used for ocean travel. While it thus remains tied to the sea, its relationship to those things named is arbitrary. The name isn't necessarily tied to the navigational instrument. It can and does move from thing to thing. *Geography* makes this more explicitly evident with the last two lines of the "1827" stanza. Having surveyed the bay, the captain leaves it with the name of his ship. Hence, astrolabe refers now to at least three things in nonverbal reality: the navigational aid, the ship, and the bay.

So too the "1871–1883" stanza reveals the problematics of naming. This stanza reveals the device of irony that Merton uses to great effect in *Geography*.[12] Miklouho-Maclay "Comes and goes" throughout the area "Exploring" and "Recording the language." That he is recording the people's language is significant given that, as a "reward" and in order "To further honor" the people and their places, he renames the land and harbor after himself and the grand duke who financed his trip. Miklouho-Maclay learned the language of the place but replaces it with his own, demonstrating that a human's name is no different from an instrument's or a ship's: it can move from object to object. Significantly, the coast is not made the possession of "Maclay," which would indicate that a thing called "Maclay" stands apart from the coast, owning it. Rather, the coast itself becomes "Maclay." As *Geography* tells it, Maclay left the coast with his own name: "Maclay Coast." Had the sentence not included the colon and the phrase to its right, one could conclude that Maclay left the coast and was still named Maclay. As it stands, however, one is left to wonder whether or not the man who gave the coast its name still has that name himself. Similarly, the man named "Maclay" "honors" the place of hospitality by providing its harbor with a new name. Importantly, this new name is linked to the president of a geographical society, pointedly revealing the relationship among geographical exploration, naming, and imperialism.[13] Foreign countries capture land and change it through the use of names.

The poem's exploration of the motility of language resonates with what Merton writes about Roland Barthes in "Roland Barthes—Writing as Temperature."[14] Merton finds in Barthes an awareness that writing is "a deadly, Zenlike stillness," that "the sign must be partly arbitrary" (146). If one fails to realize this, Barthes by way of Merton or Merton by way of Barthes tells one that "you fall back into . . . essentialist illusions." The illusion would be that words, writing, signs, penetrate "the esoteric meaning of human existence." One must read writing as writing, not as a transparent way into "the deep things of life" (146).

This notion corresponds with Merton's work on Zen; hence his reference to the Zenlike stillness of this kind of writing. Merton argues in *Zen and the Birds of Appetite* that Zen meditation seeks a "certain *kind of consciousness that is above and beyond deception* by verbal formulas. . . . Deception in what? Deception in its grasp of itself as it really is" (38). Zen, then, distrusts language. Like Barthes, it does not believe that language can reveal to one "the esoteric meaning of human existence." Language is dishonest; it lies if it claims otherwise. Hence Zen has developed language techniques that attempt to force one away from an attachment to language as something that will lead one to "ontological awareness" (Carr, *Search for Wisdom and Spirit* 81). While Zen and Merton do think that ontological awareness is possible (Carr 78–79, 81–86), both are deeply mistrustful of the claims that language makes. Merton does not, however, abandon language. While he wants people to see its limitations, he also suggests that language has an important position: it can be used to disrupt mind-sets, to help people see beyond the illusions of "reality" into what is (*Zen* 49). *Geography*'s exploration of language can, and should, be understood as Merton putting into play his own appropriation of Zen language theory and practice.

Consider Maclay. He recorded the language of the people and received their hospitality. In return, he fails to see their place for what it was prior to his arrival. In naming the coast after himself and the harbor after his benefactor, he took the fact of the geographical space, already named by the people who lived there or even unnamed and not in need of a name, and molded it to his preconceptions. He thought that it needed European naming, that it would be honored by the gift of a Western name. *Geography* deftly exposes this process of substitution and manipulation: one may give a name but the name itself is not necessary to the thing named. The name doesn't reveal the nonverbal reality, nor does it contain it. The name is simply attached to the nonverbal reality. *Geography* uses astrolabe and other words to destroy any preconception that it, or any language, necessarily refers to any one thing.

The Ambiguity of History

Flying toward San Francisco, looking at the landscape below, the narrator of *Geography* reflects: "Invent a name for a town / Any town / 'Sewage Town.'" (122). Naming is understood to be a process of invention and, moreover, the town itself isn't even important. Crucially, this reflection on the act of naming is followed by what consistently punctuates canto I of "West": the *Ashtavakra Gita* (Lentfoehr 129). In part, it reads "that the Self is Brahman and / that existence and non-existence are imagined" (*Geography* 122).

This identification of the self with Brahman in "West" does not mean that *Geography* rejects history for an ahistorical spirituality. Throughout its pages it manifests the move of the late Merton into the world and into history. It is not the work of a Bauthemly, seeking to nullify the earthly. It is an attempt to take seriously the historical dimension of human being. Just as it explores language, *Geography* delves into histories as they are particular, oppressive, and full of the necessity of responsibility. This exploration of the ambiguity of history also can and should be understood as integrally related to Merton's work on Zen.

As it mistrusts the grandiose claims of language, Zen resists the rigid form in which historical entities attempt to encase the world. It refuses, Merton holds, to force history into precut templates "to be defended against all comers" (*Zen* 6). Zen, Merton implies, refuses both a historically rigid stance and the violence that follows from such a stance. According to Merton, Zen rejects the standards provided by culture and society. It rejects, one may extrapolate, the standards of *historical* communities insofar as societies and cultures both are constituted by and constitute *history*. Zen rejects the standards of history because these standards make murky one's encounter with reality. The point of Zen is to see things as they are (*Zen* 49). To use artificially preconceived standards of culture and society is to erect a wall, a fort, a castle, which needs to be defended against those who would destroy it.

To accept and use historical standards is to place oneself into the violent ways of society and culture. One becomes a master of a fortress that needs defense. *Geography* explores both the artificially preconceived standards of society and culture and the violence and oppression they entail.

Certainly, Merton's exploration of fifty-one (and more) voices is also an exploration of fifty-one (and more) histories. People are located as living in specific places with specific concerns that are not (or not easily) universalizable. The question remains, however, whether or not the author who wrote this poem denies his own historical particularity as he creates a unified historical narrative. As such he would stand above all the particular histories: his history would be the meta-history. This, in part, is the argument made by Labrie (148). Moreover, *Geography* itself seems to verify Labrie's argument when at one point its narrator triumphantly declares "*Geography. / I am all (here) /There!*" (42).

However, Merton's work is not metanarrative, metahistory. *Geography* reveals itself as but another fragment among fragments.[15] Merton himself acknowledges as much in the "Author's Note," which precedes the poem. He claims that *Geography* "is a purely tentative draft of a longer work in progress, in which there are, necessarily, many gaps. This is only a beginning of patterns, the first opening up of the dream" (1). As it contains gaps, as it is only a beginning, it is incomplete. It can't stand as metanarrative because it doesn't contain all: parts of the narrative elude it. Moreover, Merton goes on to note, the dream "grows out of a common participation" (1). Not only is *Geography* an incomplete beginning; it is also a beginning that is dependent upon others for its construction. Merton believes that he is simply joining with other dreamers. In so doing his own voice becomes part of the sound of the other voices. But this melding of Merton and the narrator into the totality of *Geography* does not stand as unifying metanarrative, a history that denies its own particularity. If it unifies at all, it unifies what I and others have shown to be plural languages and ambiguous histories. If the narrator is all here and there, the narrator is here and there in the limitedness of linguistic and historic forms. The narrator, and Merton, fail as unifying principles just as that with which they identify fails. As Merton says in "From Pilgrimage to Crusade," there is no home.

This is an important point at a time in America when *multicultural-ism* and *diversity* are two of the words buzzing most loudly. Rhetoricians of all types, if they build on *Geography*, have three important contributions to make in this debate. First, they can and should affirm the multicultural impulse. Postmodernism, if it is nothing else, is a way of life necessarily open to many others. However, and this is the second point, multiculturalism must not devolve into relativism. While various historical and linguistic forms may be equal, they are not static. They change constantly and are always open to question. An affirmation of diversity does not entail an affirmation of inertia, an acceptance of a particular form as if that form has always and will always exist as it is. Furthermore, and this is the third point, an affirmation of diversity entails a recognition that cultures have been both oppressed and oppressors. To speak and to live in history is to participate in oppression.

Geography relentlessly explores this last point.[16] It allows for no romantic dream of liberated Edenic societies. The challenge to liberation rhetoricians like Freire and Romero could not be more pointed. This is especially so when one considers Merton's treatment of one moment of 'contact': that time when Europe invaded the Yucatan. *Geography* finds all cultures, European and Meso-American, culpable in the oppression of others. Consider, for instance, a fragment of canto XI, stanza 23 of "South," which describes the arrival of the conquistadores in the Yucatan:

> Redneck captains with whips
> Fire in their fingers
> Worse than Itzaes
> Friars behind every rock every tree
> Doing business
> Bargaining for our souls
> Book burners and hangmen
> Sling the high rope
> They stretch the necks
> Lift the heads
> Of priest and noble
> Our calendar is lost (36)

The Yucatan culture of priests, sacred books, a calendar, and souls—all marks of a culture similar to that which violently displaces it—is reported by the voice of this part of *Geography* to have been subjected to cultural tyranny and oppression. Working from a universalized notion of their own place, the Europeans, warriors and priests, destroy what they find in order to impose their system upon a defeated people. Merton's direct connection to this violent universalization of a historical particularity should not be forgotten: he was a Catholic priest.[17]

The third line of this fragment from canto XI, stanza 23 of "South," "Worse than Itzaes," reveals the extreme complexity of *Geography* and the extent to which it explores the violence of history and the tendencies all cultures have toward violent, universalizing expansion. *Geography* does not romanticize those oppressed by Western colonization; it doesn't facilely romanticize precontact, indigenous peoples as Adams and Eves still living in the garden. The Europeans simply brought their own variant of violent expansionism. They did not bring anything alien into the Yucatan, *Geography* maintains. Even precontact civilizations differed and violently forced their own traditions on each other.

Geography seeks to act within history, taking responsibility for its place in human culture. It does so in two ways: it strongly suggests that people make pilgrimage to the other, and it hints that through the defiant use of language one take responsibility for challenging oppression. Merton claims in "From Pilgrimage to Crusade" that humans are caught in a bind. They constantly are in pilgrimage, seeking home, seeking the source of life. Yet the history of pilgrimage and crusade has revealed the illusory nature of the source: there is no Eden. Still, Merton, argues, the need for pilgrimage continues. He suggests that it be redirected from a search for an Edenic place to a search for the source of life in the other. This requires a transformation in the way one thinks of the other. The other must no longer be seen as a lump of unformed matter that impedes progress (*Mystics* 111–12). As I mentioned above, Merton claims that we must find ourselves in others. Merton upholds St. Francis of Assisi as a model pilgrim. St. Francis, to Merton's delight, twisted anew the words *pilgrimage* and *crusade*. He made pilgrimage to the dreaded Muslim other of Christendom not with the assurance of his own position, Merton maintains, but with the mark of uncertainty: he was humble (112). As I discussed in chapter 2, Burke also maintains that one should seek not humiliation, but humility. Both of these postmoderns, aware of the tenuousness of history and language, return to a traditional Christian virtue in the era of the worldwide dominance of their own country. Their works counterpoint U.S. arrogance, perhaps. *Geography* can be read as an exercise in the teaching of humility. It suggests that cross-cultural encounter could be marked not by the barrier of people viewing each other as non-negotiable *ensoi*, but by humility.

Consider, for instance, The "Worse than Itzaes" line of canto XI, stanza 23 of "South," which directs one back to earlier cantos in "South." The voice of that part of the poem tells the tale of how the Yucatan natives were conquered by a foreign culture—another Meso-American people—long before the arrival of the Europeans. They were the "Itzaes" (*Geography* 31). The Itzaes, the voice reports, brought about new corn, pyramids, new Gods, and "The wail of lives" (32). They ruled for "Thirteen katuns of suffering and law" (32). Just as the European conquistadores and friars displaced one culture with their own, so too another native culture acted. Europeans are not the only ones bound by their oppressive history. *Geography* suggests that cross-cultural links may be possible based on the fact that all cultures oppress; none is pure. Hence, there is no rigid victim-oppressor dichotomy on the basis of which one culture can condemn another.

Similarly *Geography*, in "South," reports on the violence of inter-Muslim relationships.[18] "East," canto I, section 2, for instance, reveals the orthodox Muslim lack of tolerance for Shi'ite deviation; Shi'ites refuse to say the number ten, which was important to the orthodox (Schmidt 152). *Geography* reports that Shi'ite auction brokers "will not even say 'Ten' / Their brokers at auctions / When they come to 'ten' / Say 'Nine-plus-one' " (83). Upon hearing such blasphemy, the voice of this section reports that an orthodox Turk beat an auctioneer with a club, and as he wept with pain the auctioneer, in response to the demand of the Turk to say "TEN," retorts ironically " 'Ten with a club'. " As is the case with its examination of inter-Meso-American relationships, *Geography* reveals that Muslims are not a solidary people united as victims against the West. Rather, Muslims victimize each other just as they are victimized by the Westerners.

Furthermore, the auctioneer's response hints at a more active opting for historical responsibility. Merton chose to place a trope of rhetoric, irony, into the auctioneer's mouth. This ironic response is important because it shows continued resistance: the other, even while beaten, resists the demands of the oppressor. Rather than fatalistically accepting his circumstances, the auctioneer uses rhetoric, here in the play of irony, to refuse complete submission. Though his body has been beaten down, his voice rises to taunt his oppressor with defiance: "Ten with a club." He makes it known that the "ten" is forced, that it isn't sincere, that he hasn't chosen it. Even in the pain of oppression, the oppressed attempts to act responsibly, to stop the oppression.

This is a point that postmodern and liberation rhetoricians share. They affirm the possibility that language can rise out of pain in order to speak against the oppressor. With Scarry, Soelle, Rorty, and others, Burke, Merton, Freire, and Romero believe that pain destroys language and that it serves as a site of invention. Whatever differences they may have, Burke and Freire theorize the probability, necessity, even inevitability, that the oppressed will speak out of pain against the oppressors. Merton and Romero practice this. Romero, as I will elucidate in chapter 5, speaks directly from a site of pain: the suffering of El Salvador is his base. But even Merton, relatively secluded at Gethsemane, makes public the voices of the oppressed.

Rhetoricians who work with and among the oppressed would do well to remember that imaginatively defiant language can arise out of pain. A high school student teacher of English whom I once supervised certainly did. She worked with students designated by the Chicago Public Schools as "English with Support" (the lowest track), most of whom lived in Cabrini Green, a notoriously violent Chicago Housing Authority project. This student teacher refused to run from the terror in which many of her students lived. She faced their heart-wrenching stories, their toughness, their lack of focus, even their occasional weapons, with a remarkable commitment to the possibilities of language. She was certain that she could help her students speak and, by the end of her experience, she had made great strides. Short of death, language can rise from pain.

Pain

PROTECT THE LIVES OF YOUR POLICE PUT OUT THE SMALL FIRES WITH FOG OR FOAM MARK THE TROUBLEMAKERS WITH DYE MOVE THE CROWD WITH WATER-BASED IRRITANTS KEEP

THE CROWDS AWAY FROM THE CAR WITH ELECTRICITY DRIVE
THE SNIPERS OUT OF HIDING WITH TEAR GAS GRENADES
BREAK UP CROWDS WITH SMOKE (38)

This passage follows, with no explanation, no transitive link, the lyrical lament of a Yucatan elder bemoaning the invasion of his land by the European conquistadores and friars: "We count the pebbles of the years / In hiding: / Nothing but misfortune" (38). It precedes, again with no explanation, no transitive link, the continuation of the lament: "Memory of the katuns and years swallowed up by / the red moon!" (38). Linking these passages is the pain of conquest, be it by the swords and whips of the conquistadores or the water-based irritants and electricity of modern urban riot squads.[19] Geography is rife with suffering.

I count at least thirty reports of potentially painful and actually painful incidents in Geography, ranging from the "Sacred Black Brother . . . beaten to the wall" in "Prologue" (6) to Jacob Bauthemly being burned through the tongue (66) to the end of the poem where a ghost dancer prophesies that whites will burn (135). The poem manifests the pain of human being: languages of pain interweave constantly throughout its pages.[20] Geography explores the presence of pain in its study of language and history and finds in pain both a problem and a promise. The problem, which I introduced in chapter one, is the problem of the relationship between pain and language. How does one effectively rhetoricize pain? The promise is that pain perhaps provides a way by which the sense of 'we' can be enlarged.

That the poem is concerned with how one best can rhetoricize pain is seen as it rhetoricizes pain differently throughout its pages. Geography constantly explores how it is that one can, perhaps even should, speak pain, and does so through the voice of those experiencing it, in the voices of observers, and in the voice of the narrative first person. It is in this last sense that the poem explores the way pain can enlarge the sense of 'we.' In so doing, Geography both foreshadows Rorty's concerns as presented in Contingency, irony, and solidarity and provides a textual example of his suggestions. As I discussed in chapter 1, Rorty has abandoned any hope that cross-cultural crevices can be spanned by appeals to the 'true.' Instead, Rorty suggests that cultures may be linked by that which seems to be the source of irreconcilable division: pain. Geography, which may be a type of Rortian rhetoric in practice, suggests

that the other of another culture may be met in the empathetic exploration of the pain that this other is experiencing.

To begin to understand how *Geography* explores the voices of those
who are pained, consider again the poem's treatment of the conflict
between the Ranters and England's established religious authorities.
Geography presents Bauthemly's sermon about the light and dark sides
of God and the presence of Christ in him. Following the conclusion of
the sermon, section 8 opens with a list: "PROOFS EXAMINATIONS DEC-
LARATIONS / INDICTMENTS AND CONVICTIONS / ARRAIGNMENT AND
TRY ALL / DAMNABLE AND DIABOLICAL OPINIONS / DETESTABLE LIVES
AND ACTIONS" (67). This list explores the establishment's melding of
two types of rhetoric in order to condemn, convict, and torture
Bauthemly. "Proofs," "indictments," and the like point to the rhetoric
of the law court. "Damnable" and "diabolical" (and perhaps "detestable") are from the rhetoric of religion: they are words of the sermon, of
the magisterium and of the Church, which simultaneously suggest that
the Ranters can be condemned to Hell (they are damnable) and that
the Ranters are already of Hell (they are diabolical, which is to say they
have the qualities of the devil). This rhetoric leads to the violent end of
the Ranters' language. Section 10, and the whole Ranter canto finishes
with: "Burn him through the tongue!" (68). The decision of the court
to silence the Ranters seems to be final because the canto moves into
white page, and *Geography* moves on to "North," canto IV. Neither the
prosecutors nor the Ranters are heard from again.[21] This sequence
explores the imaginative constructions of a marginalized people, the
Ranters, and the consequence that imaginative reconstructions of dominant images, in this case God, can have. England's religious authorities,
responding to Bauthemly, silenced his rhetoric by burning his tongue.
Bauthemly spoke, Bauthemly was spoken to, Bauthemly was silenced by
torture.

Consider, as well, "South," canto XI. Told, it seems, in the voice
of *Chilam Balam*[22] or another Yucatan figure, this canto details the
coming of the conquistadores and the destruction of precontact Yucatan
civilization. Stanza 5, in particular, reveals the exploration that *Geography* makes into the voices of those who suffer pain. The first eight lines
read:

> They bring down all power smash man to earth make
> green skies
> Weep blood hard and heavy is the maize bread of this
>   katun
> Strangled is the flute-hero the painter Yaxal Chuen
>   the jeweler
> The Ape Ixkanyultu "Precious Voice"
> His throat is now cut gods driven out (34)

That this is the translated voice of a Yucatan native is clear: "bread" is modified by "maize"; the word *katun* is used to signify a length of time; Yucatan names are transliterated rather than anglicized. *Geography* here attempts, through translation that keeps some of the feel of the original language, to explore the sufferers' language of pain. It is important that the conquistadores slaughter not other warriors but the fruit of a peaceful culture: killed are a flute-hero, a painter, one named Yaxal Chuen, a jeweler, and "The Ape Ixkanyultu 'Precious Voice.' " This list is crucial in the description of the scene because it contrasts with the description of stanza 23, which presents the conquistadores: "Strutting and gobbling / Redneck captains" and "Book burners and hangmen" (37). Given the chance to depict the scene of contact, the voice of the Yucatan 'other' speaks in such a way as to sharply differentiate the conquistadores who come and those to whom they come. The Yucatan people are marked as 'cultured': they are named either by their position as artists (the flute-hero, the painter, the jeweler) or by names (Yaxal Chuen, Ixkanyultu). Significantly, one of those strangled is a flute-hero; this culture makes heroes not of warriors but of musicians.

In contrast, the conquistadores are marked as animals (strutters and gobblers), intolerants (book burners), and hooded murderers (hangmen). The last point is brought out with almost journalistic objectivity when the voice reports that some Yucatan people have been "strangled" and the throat of "Ape Ixkanyultu" cut. There is no melodramatic description of the painful murders; the voice simply reports, letting the acts of strangulation and throat-cutting stand without ornament against the list of artists and names.

Stanza 5 goes on to use Spanish:

> The flower dance around the rock pool
> *Canta la mujer joven*
> To call back gone man made gentle as a
> Tame animal with dance with charm
> To the sweet body lying in the water
> Covered with jungle flowers
> *Dispersados serán por el mundo las mujeres que cantan*
> *Y los hombres que cantan*
> *Y todos los que cantan.* (35)

The use of Spanish is significant: it reveals the imposition of the conquering tongue, but also the presence of an oppressed culture within a dominant one and the resistance that such residual cultures offer, using the language of their dominators. The flower dance is clearly a non-Christian ceremony but it continues in a Christian tongue, Spanish. "*The young woman sings,*"[23] the stanza reads, for lost men who were gentle (unlike the conquistadores) and for a "sweet body lying in the water." The woman sings for those of the culture who were strangled and whose throats were slit; it also sings to the body of one whom the conquistadores "contacted." The stanza ends: "*Dispersed they shall be by the world the women who sing / And the men who sing / And all who sing.*" The world of strutters and gobblers, of book burners and hangmen, separates and parts the people of the flower dance, the people who sing, the people whose contact with the conquistadores brought strangulation and throat-cutting. Yet even in the pain of death and dispersion, there is resistance: the conqueror's language is used to recall, remember, and lament the conquered. Here, *Geography* finds a call to responsibility: the language used to conquer has now become the language of the conquered who have not forgotten.

In addition to exploring the rhetoric of pain in the language of those who suffer, *Geography* also explores pain through the language of the observer. Consider "East," canto I, stanza 3. This part of "East" is taken from the journals of "Ibn Battuta" a fourteenth-century Muslim who wrote about his travel in Asia and Africa (*Geography* 146, note 82). Battuta, through *Geography*, writes of some Muslim heretics who, following their prophet, attempted to overthrow the orthodoxy in Syria with myrtle rods as swords (are myrtle rods symbols of penes?). The result was disastrous for the heretics and for the orthodox women they abused:

> They entered a town on Friday when the men were
>   at the mosque.
> They raped the women and the Muslims
> Came running out with swords
> And cut them to pieces. (84)

Battuta, the observer, offers no adjectives to dress the scene, no response of those hurt and killed, no punctuation that indicates surprise or outrage. Rather, the account is straightforward: the women were raped, and as a consequence, the rapists were cut to pieces. Battuta, through the poem, goes on to report that in further consequence "Twenty thousand heretics / Were slaughtered" (85). The sultan wished to kill the rest, but the general intervened, sparing their lives. He decided they "could be useful / Working on the land" (85). Battuta, and hence *Geography*, observes the rape of women, the cutting to pieces of the heretic rapists, the slaughter of twenty thousand more heretics, and the enslavement of the remainder with neither cringing nor exultation. Most interesting is the absence of the voice of those made to feel pain. The raped women are silent, the rapists cut to pieces are silent, the slaughtered twenty thousand are silent, the slaves are silent. Battuta and the poem pass through fields of pain, and the pain is not heard. The lament of the people of the Yucatan, their adjectival denunciation of their oppressors, is lost in Battuta's journalistic account. He sees, he does not hear. Moreover, what he sees is virtually flat: there are rapes, not bloody rapes; there are rapists cut to pieces, not insolent or evil rapists; there is a slaughter, not an earth-rending slaughter; there is an enslavement, not a wounding and bitter enslavement. The voice of the observer deals not in the sounds and sights of pain; pain is revealed quietly, without color or texture. Battuta's voice is that of an objective journalist who attempts to let the situation speak for itself.

Like the Battuta section, "West," canto I, stanza 18 explores the speaking of pain in the narrative first person. Unlike Battuta's distanced voice, however, this stanza uses the first-person singular to find in pain the possibility of enlarging one's sense of 'we.' The stanza immediately follows the fragment of the *Ashtavakra Gita*, discussed above, which proclaims that "the self is Brahman," which is to say that the self is the primal source of being. The fragment ends with a query: "what should / such a one, free of desires, know, say or do?" (122). This, not unimportantly, is a classic question of rhetoric: it asks what course of action, of thought, of speech, one should take following the realization of some truth (see Cicero, especially book 3). One presumes that the text that follows will answer the question. The text does so by asking yet another 'rhetorical' question and answering it. Crucially, it answers the question in the first person, one of the rare times the narrative 'I' appears in *Geography*. The 'I' is important because of the 'we' of pain into which it moves.

> Should the dance of Shivashapes
> All over flooded prairies
> Make hosts of (soon) Christ-Wheat
> Self-bread which could also be
> Squares of Buddha-Rice
> Or square Maize about those pyramids
> Same green
> Same brown, same square
> Same is the Ziggurat of everywhere
> I am one same burned Indian
> Purple of my rivers is the same shed blood
> All is flooded
> All is my Vietnam charred
> Charred by my co-stars
> The flying generals.

This passage seems to contradict the poem's embodiment of plurality and ambiguity. It presents the implied connections between Christ and Buddha on the one hand and wheat, rice, and maize on the other, and then provides the transitive link: the narrative 'I' declares that they are the same. "I," the poem reads, "am the one same burned Indian / Purple of my rivers is the same shed blood / All is flooded / All is my Vietnam charred." The narrative 'I' offers no argument, no pseudo-argument, no implied imagistic associations that it leaves for the reader to contemplate. It simply declares union with that which suffers.

Yet because it is an 'I' and not a royal 'we,' it does not necessarily universalize the experience. One is still left to decide whether or not one's self experiences the geography as the narrative 'I' experiences it. The experience is a sense of an expanded self, of a 'we' bound by pain but the 'I' become 'we' doesn't demand that the reader feel the union. In fact, the passage's lack of argument and detail makes it difficult for the reader to experience, even through the mediatory power of the page, the 'we' experienced by the 'I.' While the 'I' declares that these different pained beings—Indians and Vietnamese to name the two most obvious—are the same as each other and that the 'I' is the same as them, the 'I' provides no convincing reason, logical or poetic, for the reader to feel the same. Insofar as the 'I' simply declares the union, the reader is not brought into the process of unification. The 'I' has come to a conclusion, based on the 'I's' observations of the landscape and knowledge about the Vietnamese and Indians, which the 'I' doesn't share with the reader. The reader, then, is left simply to observe a transformation; the reader can't share it. Perhaps, in this way, this enlargement of the 'we' does not violate the poem's postmodern location. If one is at all attracted to the enlarged 'we' found in the 'I's' experience of pain, one must seek out a way in which one can involve oneself in the process of transformation, rather than simply reading a poem in order to gratify one's desire for an enlarged 'we' without actually having enlarged the 'we' on one's own.

Importantly, this flux between the 'I' and the 'we' reveals the poem's connection to Merton's work on the Zen koan and in so doing presents itself as a Zen rhetoric. The audience is not given an answer, a directive, but rather is invited to take part in the process of the question.[24] Merton argues that one reaches "the heart of the *koan*," which is an enigmatic question upon which followers of *Rinzai* Zen meditate, when one realizes that the "answer is the *koan*, the question, seen in a totally new light. It is not something other than the question. The *koan* is not something other than the self" (*Mystics* 236).[25] *Geography*, in raising this dilemma of the 'I' and the 'we,' requires that its readers embody the question, answer the question for themselves. Unlike Bauthemly's sermons or the rhetoric of his prosecutors, the poem offers no sure answer concerning the nature of the world. In this way, *Geography* comments upon those rhetorics it considers throughout its pages. It explores self-assured rhetorics that offer sure answers, which assume the monological supremacy of their own voices, but it demonstrates that none is supreme: there only exists a plurality of voices. As its juxtapositional technique shows, *Geography* itself offers no answer, no assured monologue concerning the world. Rather, it invites one to involve oneself in the process of construction, in the process of answering the questions concerning the nature of human community. It offers such koans as this: Who is the Blackfela Christ? Who is the conquistador? Who is the conquered? How are you Vietnam charred?

The problem and the promise of pain as manifest in *Geography* have the mark of Merton's understanding of Zen. Merton, as Carr argues, maintains that suffering is part of human existence and that it should not "be brought under human control" (*Search for Wisdom and Spirit* 82). In accord with its mistrust of language, which attempts to falsely contain reality, Zen (and Christianity), Merton maintains, advocates that "the only thing to do about" suffering "is to plunge right into the middle of contradiction and confusion in order to be transformed by what Zen calls the 'Great Death' and Christianity calls 'dying and rising with Christ' " (*Zen* 50).

Geography explores various ways of rhetoricizing pain and in so doing plunges into the contradiction and confusion pain brings about. To present pain in one voice and one language would have the effect of containing the pain, because such a rhetoricization would falsely presume that pain has one voice, one language, one experience. Instead, *Geography* tries on, so to speak, various rhetorics of pain, thereby revealing the contradiction and confusion of suffering.

Moreover, if one is transformed by the Great Death of Zen or the dying and rising with Christ of Christianity in one's encounter with the chaos and confusion of suffering, one's sense of 'we' is necessarily expanded, insofar as Merton understands this expansion to be the primary effect of the Great Death and the dying and rising. He writes of this self who has died/died and risen: "Its existence has meaning in so far as it does not become fixated or centered upon itself as ultimate, learns to function not as its own center but 'from God' and 'for others' " (*Zen* 23–24). This notion, not incidentally, reflects "From Pilgrimage to Crusade." In the new pilgrimage for which Merton argues one moves to the ends of the earth to meet the other whom one previously treated as lumped mass. So too, in the Great Death and in the dying and rising with Christ one's sense of self is transformed beyond the small, false self of modern consciousness (*Zen* 22) into a self that finds 'I' in the 'them.'

Imagination

A postmodern rhetoric deeply concerned with the problem and possibilities of pain, *Geography* also concerns itself with the realm of imagination. It promotes what I have called in chapter 1 the "object-oriented imagination" and moves through this into a Zen-influenced "process-oriented imagination." It challenges object-oriented imagination in order to undercut the parochial surety that Merton finds to be the cause of oppression.

It is important to note that *Geography*, in its move toward the process-oriented imagination, embodies Merton's criticism of liberation rhetorics. As I discussed in chapter 2, Burke criticizes what I call "liberation rhetorics" because he believes that they accept the values of a given system and simply use these values in order to violently wreak vengeance within the system. Merton, in contrast, criticizes liberation rhetorics for a different reason. To their credit, Merton holds, liberation rhetorics are "iconoclastic" when they challenge the language of an oppressive establishment and are better than establishment discourse because they are closer to "the hard realities of poverty, brutality, vice, and resistance." Nonetheless, liberation rhetorics are "fully as intransigent as the language of the establishment" and are languages of "self-enclosed finality" ("War and the Crisis of Language" 247). They break icons only to announce and defend their own iconographic system.

The images in *Geography* are revealed to be what they are: constructions for interpreting that to which they point. They are not, *Geography* shows, reality itself. Whose God, for instance, is God? In his essay "Cargo Cults of the South Pacific" Merton argues that "On the basis of his observation, the native evolved cults of symbolic activity, hoping to put himself in contact with the source of Kago, thereby bringing about a situation in which Kago would come for him and not just for the white man" (82). As I discussed above relative to the figure of Jesus Christ, one of the cargo cults' symbolic activities is that of refiguring, reimagining Christ as one who ran a cargo-bearing "Blackfela" steamer and as one who would change brown skin to white. The Christ of the cargo cult doesn't exist in the nonverbal world; but, within the verbal world of the cult, he is vibrantly alive. His birth was dependent upon the ability of the cargo cultists to gather their own desire for Western goods and skin color, along with the Jesus to whom they had been introduced by the missionaries, and synthesize these elements in such a way that their own imagined Jesus appears. But this imagined Jesus fails: he doesn't deliver the goods, and the final cargo song trails off, unanswered, into the white space of *Geography*. The object-oriented imaginative activity of the cults, which creates a new image of the figure of Jesus Christ, fails and shows that its image of Christ is an image that is simply an image and nothing more.

On the whole, *Geography*'s 'Jesus Christ' can and should be read as a Zen use of a "language against itself" in order to reveal that images are used to "see only what conveniently fits our prejudices" (*Zen* 49). The image's definition and characteristics are changeable and changing, at one moment representing an inner presence, as with Jacob Bauthemly, at another representing a master merchandiser, and at still another a carpetbagger white man mistrusted by the "Niggers." Jesus Christ changes and is changeable because, as an image, it is only an image, nothing more or less. Whose Christ is Christ? *Geography* demonstrates the inadequacies of all Jesus Christ images. The poem takes that Zen aphorism, 'if you meet the Buddha on the road, kill him,' and gives it life by replacing the iconic Buddha with Jesus and killing this Christian icon. The multiple and contradictory imagining of Jesus Christ in the poem serves as a point of exploration into the imaginative process. No one image is Jesus Christ. Important to consider is that all of these images of Jesus Christ are implicated in painful situations. Bauthemly's Christ placed him in contradiction to the English establishment, leading to his imprisonment and torture. The carpetbagger Christ is mistrusted by the "Niggers" because it is the representative of an oppressive system. This white Christ often justified the oppressive pain lived by the enslaved and free African Americans, the poem implies. Such a killing of Christ challenges the Church of which Merton was a monk and priest. The Roman Catholic Church, it hardly needs to be argued, claims that, as the hierarchic institution, it proffers the true image of the incarnate God. *Geography* indicates that no image is the true image. It is significant that the challenge posed by the poem is informed by Zen. Not only does it challenge the Church; it does so influenced by another religious tradition, thereby calling into question the Church's claim that it is universal. Just as Burke offers a counterversion of Christianity in the guise of the comic Christ, so Merton offers a counter-version in the guise of a Christ killed on the road. Significantly, neither Burke nor Merton rejects Christianity, refusing to acknowledge its power and importance in Western culture. Rather, they accept the givens of their system, one of which is Jesus Christ, and seek to subvert Christ in order to use the figure for their own purposes.

This unveiling of the limitations of imagination informs every act of object-oriented imagining in *Geography*. The gods of the Itzaes, the people who conquered the people of the Yucatan prior to the invasion of the conquistadores, are shown by the poem to be subject to a process of object-oriented imagining that leads to a displacement by the gods of the conquistadores. When they first came, the Itzaes were seen to be "Fathers" who ruled a paradise: "3. Sunrise. New Kingdom. / Fresh wakes sweet tropic earth! / Tribute paid in cotton / For the Four men / (North South East West) / In Chichen" (31). As Fathers, the Itzae were the hierarchical representatives of the Four Men, the gods of the geographical directions, to whom the people were required to pay tribute. But this new society, based on the exaction of tribute by these gods, was a good society, a society good enough to evoke "sweet tropic earth!"

However, wealth brought by tribute subjects the Itzae's gods to a reimagining: "Then the Lords / Rich in cotton / Meet Gods / Equal in voice to Gods" (31). It seems that the Itzae Fathers came to identify themselves with their gods and subjected the people to oppression: "And those whose voices / Were not equal to God's voices / Were thrown into the well / To cry louder" (31). What followed this was a furthering of the object-oriented imagining: pyramids were built, laws decreed, deals made with "the Raingods" and finally the Itzae claimed that "Our Gods have grown bigger" (32). This line reveals, explicitly, the object-oriented process of symbolic imagining integral to a culture's construction of reality. The gods began as directional markers overseeing a sweet tropic earth. Through the process of object-oriented imagining they grow and grow until they have grown bigger than the initial imaginings.

At this point, the voice of the poem declares, "Then bitter times began / The plain smoked / All the way to the sea" (32). The Itzae's object-oriented imagining of their gods led to a point where their gods were big—so big that oppression came as a result. They reigned for "Thirteen katuns" until they were "Driven from their cities into jungle" in "4 Ahau" (32). The oppressive society based on the object-oriented imagining of the gods was destroyed, revealing the gods to be less than all-powerful: they were not big enough, perhaps.

On the large scale, then, *Geography* reveals object-oriented imagining as highly problematic. The elaborate construction of gods, whether it be to seek liberation or to justify oppression, finally dissolves into nothing: the images so carefully constructed simply don't withstand the movement of history. So too on the small scale *Geography* demonstrates the instability of object-oriented imagining. Consider, for instance, a fragment of "North," canto I, stanza 20:

> 20. Gryphon rends slipson two piece pioneer. Wave checks
> a gonerful went. Fully lined savings bake clam tide. Cli-
> mate is always holy here in Rum. Roses of life come out
> like flags to welcome police stranger. You can't go wrong
> with our guard. You add accessories toptop create. Dreamy
> glassass boats over the ride you fishface. Him boss vanna
> lighterage. Bovers. Oxers. Beefteas. Stews. Dead hightides
> climate Duggle Stone Club. Pantry party in the wastelands
> of Mugg. Up went ten rebels through the viewfinders with-
> out flash. Won checks overwhelming barques. Cutty-life
> still-Sark clambake in editor's home. Much president leads
> quintet. (Couplet under the bed.) Red forefathers wet the
> tent. . . . (51)

This passage, which is characteristic of the entire canto I of "North," presents images only to undercut them one after another: object-oriented imagining is repudiated the moment in which the poem glories in it. This stanza is Burkean verbal manipulation par excellence. It places together a wild menagerie of images that seem to point to the construction of a new, larger object: a segment of the poem's "North." But this object is not a comprehensible object; it is not even imagistically satisfying. The fifth sentence, for instance, promises a wild surrealistic image that is never developed. Who is the police stranger? How do roses come out like flags? The sixth sentence wrenches one away from the promise of the fifth into an impenetrable image: Who is the guard? What is the situation in which one can't go wrong? Even the most titillating part of the fragment disappoints: "(Couplet under the bed)." Following a sentence concerning a presidential quintet (what president, what quintet?), Geography implies that a presidential couplet is under the bed, engaged in whatever it is in which presidential couplets engage under beds. Much is presented, nothing is developed. The stanza simply does not allow any movement through its language to either more developed language or to nonverbal reality. Object-oriented imagining is gloried in only to be denied. At this point Geography practices that kind of writing with which Merton identified Roland Barthes, that kind of writing which, as I discussed above, reveals the plurality of language. The writer of this kind of writing, Merton argues, "must practice writing 'without alibi, without thickness, and without depth . . . The exact contrary of poetic writing.' Here language no longer 'violates the abyss' but slides away from us across an icy surface" ("Roland Barthes" 145).

Just as Merton distrusts the ability of language to point to the abyss, so too he doubts the place of images and imagination. While he claims that the imagination is important (Contemplation 343–48), he also claims that the imagination and the images that it produces are finally a hindrance if taken too seriously. He writes in Mystics and Zen Masters: "He who insists on 'imagining' something like the invisible and uni-maginable object (of faith) only deludes himself by clothing his mind in 'coverings,' whereas the consciousness of 'pure faith' (and hence of mystical contemplation) is naked and obscure" (242). This is precisely the point of Geography: it explores the various imaginings of the world in order to debunk them, to show how all are finally inadequate expres-sions of 'reality.' Whose image of God is God? As far as Geography is concerned, no image of God is God: all rise, all fall.

As Merton writes concerning the experience of satori (enlighten-ment) to be achieved through Zen: one knows that "one is Buddha and that Buddha is not what the images in the temple had led one to expect for there is no longer any image, and consequently nothing to see, no one to see it, and a void in which no image is even conceivable" (*Zen* 5). This denial of the final efficacy of the object-oriented imagination leads one back into Merton's postmodern Zen rhetoric. All images are limited because they are inevitably the products of imaginations bound by and within languages and histories. One cannot presume that the presentation of an imagined object, be it God or another human, is correct. One must not allow oneself to be finally convinced of the truth of anyone's imagining. One must, instead, take on the process of discovery for oneself; one must become the question. What is language? What is history? What is pain? What is imagination? What is rhetoric? Only then, so *Geography* would have one believe, can one know. Or as Meister Eckhardt says through Merton: "to discover nature's nakedness you must destroy its symbols" (*Zen* 13).

4

Zoon Phonanta: Freire's New Human

> I was very moved by the book Freire did with Antonio Faundez, *Learning to Question*. That was the first book of dialogues to introduce me to the notion of collectivity. And one of the things I've been thinking about as an intellectual, as a Black woman intellectual revolutionary thinker, is what does it mean to engage in some kind of collaborative response? What does it mean for us to talk to one another?
>
> —bell hooks and Cornel West, *Breaking Bread*

Paulo Freire, for many who work for the liberation of oppressed peoples, is a symbol of the revolutionary theorist. bell hooks, a self-described U.S. "Black woman intellectual revolutionary thinker" who has dedicated her professional life to the liberation of African Americans and women, is one such person. She calls Paulo Freire her "mentor" (hooks 2). hooks wants to know what it is to speak, what it is to speak as a Black woman intellectual, what it is for Black men and women to speak together (3), what it is for many kinds of oppressed peoples, such as gays, lesbians, and African Americans, to speak together (85). In Freire she finds an exemplar of liberation rhetoric, one who teaches how it is that oppressed peoples can speak to each other and to speak together against the oppressors of the worlds in which they live.[1]

Central to Freire, as one of the world's preeminent literacy theorists, is the word. Freire has devoted his life to helping the oppressed learn to speak with each other and against their oppressors by helping them learn to read and write. Yet this word, for Freire, is not simply the secular word of modern education, not the secular word of one-time First Lady Barbara Bush and her well-intentioned but highly ineffective campaign for literacy in the United States, not the word of high schools and colleges throughout America that are decrying their students' inabilities to read and write. Freire's word is the Word that imbues all words.[2] As I suggested in chapter 2, Kenneth Burke offers a version of counter-Christianity in the guise of the comedic. Similarly, as I argued in chapter 3, Merton accepts the Christianity of his culture and of his vocational commitment but, with the aid of Zen, transforms it in order to offer a different model to his readers. Likewise Freire, working originally in Brazil, takes the Catholic religious vision into which he was born and revises it. Central to Freire's work is a rhetorical theology of the Word that allows humans to speak pain and imagination within history. It is this Word that enables Freire's oppressed to speak to each other and to speak against their oppressors and thus create themselves, and the world, anew. Though I've no doubt that Freire believes in a God that is more than humanity, the Word that comes to Freire's oppressed through his program of literacy ultimately allows his oppressed to rival God by becoming creators.[3]

In regard to the Word, the social critic, philosopher of language, and literary theorist George Steiner speculates that

> According to the Neo-Platonic and Johannine metaphor, in the beginning was the Word; but if this *Logos*, this act and essence of God is, in the last analysis, total communication, the word that creates its own content and truth of being—then what of *zoon phonanta*, man the speaking animal? He too creates words and creates with words. . . . Does the act of speech, which defines man, not also go beyond him in rivalry to God? (37)

This is a question common to both Hebrew and Greek worldviews. If God is Word, if Word is made flesh, if humans are both flesh and Word, then how is it that humans are not God? In Freire's system, it isn't clear that they aren't. Founded upon and permeated with Word and human as *zoon phonanta*, Freire's theory certainly is within the neoplatonic and Johannine tradition, not to mention the tradition of the Hebrew Bible as well. It is, after all, *zoon phonanta* who names the animals in the second creation story in Genesis; it is *zoon phonanta*, as Steiner points out, who built Babel, rivaling God (36).

Written by Freire after he was exiled from Brazil by the 1964 military junta, *Education as the Practice of Freedom* makes clear that Freire sees Word as central to human existence. He writes: "Our traditional curriculum, disconnected from life, centered on words emptied of the reality they are meant to represent, lacking in concrete activity, could never develop a critical consciousness" (37). The positive implication of this negative example is that Freire seeks words that are full of the reality they are meant to represent, words that help students develop critical consciousness. He seeks, then, to help *zoon phonanta* find words that will help them become critically conscious, by which he means, in this text, people who are integrated with reality, people who critically understand the web of causal and circumstantial correlations in which they live and by means of which they can transform the world (44). Such words, he argues in *Extension or Communication*, are *logos* (119). Freire means by *logos*, which here I equate with the tradition of the Word to which Steiner points, two things: an understanding of one's place in the world; and an understanding that one can transform the world by naming it (Stanley 387–88).

To be oppressed, as Freire understands it, is to be the "B" of "any situation in which 'A' objectively exploits 'B' or hinders his pursuit of self-affirmation as a responsible person" (*Pedagogy* 41–42). Liberation from oppression means that one understands that history is open to change and that one can help to change it. In this dimension, the responsible apprehension of the nature of reality, humans know that they can shape the world and become human in the process of shaping it. Oppression, then, is to deny people a hand in the shaping of the history in which they live. Central to this transforming action, Freire goes on to argue, is the nondeceptive word, the Word that enables the oppressed to name their worlds, to name the historical reality in and for which they are to become responsible (73–76). This is entirely the point of Freire's pedagogy of the oppressed; it is, finally, what Freire means by liberation. People come to know that they are historical beings, that they can shape history, and that history is shaped through language. Or, as Peter McLaren writes: "language is that sociolinguistic territory in which history both rehearses its nightmares and dreams its liberating possibilities" (232). This is the moment of *logos*, the moment at the end of the literacy process that Freire calls *conscientização* (*Pedagogy* 73, 94–95, 101–18; *Pedagogy in Process* 67–68; *Education as the Practice* 3–6, 49; *Cultural Action* 14, 21; *Literacy* 67–68).

This pedagogical focus is Freire's genius. While Burke theorizes at length and merely hints at the pedagogical activity that his theory implies, Freire always is concerned about the fate of his theory in the lives of students. He doesn't theorize simply to determine the structure and possibilities of rhetoric; he theorizes in order to help his students liberate themselves. His work is driven finally by the educational needs of his students. This, perhaps, marks the greatest distance between postmoderns and liberationists. Postmoderns tend to work adrift in the world. So aware are they of the heterogeneous nature of humanity, no particular people impel them to speak, no specific communities demand their attention and energy. Conversely, liberationists like Freire (and Romero, as I will discuss in chapter 5) identify themselves fully with their people. The oppressed condition of his people is the situation out of which Freire's work arises, the situation to which his work always returns.

Freire's pedagogical impulse separates him even from a postmodern like Richard Rorty who, to his credit, is deeply concerned about the suffering of earth's peoples and even suggests ways in which pain may be able to serve as a point at which cross-cultural divisions can be spanned. However, Rorty finally argues, as I discussed in the first chapter, that only a cultural elite should be educated to be aware of ambiguity and plurality fully. Freire, in contrast, democratizes his education. He argues that all peoples, regardless of their class, must become literate in his sense. Whereas Rorty fears the effects of postmodernism socialized throughout all levels of social order, Freire welcomes the day when all levels of a society have come to know the word as he wants them to know it.

The coming to *logos* of liberation occurs through the process of literacization that was developed by Freire first in Brazil and later within the context of numerous revolutionary struggles. The Appendix to *Education as the Practice*, from the late 1960s, best shows the Freire literacy program itself. *Literacy*, from the late 1980s, provides the most extensive recent development of what Freire has come to call "emancipatory literacy" (145–60). Most commentators, following Freire's self-description, discuss him within the context of literacy education and theory. My claim, however, is that Freire is best understood as a religious liberation rhetorical theorist.[4]

One problem with any attempt to claim that Freire is a rhetorical theorist is that he treats the word *rhetoric* pejoratively and also denigrates what has been commonly held to be a key characteristic of rhetoric: persuasion. Whenever he treats the word pejoratively, he claims that rhetoric is language unconnected to reality, unconnected to the world to which language points: it ignores the dialectic that exists between words and the material world. Therefore, rhetoric is deceptive and meaningless (*Politics* 99–100, 123, 130; *Literacy* 39; *Pedagogy in Process* 32, 116). This misunderstanding of rhetoric has existed at least since the time of Plato (Swearingen 5–6, 224–25) and Freire is simply a contemporary representative of it. Whenever he denigrates persuasion, Freire claims that any educator who attempts to persuade the learner ignores the dialectic that exists between teacher and student (e.g. *Extension* 97, 114; see also Goulet xiii).

One could argue that Freire too easily dismisses rhetoric as lying. One could also pursue that inherent link between rhetoric and literacy. They both arose simultaneously in the West: one cannot think of rhetoric without thinking of literacy and vice versa (Swearingen 9). It is also possible to argue that Freire's theory is rhetorical theory, whether he knows it or not, because he theorizes synecdoche and metaphor, both figures of rhetoric. Echoing Burke's discussion of synecdoche, Freire holds that his literacy pedagogy will help students understand the relationship between the part and the whole. Freire claims that humans know their worlds only when they are able to discern the ways in which seemingly disparate elements are actually constituents of a whole. His method of codification, which develops a broad picture in order to help the students understand a specific word, is fundamentally an education in synecdoche. His students would learn to manipulate parts into wholes and wholes into parts (*Pedagogy* 94–96; see also *Cultural Action* 13–14; *Literacy* 67–68; *Education as the Practice* 51–52). So too Freire's literacy pedagogy instructs students in metaphor (*Cultural Action* 25).

While an exploration of the role figures play in Freire's work, both as he theorizes them and uses them, would be exciting, it is not to the point here because I do not, as too many do, exclusively define rhetoric in terms of figures (e.g., Ramus). Rather, as I discussed in chapter 1, I identify rhetoric as the dialectic of language. Freire, as many have argued, is a dialectician concerned, primarily, with the way language can help liberate the oppressed (*Politics* 130; Berthoff, Foreword; Knoblauch; Schipani).

Each in his own way, Burke, Merton, and Romero foreground the dialectic of pain and imagination. Freire leaves it in foundational sub-strata, only at times revealing it in its full force. Freire himself argues, and commentators have followed his lead, that the primary dialectic of this historical epoch is that of domination and liberation (*Pedagogy* 93; see also Schipani 5) and it is within this dialectic that his literacy programs are shaped. I suggest, however, that beneath this dialectic is that of pain and imagination. In *Pedagogy* Freire develops his notion of epochal units, units that contain the themes of regions, nations, conti-nents, and the like. He envisions them as concentric circles, the smallest contained within the next and so forth. The broadest epochal unit, Freire claims, "contains themes of a universal character"; he considers the "fundamental theme of our epoch to be that of *domination*—which implies its opposite, the theme of *liberation*, as the objective to be achieved" (93). The point of the process of *conscientização* is the coming to *logos*. At this stage the oppressed recognize domination/liberation as the primary dialectic and opt for liberation rather than domination. However, Freire's theory of *conscientização* is concerned with the dialec-tic of pain and imagination as much as it is concerned with the dialectic of domination and liberation, if not more so. Perhaps it is best said that the theme of liberation is itself constituted by the dialectic of pain and imagination. The oppressed need liberation because they suffer pain; their liberation is based on the imaginative use of language and directed toward an imagined paradise. The dialectic of pain and imagination is more fundamental than the dialectic of domination and liberation: it is the dialectic that names domination and generates liberation from domination.

At its base, Freire's literacy theory is a theory of religious liberation rhetoric informed by the dialectic of pain and imagination. He propa-gates literacy because he wants people to be able to name their pain and imagine a painless world. Unlike Burke, Merton, and Romero, Freire emphasizes the object-oriented imagination. The process of imagination serves not itself but an objective end: utopia.

Pain

One cannot turn to Freire's work and find sections labeled "literacy and pain" or "suffering and *conscientização*." Rather than giving it an explicit position in his theory, Freire mostly assumes the reality of pain in the lives of the oppressed. Pain generates his theory, but does so only implicitly. One must attend carefully to Freire's efforts in order to discern the dialectical force of pain. Close attention to his theoretical efforts discovers this: pain predominantly characterizes an oppressive situation; it is the crucible of purification for both oppressor and oppressed; and it is a fundamental part of the literacy process, of the coming to Word.

As I discussed above, Freire understands oppression to be "Any situation in which 'A' objectively exploits 'B' or hinders his pursuit of self-affirmation as a responsible person." And central to oppression, for Freire, is class conflict.[5] Through the literacy process, the oppressed separate themselves from their oppressors and come to realize that they are "co-equal contradictions of the dominant elites" (*Pedagogy* 162–64; see also *Literacy* 52–54). Freire is aware that he may be accused of a naive Marxism that reduces the forms of historical ambiguity to class (Shor and Freire 111–12), but he nonetheless argues that class is central to historical struggle and that people who would want to change history must understand this and act accordingly (Freire and Faundez 74; see also *Politics* 135–37; *Pedagogy* 46–47, *Cultural Action* 52). While Freire invokes the figure of 'class' without adequately addressing its complexities,[6] and while he is extremely vague as to what he means by the trope, it is possible to glean from his work at least some characteristics of class as he understands it. On the surface, he appears to follow a stereotypical Marxist line. Deeper, however, one discovers that oppressive class relationships, for Freire, are marked by pain.

Throughout his books, Freire invokes Marxist figures to explain what he means by the classes. Speaking in terms of "workers," Freire looks for a society that employs all citizens to make goods of value to society and for labor that is not sold but committed to the good of the community (*Pedagogy in Process* 107–9, 157). While Burke, as I discussed in chapter 2, rejects the European figure of 'worker' as inadequate to the task of American rhetoric,

Freire chooses to import it into the Brazilian situation. It marks, for him, the reality of class conflict.

In Freire's system, the oppressor class, by implication, has the marks of the capitalist. It would want to prohibit the rights of workers, thwart full employment, engineer the economy so that it concentrates on the production of socially useless goods, or what Freire calls "value goods" produced in order to enhance their own comfort (107–9), and maintain a wage labor that leads only to the sustenance-level reproduction of the working class, not their flourishing (107–9). The classes, then, are marked by an economic dialectic. The oppressed are those who labor; the oppressors are those who purchase labor. Each struggles against the other over a variety of issues defined by the parameters of economics. Beneath this dialectic, however, is pain. As those who are forced by an economic system to become wage laborers, the oppressed suffer under the weight of the system and at the hands of those who purchase their labor. The oppressors, as those who purchase the labor of the oppressed, either allow the suffering to occur or directly inflict pain upon the oppressed so that they, the oppressors, may live comfortably, without suffering.

In *Cultural Action* Freire claims that societies in Latin America are formed "by a rigid hierarchical structure" and are marked "by high percentages of illiteracy and disease, including the naively named 'tropical diseases' which are really diseases of underdevelopment and dependence; by alarming rates of infant mortality, by malnutrition . . . by low life expectancy" (35–36). These passages indicate both the surface and deep levels involved in Freire's understanding of class relationships. One segment is educated and presumably enjoys the comforts the system provides. The other remains illiterate and does not enjoy the system's largesse. Rather, this segment suffers from myriad physical afflictions, all of which lead to "low life expectancy." Within the class relations of oppressor/oppressed, it is the oppressed class that is understood as the one that suffers, that is in pain. Unlike the postmodern Merton, whose *Geography* reveals a world in which oppressed and oppressor alike inflict pain, thus blurring the distinction between oppressor and oppressed, Freire maintains that a, if not the, key difference between oppressor and oppressed is that the oppressor inflicts pain upon the oppressed.

Freire returns to this theme in *Pedagogy*, which was written after *Cultural Action*. He presents as self-evident the pain in which the people of his own country—Brazil—and the people of other countries live. They are wracked by terrible diseases that do not bother the elites of Latin America. These diseases, moreover, are not simply a result of "nature." Rather, they are the "myriad diseases of poverty" (172; see also *Cultural Action* 35–36). These "diseases of poverty" are called "tropical diseases" in the "terminology of the oppressors" (172). They are not inevitable, Freire claims. Rather, they attend poverty that is the result of oppressive class relations structured into an unjust economy. The oppressors, however, mask this with metaphor. They think of the diseases of poverty as having originated in the natural landscape in which people live—the tropics—rather than in an unjust order. Freire offers a countermetaphor in order to locate these diseases in their proper place: poverty born of an unjust economy. The metaphor used by the oppressors attempts to hide what for Freire is the second characteristic of the oppressive class relationships. The first is that the oppressed class suffers. It suffers—and this is the second characteristic—at the hands of the oppressors. The oppressor class inflicts pain.

As that which owns "the world" (*Politics* 123), the oppressor class is triply implicated as that which inflicts pain. First, as it lives a life marked by good food, fine clothes, global travel, broad education, and Beethoven (*Pedagogy* 43), the oppressor class simply ignores the suffering of the oppressed class. It leisurely plays while most people labor in pain until they die (43). As inflicters of pain, the oppressors are implicated because they show no care for a painful situation. They ignore suffering.

Second, as that which owns the world, the oppressor class holds in its hands the oppressed (*Politics* 123). The oppressors are not implicated simply because they ignore suffering while they pursue comfort. They also are directly responsible for the suffering. At the top of the socioeconomic hierarchy, they maintain an unjust order that oppresses others. "The oppressor knows full well," Freire tells his readers, "that what is in his interest is for the people to continue in a state of submersion, impotent in the face of oppressive reality" (*Pedagogy* 37–38). By "submersion" Freire means a state opposite that of *conscientização*. It is the state from which literacy education seeks to help the oppressed emerge.

Finally, the oppressors are implicated as those who argue that "the pain and degrading discrimination" suffered by the oppressed "should be accepted by the dominated as purification for their sins" (Freire, Foreword viii). The oppressors do not simply ignore suffering nor inflict it within the hierarchy. They also attempt to convince the oppressed to accept pain as both just and helpful. The oppressed deserve it because they sin and it will help cleanse them of their sin.

Often, Freire claims, the oppressed accept this vision of their pain. They may come to accept what the theologians of the dominant classes have taught (Foreword vii); they may fatalistically think that God has ordained their suffering. This reluctance on the part of the oppressed to deny that their suffering is part of the just order is one of the great difficulties, Freire holds, which his system of literacy education faces (*Pedagogy* 48–52). The oppressed, as those most pained, are those most in need of *conscientização*. However, the oppressed, as those most pained, are often reluctant to move beyond their suffering within an oppressive class relationship. They have difficulty understanding, Freire argues, that suffering isn't a means of purification. This suffering, understood properly, is what prepares the oppressed to subvert the order of things and lead the entire society to a new, just order. Suffering provides the oppressed with a privilege: they understand the sins of the system better than anyone. Thus, they have the right to claim leadership in the revolution. The suffering of the oppressed prepares them not for heaven but for action on earth (29). Freire's program is intended both to help them know that they suffer as a result of an unjust order dominated by oppressive elites and to help them use this suffering as a crucible in which they form themselves as subversives of the oppressive order, as pained leaders looking beyond their pain.

Freire also holds that the pain of the oppressed is the crucible into which the oppressors must place themselves if they too seek liberation for the oppressed. While societies are structured by antagonistic classes, Freire maintains that it is possible for individual members of the oppressor class to give up their positions and commit themselves to the oppressed. Those educators, for instance, who would work with those most in pain, must be more than informed by the memory of the oppressed's suffering. They must immerse themselves in this suffering and be converted by it, converted so that they identify with the oppressed. The general phrase that Freire uses to describe this process is "class suicide" (46–47; *Pedagogy in Process* 16).

The oppressors who opt for liberation must commit suicide because it is, finally, the oppressed who must lead the way to transformation. They, better than anyone, understand what it is to need liberation because better than anyone they understand what it is to suffer (*Pedagogy* 29), what it is to be held torn and broken in the oppressor's hands. The dominant dialectic of the epoch, according to Freire, is that of domination and liberation. The oppressed, who are the most dominated and the most in need of liberation, understand the dialectic as nobody else because they understand better than anybody one of the dialectical pair that informs liberation itself: pain. Freire indicates three general ways by which such suicide can be committed.

First, Freire boldly borrows a figure from Christianity: to commit suicide, educators must experience Easter fully (*Politics* 105); educators must find in the pain of the oppressed an Easter experience that can transform selves (123). In this dimension, class suicide is accomplished imaginatively and leads to a change in the oppressor's psyche. The educator is to replace the figure of the suffering Christ with that of the suffering oppressed. Just as the educator experiences the persecution and death of the Son of God, so too the educator should experience the travails of a crucified people. So too the educators, focused on the suffering oppressed, will be reborn with them as they struggle to liberate themselves and thus the world (123). The imaginative entry into the lives of the oppressed through an icon occurs in the process of the struggle for liberation; the educator cannot simply remain distant.

This discussion of people's self-metaphorization as Christ has important implications for all types of rhetoricians. Self-transformation is made possible through a change in self-description. What allows the change in self-description are models of self that serve as guides. The postmodern rhetorician's liability is that there are so many models that they cancel each other out. This, no doubt, is the energy behind Burke's battle over 'worker' and 'people.' He wanted the latter, others the former; neither caught on. So too with Merton the models are conflictual: all are interesting, but all are inadequate. Freire, in contrast, is able to offer a model for self-metaphorization. As a Roman Catholic operating in a predominantly Roman Catholic context, Freire knows that Christ is a sure metaphor. The same is true, as I will discuss more fully in chapter 5, for Romero. In Brazil and El Salvador, people can take on Christ because it is already part of their selves. While Freire and Romero only have to attempt to change the meaning of a single metaphor, Christ, postmoderns must adjudicate between many competing metaphors.

Freire also suggests that the experience of psychological suffering allows one analogically to enter into the crucible of the oppressed's physical pain. He tells the U.S. educator Myles Horton that "We have the right to say that we are suffering; we have the right to express our pain. When Elza died, I had the right to stay home, suffering. . . . But I asked myself during those so difficult days for me, how many workers could cry about *their* loss?. . . we have to get the right to express our suffering because, look, the workers suffer" (Horton and Freire 215). This statement, perhaps, is the result of a conversation between two old men, one of whom, Horton, is dying. It begins with a general reflection on the place Freire would allow pain in the discourse of workers. Freire then moves from this general level to a particular: his own suffering at the death of his first wife, Elza. This pain is primarily psychological, the psychic anguish one feels at the death of a spouse. But this pain, Freire notes, did not allow him to wallow in himself and his own suffering. Rather, his own pain reminded him of the pain of those to whom he has dedicated his life, the workers. He knows that they suffer and need to be able to speak this suffering. No doubt, this suffering can be psychological, like Freire's at the death of Elza. Yet the pain of the workers about which Freire is concerned is primarily physical. It is the pain brought about by and within unjust economic systems; is the pain of the diseases of poverty. Not incidentally, Freire, in the above quotation, is concerned about the expression of suffering. He affirms that those who suffer have the right to express their pain. As I will argue below, Freire makes pain integral to *conscientização*. As the workers come to *logos*, they will learn to express their pain.

In addition to the imaginative entry provided by the transfiguration of the Easter trope and the analogical entry provided by mental suffering, Freire suggests that educators can enter the oppressed's crucible of pain through physical encounter. He claims, for instance, that what helped him to meld Christianity and Marxism was the suffering of the oppressed (243–47). He went to the slums, he reveals, because of his

Catholic upbringing; his mother, in particular, had taught him that there must be consistency between faith and acts and that Christianity demanded compassion toward those who suffer (245). Once in the slums, in the midst of the "misery" of the oppressed, Freire was led to Marx; he was convinced that "the structures of reality" would have to be changed and that Marxism, combined with Christianity, would enable him to design a literacy program that would lead to such a change (245–46). The suffering of the oppressed, then, seems to have served for Freire as a cauldron of conversion: it politicized him and led to a further commitment to the plight of the oppressed in misery.

Pain has a third role in Freire's theory, in addition to characterizing oppressive situations and serving as the crucible of transformation. It is also integral to the process of *conscientização*.[7] Freire includes the recognition of pain as part of the process of *conscientização*; his program attempts to counter the theological fatalism that too often engulfs the oppressed. It does so first by the choice of "generative" words that form the basis of the literacy project; Freire does not discuss explicitly the presence of pain in the generative words.[8] Central to the Freirean project is the gathering of these words. Rather than imposing a primer upon their students, literacy educators research in detail the oppressed's discourse until they identify fifteen to eighteen words that have struck them as being worthy to form the basis of literacy education in a given area. These words must be phonemically rich, phonetically difficult, and pragmatically important. It is the last which is most crucial for the inclusion of pain as part of the process of *conscientização*. As Freire writes, the pragmatically appropriate word "implies a greater engagement of a word in a given social, cultural, and political reality" (*Education as the Practice* 51). The generative list from the "vocabular universe" of the state of Rio de Janeiro well indicates how it is that pain is included in the most fundamental part of the process of *conscientização* (82–84). By "vocabular universe" Freire means the oral system in which a group lives. The words must be from the oral system. They cannot be from outside the lives of the students.

The first word from the Rio list, for instance, is the Portuguese *favela*, "slum." Freire holds that before the educator helps the students explore the syllabic combinations of the word, the educator must first help the students study the word's context. They are to discuss housing, health, nutrition, and clothing as they impact upon the word. The specification of *favela* into the subunits of food, clothing, health, and education would necessarily lead into a discussion of the pain of the people's lives. Food is a topic of concern because they lack it or lack food of quality; health is a topic because the oppressed suffer from the "diseases of poverty." This generative word is meant to help the *favela* dwellers name their pain in order to name the reality in which they live.

The same process applies to the other words on the list: rain, plow, land, food, Afro-Brazilian dancing, well, bicycle, work, salary, profession, government, swamplands, sugar mill, hoe, brick, wealth. Freire suggests a way to study each word, and it is instructive to analyze these in order to further understand how the painful dimensions of the generative words are meant to be made available to the learners. Consider, for instance, the word *profession*, which is seemingly innocuous. Freire proposes that these topics are crucial: "The social sphere. The problem of business. Social classes and social mobility. Trade and unionism. Strikes." The painful dimensions of the relations between social classes in the Freirean system have been discussed above; presumably Freire would want his teams to help the students come to know the general reality of the relationship as he enunciates it in his theory in general. Freire would be the first to admit that the specifics of class relations would vary from locale to locale. However, he also adamantly insists that there is a universal dialectic between domination and liberation; as I have demonstrated, pain is one of the deep dialectical partners that informs this surface dialectic. So too the final word *wealth* would open up the painful dimension of *conscientização*. This word, in particular, is rife with dialectical pairs that serve as the suggested aspects for discussion. One, perhaps not surprisingly, is "Dominant nations and dominated nations." The way in which Freire understands this relationship to be informed by pain needs no further rehearsal.

Pain as a part of the process of *conscientização* is found not only at the level of the generative words. It is also a part of "codification," which accompanies the initial introduction and discussion of a word. By codification Freire means the construction of a "representation of typical existential situations of the group" which includes the generative words in one way or another (51–52). Consider, for instance, one of the original codifications used in the Freire-led literacy program in precoup

1964 Brazil (77; see also *Cultural Action* 14). The picture is of a book, open to two pages. The page on the left is the picture: a crowded montage of mushrooms, people, and a dove in the center near the top. On the opposing page a poem, "A *Bomba*," reads " 'THE BOMB: The terrible atomic bomb / And radioactivity / Signify terror, / Ruin and calamity. / If war were ended, / And everything were united. / Our world / Would not be destroyed.' " Freire tells his readers that the discussion of this codification proceeds in two phases. In the first, the group is to discuss the nature of poetry as it relates to the question of culture. In the second, the text becomes open to group discussion. Inevitably, one may presume, the discussion would center on the presence of potential pain, actual pain, and the extinction of pain through the extinction of human existence through atomic warfare. Another literacy program might, for example, choose a Jack and Jill type rhyme in order to engender a discussion about the nature of poetry. Freire, however, chose a codification of the possibility of atomic war and the "Ruin and calamity" it would bring. The implications for American literacy education, at all levels, is obvious. Educators must decide if they will engage their students in the monumental problems of the world or if they will offer abstract and pat educational programs.

The codification and the poem also include the possibility of peace and the construction of a new world order that would end the threat of atomic war. Because it is uncrowded and centered near the top of the page, the most distinct figure of the picture is a flying dove among the crowded montage of mushrooms and people. Furthermore, the poem presents the thought that war can be avoided if "everything were united." While Freire does not explicitly say that the educator must direct the students to the possibility of peace, it is not by chance that the codification presents the possibility of a world order different from the one in which the ruin and calamity of atomic war is a possibility. The process of *conscientização* leads the oppressed to name the pain of the world in order to transform it. Atomic war is not inevitable; it can be avoided if the people who come to be *logos* so choose. Counterposed to the pain that comes to be known through the process of *conscientização* is the possibility of a new world. The process attempts to inculcate the imaginative capabilities. Freire seeks to teach the oppressed that their suffering is not necessary and ordained by God or fate and that they can actually change their lives. One of the steps toward change is to imagine a new future (Foreword ix). Just as the oppressed who come to *logos* are to grasp the pain that informs the need for and hope of liberation, they are to grasp the powers of imagination which can create an alternative, which can direct their liberation, which can be the end of their deeds of liberty.

Imagination

In Freire's theory, pain surfaces only occasionally and requires one to dig for it. Imagination is much more visible. Still, Freire has neither highlighted nor systematized imagination. While more evident than pain, it still subserves other issues. Freire has not, as is the case with pain, pushed his theory to its imaginative limit. For Freire, the imagination is both potentially and actually positive and negative: it can serve either domination or liberation. The oppressed and their educators must discern its dominating dimensions and enact its liberating possibilities.

Concerning its negative dimension, Freire criticizes conceptions and uses of imagination that function to keep the oppressed submerged in either nature or the myths of the dominant class. Some imaginative praxes, Freire argues, inculcate within people a longing for an imagined reality that will not overcome the systems of oppression (*Cultural Action* 1). To counter this, Freire places imagination at the center of the process of *conscientização* . The ability to discern and discuss images under the figure of synecdoche is both central to the process of literacy training and a proper result. Further, central to coming to *logos* are the ability to imaginatively abstract away from material reality and the ability to recombine words and sounds. Finally, and perhaps most important, Freire posits that the ability to reorder reality to create the future is the goal of the process of *conscientização*. Freire wants the oppressed, newly come to Word, to imagine and create utopia.

What has not been clearly delineated by Freire commentators, nor by Freire himself, is that Freire distinguishes two broad types of oppressed people in need of the imaginative power of *conscientização*: the rural oppressed and the urban oppressed. The former is marked by its submersion in myths of nature and its self-assumed similarity to animal life; the latter is marked by its submersion in the myths of industrial urban societies.

Freire criticizes any system that would lead human beings to accept the world as animals do or even imaginatively explain it by reference to myths of nature common to primal peoples. He argues in *Cultural Action* that human beings are not animals. The latter are limited because their imaginative process allows only for images presented by the senses and perhaps some minor manipulation of these images. Humans, however, can think: they can gather what is presented by the senses and reorder it in order to create worlds after worlds (6). What distinguishes humans from animals is the coming to *logos*, the coming to language that allows humans to transform the world. Humans, Freire tells his readers, are not meant simply to associate sense images with one another; they are meant to move beyond this stage of simple image association common to animal life and act, in *logos*, to create the world anew. As with Coleridge, and Burke for that matter, Freire looks to a level of imagination informed by the creative impulse itself. Freire would push his students beyond the levels of memory and fancy into a level of wordplay that echoes creation itself.

Similarly, humans are not to rest content with having moved beyond the level of animals to that of primal peoples who typically explain reality by reference to myths of nature and magic. While this stage may be an improvement upon the stage of animal image association, it is inadequate. Freire applauds Cabral, the revolutionary leader of Guinea-Bissau, who said to his people that "we can no longer believe in imaginary things," that people must have a scientific understanding of the world, that people must not explain natural occurrences like thunder and lightning by reference to imaginary myths, that people must not seek in amulets protection from bullets (*Pedagogy in Process* 134–35). Freire himself elaborates on this in his earliest work, identifying "magical" thinking with "semi-intransitivity." Magic and semi-intransitivity are characterized by the belief in superior powers that control the world, fatalism, and the inability to perceive authentic reality (*Education as the Practice* 20, 44). Freire claims that Chilean peasants, for example, who are caught in the magical dimension, construct imaginary systems in order to deal with the difficulties of rural existence. One group, Freire notes, makes a fire, throws ashes into it, and says "words of power" in order to halt hail. Another group, whose crops are being destroyed by rodents, waits for the priest and the priest's prayers to drive the rodents away (*Extension* 103–4). While Freire respects the logic that informs these systems (104; *Cultural Action* 36–37), he thinks they are finally inadequate; they are not the systems of people who have come to *logos* (*Extension* 106–7).

In addition to the rural populace who are similar to animals, Freire writes of the urban oppressed who are submerged in the myths of the oppressors. This is not to say that this group is entirely distinct from the rural oppressed. In fact the urban oppressed, whom Freire calls the "urban proletariat," using a Marxist figure (*Pedagogy* 145), are submerged in these myths after they "have begun to be conscious" (145). The urban oppressed, while suffering a form of oppression that differs from that of the rural oppressed, exist on the same line of historical development as the rural oppressed.

Freire argues that the social processes that move people away from their magical worldviews must do more than remove the magical rites; the sources of the rites must be removed as well. If they aren't, the sources will continue to thrive and come to mythologize technology. If this happens, people will simply use technology much as they used magic: technology will become the force that rules their lives (*Cultural Action* 37). Freire, who clearly believes that the modern move away from submersion in nature and magic is good, fears a new type of submersion. If not done properly, with an eye toward liberation, modernization will simply replace one set of problematic images with another. Technology, one of the marks of modernity, is capable of replacing magic as a mythic image. It can easily be turned into a god that resides in an inner sanctum, controlled by an elite priesthood (37).

In addition to this mythological imagining of technology as a god, modern societies have other imagistic ways of controlling the oppressed as they emerge from nature. One is by teaching the oppressed that the oppressor's history is the most important, if not the only, history. Freire notes that in Guinea-Bissau the Portuguese colonialists did just that: they taught that the history of Guinea-Bissau began with their arrival (*Pedagogy in Process* 14). This mythologization of history, Freire argues, is especially a problem for the urban oppressed since the social structures of modern urban existence encourage and depend upon historical con-struction (126).

Other ways of halting the process of *conscientização* include the use of mass media to induce people to believe only what they have heard on television and radio (*Education as the Practice* 34) and the propagation of the "myth of the possibility of ascent" (*Pedagogy* 144–45). In the latter instance, the oppressors teach the nearly historicized urban oppressed that personal success is achievable if only one works hard enough. What it fails to teach is that individual ascent is rare, and that class ascent is impossible. Common to all these ways of retarding the historicization of the urban oppressed is the inculcation of the image of the oppressor into the oppressed. The oppressed come to identify themselves with the oppressor, taking the oppressor's history as their own. As a result, the oppressed come to fear freedom because it would require them to destroy the image of the oppressor with which they have identified (31).

In a modernized society, truly insidious is the fact that the images of the oppressors determine the being of the oppressed even after the oppressors have been vanquished. Consider Freire's discussion of the literacy program in revolutionary Guinea-Bissau. He argues that this country chose Portuguese rather than Creole as the language of the national literacy campaign because the elites who determined policy in post-revolution Guinea-Bissau had internalized the oppressors' myths and chose to continue to propagate them: the elite believed that Portu-guese and its attendant images were superior to Creole (*Literacy* 118). They did so despite the new system of education, which Freire helped develop, which countered the colonialist mythologization of Guinea-Bissau history. The Freirian system calls upon the oppressed to be courageous, not to fear reimagining themselves. This means that the oppressed, who come to *logos*, will need to reject the images given to them by the oppressors (*Pedagogy* 163). However, as Freire illustrates with his discussion of the literacy campaign in Guinea-Bissau, the oppressed often refuse to reject the oppressor's imprints.

Well aware that the oppressor class uses images and the imagina-tion to maintain its position of domination, Freire makes images and the imagination central to the process of literacy he proposes. Just as the oppressed are, in part, to be kept in their pained condition through the manipulation of their imaginations, Freire seeks to help them use their imaginations for liberation. Freire holds that his system will lead to "knowing the denounced reality at the level of alphabetization and post-alphabetization" through "the continual problematization of the learners' existential situation as represented in the codified images" (*Cultural Action* 21). He continues with this: "Little by little, as these possibilities multiply, the learners, through mastery of new generative words, expand both their vocabulary and their capacity for expression by the development of their creative imagination" (22). These quotations point to the way in which Freire makes imagination central to the process of *conscientização*. It teaches the oppressed the process of imagination and the end for which Freire works: utopia.

The first quotation refers to the phase of codifications, discussed briefly above. These codifications, these representations, these images, are indispensible to the process. They help the learners objectify their own situations, and abstract themselves away from their own locations so that they can emerge from the images of human being that dominate these locations. Freire tells of a discussion, for instance, among peasants in Monte Mario. The generative word was *bonito* (which is the name of a fish and in English means "beautiful"). The codification was an image of the town in which the students lived; the image was a design including vegetation, houses, boats, and fishermen holding *bonito*. Freire reports that the students studied the image, looked out the window, again studied the image, and one said to another: "'This is Monte Mario. Monte Mario is like this and we didn't know it'" (*Literacy* 67–68). Freire, not content to let the point go uninterpreted, remarks that "through the codification these participants could achieve some distance from their world and they began to recognize it. It was as if they were emerging from their world to know it better" (68). The graphic dimension of *bonito* allowed the students to abstract themselves away from the universe in which they only knew the phonic *bonito*. The graphic image, which is the written word, helped the students separate themselves from their universe. The codification of the oral and written word intensifies this process. The image of their town in which *bonito*, in its phonic and graphic forms is a part, becomes objectified. With the help of the image they separate themselves from the town as subjects. Like Burke, Freire understands the ability to abstract as crucial to human being and therefore rhetoric as one of the primary functions of human being.

The codification and poem "A *Bomba*" serve the same purpose. The images of the mushrooms, the crowded people, and the dove help students emerge from a world where they don't know the potential ruin and calamity that would come from atomic war into a world in which the pain is known and named. Visually interesting and appealing, the image of the war to come brings people into a state of consciousness in which they know of the pain that would result from the use of atomic weapons. Imagination and pain work together in the process of *conscientização*; they help bring the people to *logos*; they help the people opt for liberation.

In addition to training them to abstract themselves away from their worlds in order to clarify their relationships with them, this phase of the process also trains students to think synecdochally. Like Burke, Freire makes the process of abstraction central to rhetorical education. He also favors the figure synecdoche, which is vitally important to Burke, and which Burke identifies as one of the four most important tropes (*Grammar of Motives* 503). Trained synecdochally, students learn to move between wholes and parts, parts and wholes: between their own lives and the lives of the community; between words and global images that contain the word. The codification of *bonito*, for instance, is part of an activity of abstraction, to help students separate themselves and their world into discriminated parts. They are to come to know that they are not submerged in the town, that they exist as entities independent of other entities with which they come into contact. Yet the codification also teaches the students that they are not simply discrete parts. They exist as parts of a whole. They may be fishermen, as opposed to vegetation, but both fishermen and vegetation are part of the larger category: Monte Mario. So too "A *Bomba*" teaches synecdochal thinking. The learners come to know that even though they may live in countries that do not have nuclear weapons, they, as human beings, are part of a nuclear order that threatens their lives. The learners aren't allowed to compartmentalize nuclear weapons as if the weapons belonged to a system apart from their own. The learners themselves come to think of themselves as members of a nuclear world.

The second quotation, from above, which tells Freire's readers that *conscientização* helps students use words imaginatively, also reveals the way in which it makes imagination central to itself: "Little by little, as these possibilities multiply, the learners, through mastery of new generative words, expand both their vocabulary and their capacity for expression by the development of their creative imagination." The generative words, upon which the codifications are based, are meant to be combined and recombined. They serve as the seeds of new words, which the learners create for themselves. Portuguese is a syllabic language, and the original Freirean system used this to help the students learn to create vocabularies. Consider, Freire tells his readers, the word *tijolo*, "brick" (*Education as the Practice* 53–54). Once it has been discussed with a codification, it is broken down into its syllabic components: *ti - jo - lo*. The students take each element and learn its phonemic family: *ta - te - ti - to - tu* and so on. They are then asked to take all the phonemic families and create as many words as they can, such as *tatu* (armadillo) and *lajota* (small flagstone). This process has at least two effects. The first is that, like the codifications, it helps the students emerge from an oral universe and "recognize" that language can be studied and is created by humans (55). Furthermore, according to Freire, it teaches them how to create their own discourse. Language itself becomes the object of imaginative combination and recombination. To use Burke's phrase, Freire's students learn the intricacies of "verbal manipulation" at a very fundamental level: syllabic organization. Just as the students will learn how to use language to name the world and transform it, they now use language to name and transform language. It is not incidental, certainly, that the generative words, as I discussed above, are words that are filled with pain.

Freire does not place imagination at the center of the process of *conscientização* as an end in itself. Students do not learn how to abstract themselves from the world in order to name it and understand its pain simply for their own sake. Neither do they learn how to think synecdochally nor how to combine and recombine phonemic elements simply to be able to think and act thusly. The process of *conscientização* is meant to prepare students to imagine a new world, a world free of oppressive pain.

Concerning transcendence, Freire writes that it is "the capacity of human consciousness to surpass the limitations of objective configuration" (*Cultural Action* 28). He discusses transcendence in order to draw more clearly his distinction between animal life, which only associates sense images, and human life, which must do more. The more it must do, as I have discussed above, is to take the world, be it language or the society in which the oppressed live, and reshape it with imaginative creativity. The human come to consciousness surpasses the limits of the world, be it language or society, and can thereby create it anew. Though a bee, Freire tells his readers in two places (*Learning* 59; *Cultural Action* 31–32), shames many an architect with the complexity of its hive, the worst architect is still more conscious, more human, than the bee, because the architect builds with mind and paper before using bricks and mortar. This ability to imagine the construction of something, be it a house, a language, or an entire society, is what makes humans human. What Freire wants the oppressed and their educators to imagine, above all, is a transformed world, a recreated society (*Learning* 59; Shor and Freire 186). The oppressed discover the pain and imaginative possibilities of their world in the process of *conscientização* in order to envision a new world, a new Eden. The recognition of pain that would destroy imagination and the recognition of imagination that would alleviate pain work together to bring the oppressed to *logos*, to make them *logos*, so they can speak the word that will transform the world, redirecting the movement of history. Freire tells Ira Shor: "This is Utopianism as a dialectical relationship between denouncing the present and announcing the future" (187).

The aim of transformation, as Freire understands it, is the birth of a new man and woman who exist in a society that is not marked by oppression. *Conscientização*, then, means that the oppressed class must work toward a society that does not mirror the oppression of the society in which it currently exists. Freire writes that as tempting as it may be for the oppressed to mimic the oppressors and become oppressors themselves (*Pedagogy* 29–30, 84), the oppressed must not do so. They must, rather, give birth to the new humanity, the new man (29–33), the new man and woman (*Pedagogy in Process* 105) as part of the nonoppressive new society (157).[9] The coming into the *logos* of *conscientização* means that the oppressed will enable humanity to rebirth themselves, following a metaphor common to the Christian tradition, as the new Adam and Eve; the coming into *logos* of *conscientização* means that the oppressed will enable humanity to reenter, if not re-create, Eden. As Freire writes, "it is necessary for education to give body and spirit to the model of the virtuous human being, leading to a beautiful and just society" (*Literacy* 41–42). The coming into *logos*, as Steiner suggests, allows humans to rival God. Humans become and speak the Word that creates.

Like many utopian thinkers, Freire is vague concerning the exact characteristics of the new man and woman, even of the new society. It is perhaps most clearly envisioned in a primer used in the literacy process of postrevolution São Tomé and Príncipe. The primer is based on Freire's theory, and was developed with his support, if not guidance, when he worked with the World Council of Churches. A part of it reads as follows:

> What is a new society without exploiters or the exploited? It is a society in which no man, no woman, no group of people, no class exploits the work force of others. It is a society in which there are no privileges for those who work with the pen and only obligations for those who work with their hands on the farms and in the factories. All workers are to serve in the well-being of everyone. (*Literacy* 82; see also 79, 85; and *Pedagogy in Process* 157)

This image is both a product of Freire's and others' imaginations and is meant to become part of the imaginations of the students who use this primer. As they come to Word they are to imagine themselves as humanity reborn with the power of God. As literate, they can create, anew, a world without the pain of exploitation.

Freire, finally, emphasizes an object-oriented imagination over a process-oriented imagination. While he painstakingly details the process in which students should be engaged—encounters with pain and abstraction through synecdoche and metaphor—Freire seeks to end the process with and in utopia. Once utopia has been achieved, the need for the process will no longer exist. People will live harmoniously, thus precipitating the end of the pedagogy of the oppressed.

Language and History

The dialectic of pain/imagination that informs that of domination/liberation occurs, as Freire understands it, within the context of language and history.[10] He argues that "the process of liberation of a people does not take place in profound and authentic terms unless this people reconquer its own word, the right to speak it, to 'pronounce' it, and to 'name' the world" (*Pedagogy in Process* 126). Language and history, Freire maintains, is a site of struggle between oppressor and oppressed. In addition to imposing their own history upon the colonized, as I discussed above within the context of imagination in Freire's theory, colonizers impose their own language. The propagation and inculcation of imperial language are central to the colonial project: the colonizer forms the colonized's identity by forcing the colonized to speak the colonial language. Moreover, it is often this language that marks the dominating presence of the colonizer in the postcolonial period. Technically, a colonized people may have achieved liberation, but as long as they speak the colonial language, they remain, at least partially, within the colonial system (126; also *Literacy* 152; Freire and Faundez 74, 80–81; Shor and Freire 149).

Thus Freire, like any liberation rhetorician, can be read as having affinity to the basic postmodern project: language and history are central to his project. However, while Freire shares postmodernism's concerns with these categories, he differs from postmodern rhetoricians because finally, for Freire, history is not completely ambiguous, language not completely plural. The history and language of the oppressed serve as foundations upon which Freire judges, and wishes to rebuild, the world. Freire argues that the history and language of the oppressed must serve as the final foundations because they, uniquely, understand the ways of the world. Their vantage has allowed them an understanding of the world that the oppressors *qua* oppressors simply cannot have. As they come to Word the oppressed become the linguistic and historical ur-class that is capable of transforming the world.

The process of literacy that leads to *conscientização* and allows the oppressed to emerge from their submersion in nature and the myths of industrial society and enter into history makes the oppressed into *logos*, in particular *logos* as noun and verb. Freire writes in *Pedagogy*:

Human existence cannot be silent, nor can it be nourished by false words, but only by true words, with which men transform the world. To exist, humanly, is to *name* the world, to change it. Once named, the world in its turn reappears to the namers as a problem and requires of them a new *naming*. Men are not built in silence, but in word. (76)

This quotation points to what very few have noticed in Freire. Human beings are able to name the world and thereby transform it only because they themselves are built in word. They are taught to name, they name, the world changes, the world demands a new naming, humans name it anew, and the cycle continues. People build the world through naming and are dialectically built in word by the world they have named.[11] Nowhere is this more evident than in Freire's discussion of the process of *conscientização*. Each stage is understood by Freire to be a stage of coming to language, particularly coming to verb. This process has already been summarized by many of Freire's commentators. What all miss, however, is the way in which the process is a process of coming to language in history.[12]

As Freire understands it, the literacy process of *conscientização* is marked by three essential stages of consciousness: semi-intransitivity, naive transitivity, and critical transitivity (*Education as the Practice* 16–18). These have been well detailed elsewhere and need no further explication in terms of their characteristics (Elias, "Social" 7–9; Schipani 12; Ordonez 116, 186; Collins 59–64). What is important to emphasize is that they are 'transitive' dimensions of consciousness, which is to say that they are verbal levels of consciousness. As the oppressed move through the literacy program, they become more and more transitive until they become critically so: they become critically transitive *logos*.[13] Freire seeks to help the oppressed become *logos*, that is to say, become conscientized as verbs. It is as verbs that they are able imaginatively to act in history as agents of the transformation of their pained lives.

Like his postmodern counterparts, Freire emphasizes the idea that humans as linguistic beings must take responsibility in history and for history; the difference, again, is that Freire privileges the historic role of the oppressed. Whatever the situation from which they emerge, be it the submersion in nature common to the rural oppressed or submersion in industrial myths common to the urban oppressed, Freire argues throughout his published writings that the oppressed, through the process of literacy that leads to *conscientização*, will and must become responsible for history. He writes in *Pedagogy*: "Men emerge from their *submersion* and acquire the ability to *intervene* in reality as it is unveiled. *Intervention* in reality—historical awareness itself—thus represents a step forward from emergence, and results from the *conscientização* of the situation" (100–01). Yet the oppressed must do more than simply accept historical responsibility. It is responsibility of a certain kind. Their acceptance of responsibility, according to Freire, also means that they will both recognize the themes of the epoch in which they live and choose liberation as the theme that will guide their responsible action of transformation not only for themselves but for the world (91–93; *Literacy* 156; *Education as the Practice* 5, 43; *Pedagogy in Process* 20, 23).

As if to anticipate postmodern criticism, Freire sometimes reveals a hesitancy to declare the superiority of the language and history of the oppressed. This is just as true of his discussions of oppressed peoples relative to each other as it is of his discussions about the relationships between oppressed and oppressors. However, the disclaimers do not, finally, contradict his primary argument that the language and history of the oppressed are to be privileged.

Concerning literacy programs among the "so-called indigenous populations" of Latin America, Freire writes that any "literacy program that negates the plurality of voice and discourse is authoritarian, anti-democratic" (*Literacy* 57), and any democratic society is authenticated by the "legitimation" of "different discourses" (56). One of the problems with the literacy program in Guinea-Bissau, he argues, is that its leaders did not respect the plurality of voices among the oppressed (over thirty languages and dialects) despite Freire's protests (110); they chose instead to impose Portuguese as the language of literacy education, dooming the program to failure. It did not, Freire claims, account for the plural languages of the people (112–13).

Freire, as well, recognizes that history is ambiguous to a certain extent. His actual practice in Brazil was marked by an awareness of the ambiguity of the language communities of that country. Rather than choosing a universal primer that presented a given number of words, the Freirean program emphasized the contextualization of the programs in the divergent language communities of the oppressed (Brown 227; Appendix, *Education as the Practice*). Based on what Freire calls "generative words," the literacy program differed from area to area because the literacy workers would investigate the words used orally by the communities and only then choose ones that were important to the life of the people. While some words were common to the various area (such as *favela*, "slum"), no two lists of generative words were identical. Freire recognized that the oppressed lived within different oral language communities, and he attended to this in the praxis of his literacy programs.

Thus, Freire avoids the criticism Lyotard levels against European communism, which I discussed in chapter 1. The European Communist Party, Lyotard argues, erred by ignoring the heterogeneity of 'workers.' It insisted that there was one type of worker and that it, the Party, defined the term. Freire, like the Party, demands the term *worker*. Yet his literacy program allows the heterogeneity of workers to speak. Rather than imposing a vocabulary decided upon by a central office, Freire insists that his literacy teams discover, within each particular locale, the worlds of the workers.

This is not to say that the worlds of the workers are primary. Freire argues that the oppressed must become masters both of their own language and that of their oppressors (*Literacy* 151–52). He recognizes that people simultaneously exist in different worlds and seems to relativize the commitments that they must make to these communities. He maintains that the oppressed must master the oppressor language so that they are not imprisoned in a linguistic ghetto. They must learn to interact with the world that oppresses them if they are to liberate themselves. The oppressed must master their own language so they may use it as a tool of resistance. Once mastered it can be fashioned into a revolutionary grammar and syntax in order to counter the oppressor language (128–29, 154; Freire and Faundez 45, 80–81).

Finally, though, Freire advocates monological contestation. While he recognizes that the languages of the oppressed, be they the language of the rural oppressed in Chile (*Extension* 104–6) or the language of the African-American urban oppressed in the United States (*Literacy* 126–28, 151–55), are logical and rule-governed, he regards his model of literacy as the superior language of the oppressed. The plural indigenous languages of the oppressed are finally inadequate to the task. The oppressed must go through the process of *conscientização* in order to become *logos*. Pre-*conscientização* being is, finally, too permeated with either animal existence or the images of the oppressors to allow the oppressed to liberate themselves. As Freire writes in *Extension*, he wishes to substitute a critical way of thinking for the magic way of the peasants (106). Or, as he discusses in *Literacy*, "emancipatory literacy" is what can help the oppressed become Word and transform society (156). This dimension of Freire's thought was most clearly and definitively enunciated in the final paragraph of *Cultural Action* (52). Speaking of the oppressed globally, Freire claims that conscientization is necessary if they want to achieve "the 'maximum of potential consciousness' " that will enable liberation (see also Shor and Freire 150–51, 181–82).

Similarly, Freire opts for the language and history of the oppressed as superior to that of the oppressor class. While he wants students to master both their own system and the oppressors', he argues that

> the ruling classes, as is the logic of the class system, prohibit the dominated classes from *being*. In this process the ruling class itself ceases to *be*. The system keeps them from rising above the contradiction, from any movement that would end their alienation as well as that of those they dominate. The dominated alone are called to fulfill this task in history. The ruling class, as such, cannot carry it out. (137)

For Freire, only oppressed classes must universalize themselves: only they can help both the oppressors and themselves become human beings.[14] In fact, Freire claims that the oppressed must not be ambiguous (*Pedagogy* 50, 121–22; *Politics* 135; *Literacy* 95); they must discover and assert their identity as an oppressed class in order to separate themselves as a class from the oppressor class and thus act to transform oppressive societies.

One practical implication of this theory is that Freire opposed the choice of Portuguese as the language of literacy education in postrevolution Guinea-Bissau (*Pedagogy in Process* 125–27; *Literacy* 111–13). As a World Council of Churches consultant, he urged the revolutionary government to choose Creole instead because Creole was the lingua franca of a nation marked by linguistic pluralism. The choice of Portuguese, Freire argued, simply furthered the pattern of colonization. Portuguese was the language of the colonizers and of the colonized elite who had internalized the myths of the mother country. It was not the language of the people; it did not manifest their lived history. Portuguese, in the case of the literacization of Guinea-Bissau, could serve only domination. Creole, in contrast, was that language rooted in the lived experience of the oppressed, that language through which pain and imagination could serve liberation. This, Freire holds, is the reason for its superiority. It is the medium of liberatory rhetoric.

5

Romero's Pastoral Letters: 'Goodtidings to Those Who Suffer'

here fascism and Auschwitz haunt our nights; tomorrow cocktails of bacteria and neutrons will perhaps be the last cups from which we drink.

—France Qúeré, *The Book of Christian Martyrs*

To the rear billow the clouds of the six million, in front the clouds of the nuclear holocaust. History is marked by these events of almost unspeakable pain and cataclysmic death. How can one write the death of the six million? How can one speak the mushroom cloud made worldwide? Their scope and intensity seem to defy discourse and, thereby, history. Yet it is important to keep in mind that they are *almost* unspeakable. Humans can speak the cataclysmically painful moments of history, as the epigraph demonstrates (Qúeré 13). The six million become ghosts who haunt our nights, specters only wispily present. The nuclear holocaust becomes an early evening scene of ironic macabre.

It is within this frame of ghosts and radiated cocktails that this book finds itself and that the subject of this chapter, Oscar Romero, spoke.[1] Romero was the archbishop of San Salvador, El Salvador, from 1977 until his assassination in 1980. As a Western Christian, Auschwitz was certainly Romero's legacy; the nuclear holocaust was his potential destiny, as it is for all creatures. But unlike many in Western Europe and North America, such as Burke and Merton, Romero's life and death as archbishop were bound by an even more immediate cataclysmic frame: that of the lives and deaths of his people. Attention to the life and death of Romero does not erase the frame of the six million and the nuclear holocaust; it does, however, momentarily bracket it. To read Romero is to read within the painful frame, the hopeful frame, in which he immediately lived.[2]

As he worked within El Salvador, Romero adhered to the global Roman Catholic community defined by its social teaching and to a specific, local manifestation of the Church, namely the liberation theology endorsed by the Latin American hierarchies at Medellín and Puebla.[3] While liberation theology was, and is, held suspect by the Catholic hierarchy, Romero believed liberation theology to be not an aberration found in a particular community at a particular time but, rather, fully consonant with the history of Roman Catholic social teaching. James Brockman claims that the first Letter "is heavy with quotations, as Romero labored to make clear that he was following the teaching of the universal church" (24); this is true of all the Letters. Romero simultaneously claims membership and leadership in the Salvadoran community and in the global community of his church. It is within this overarching dialectic, Romero as both Salvadoran liberation theologian and follower of Roman Catholic social teachings, that his Pastoral Letters work the dialectic of pain and imagination.[4] These Letters move, as do the rhetorics of Burke and Merton, toward a painful, process-oriented imagination. Unlike his fellow liberationist Freire, Romero seeks to engage his people not in an objectified end, but in the ongoing process of imaginative activity.

While the dialectic of pain and imagination in the Letters is thematically intriguing, the Letters' discursive strategy is my primary concern. They well manifest the dilemma and promise of rhetoricizing pain and imagination. As they speak the dialectic, they vacillate between the lived experience of the Salvadoran people and intertextual allusions and quotations. By intertextual I mean that Romero's Letters invite, even demand, their readers to enter into a labyrinthine exploration of texts that exist outside the Letters.[5] The readers are directed beyond the Letters and El Salvador into textual worlds such as those of the Bible and church documents. Romero, in effect, tells his audiences that if they want to begin to rhetoricize the dialectic of pain and imagination, they must move from the pain of El Salvador, from his words and images, to the words and images of other texts; be it those of the Bible or church documents. Romero calls his people to become a textual people, to discover in his texts and in the texts to which he directs them the ways in which they can understand and eventually verbalize their pain and their imagination.

This intertextuality serves as both an invitation and obstacle to shared discourse. Romero, who lived in the pained world of the people of El Salvador, lived as well in the world of the literate word. Romero wrote Letters whose meaning depends upon the ability of readers to move through Romero's literate, intertextual world. If the readers of the Letters are to participate with Romero in the dialectics of pain and imagination, history and language, the readers must move with Romero through the texts to which the Letters allude. If the readers won't, or can't, they are then distanced from the process in which Romero wants them to become engaged. If they can and choose to, they become involved in an intricate and complex intertextual world that transcends Salvadoran space and time.

The implications of this dialectical vacillation are enormous when one considers the intended role of the Pastoral Letters. Unlike Burke's theory, geared toward an academic audience, or Merton's *Geography*, accessible mainly to a literary elite, the Letters are pastoral. They are meant to be teaching documents for an archdiocese composed of educated and uneducated, literate and oral peoples. Yet as the Letters speak pain and imagination, their strategy implies a reader who is fully comfortable or who is willing to become fully comfortable in both the lived reality of El Salvador and in the vast complex of texts that exist outside of and independent of El Salvador. The Letters, at least in their intertextual dimension, presume a high degree of literacy. Thus, the Letters transcend Salvadoran space and time. In their intertextual dimensions, independent of the lived reality of the country, they are accessible to, and perhaps written for, a global literate class.

The first of the Letters certainly manifests this global intent. While addressed especially to his friends in the Salvadoran community who acknowledge both the local and the global Roman Catholic community with their acceptance of him as archbishop (*Voice* 54), the first Letter also claims that the church lives to save the world by bringing to it the meaning of Easter (54, 59). The saving act, in the first Letter (and in those that follow it, though less obviously), is marked by Pentecost, which is Easter made complete (57). Pentecost is the reversal of Babel, it is the moment when the apostles were able to speak to all peoples in

all tongues. It is a moment of linguistic unity in a linguistically fragmented world. Romero understands the Letters to speak beyond the
Salvadoran community, beyond even the global Roman Catholic community. They address all peoples. As they speak for the Church, which
finds its fullness in Pentecost, in the reversal of Babel, they speak as the
unifier of a linguistically, and thereby socially, fragmented world. Like
Burke, Romero places the rhetoric of his Pastoral Letters within the
lapsarian state of Babel: rhetoric's place is to be found amongst the
painful scramble of divided peoples.

Before turning to the Letters in detail, however, it is helpful to
examine a Lenten sermon that Romero preached twenty-two days before
his assassination at 6:30 P.M. on March 24, 1980. It addresses the feast
of the transfiguration, the festival that marks the illuminating glorification of Christ on Mount Tabor. The transfiguration, for Romero, is a, if
not the, root metaphor of the Salvadoran experience: it reveals the pain,
the imagination, the history, the language of his people. Thus, it is not
simply coincidental that the second, third, and fourth Letters were
written for that feast. These Letters are meant to mark and be marked
by 'El Salvador' in its many dimensions: as the name of the country, the
title of Jesus Christ, and the titular patron of both church and state
(Brockman 80). This is true, as well, for the first Letter, though it was
written for Easter. Romero's Lenten sermon concerning the transfiguration demonstrates that Romero linked the Easter event and the glorification of Jesus on Mount Tabor. It ended with this:

> We pray, brothers and sisters: the situation of our country is very
> difficult but the figure of Christ transfigured in full Lent is not far
> from us; it is the way that we ought to follow. The way of the
> transfiguration of our people is not far. It is the way that marks, for
> us, the Word of God this day: the way of the cross, of sacrifice, of
> blood and pain, but with a view full of hope set in the glory of Christ
> who is the Son chosen by the Father in order to save the world. We
> must listen to him! (*Su Pensamiento*, 3: 306)[6]

The country's troubles have an aural, rather than visual, quality
that calls Romero and the people. The call of language is critically
important to Romero, critically important to the people for whom

Romero has chosen to speak. The book that contains the Pastoral Letters, in both Spanish and English, is deliberately entitled *Voice of the Voiceless (La Voz de los sin Voz)*. Romero understood himself, and was understood by others, to be the one who spoke for the voiceless oppressed. As Jon Sobrino writes: "he presented his prophetic view of society divided into 'those who have too much voice,' and who detested him, 'and those who have none,' whose voice he was determined to be" (*Archbishop* 129).

The portion of the sermon quoted above manifests Romero's understanding of the place of his voice relative to the voice of the oppressed. He, and with him his parishioners, hears the country, and he takes it upon himself to interpret what he hears, to mold it into the image of the transfigured Jesus "in full Lent" (*en plena cuaresma*). This image analogically links itself to that which Romero hears: as the country suffers so does Christ; as Christ suffers so does the country.

Romero also introduces a visual dimension to this glorification of suffering: he and his people hear the suffering of the country and link it analogously to the image of the Lenten Jesus. In so doing, and by way of asking his people to accept the way of the cross as their own, Romero directs his hearers to the sight of the glorious Christ. Romero's analogical link between the image of the transfigured, Lenten Jesus and his people reveals a significant difference between his own painful rhetoric and the rhetorics of Burke, Merton, Freire. These three find nothing particularly redemptive in physical pain. Moreover, Freire condemns religion for teaching that physical suffering is a part of God's plan. Romero, in contrast, asks his people to understand that their own material suffering is analogous to the suffering of Jesus. Romero wants them to internalize the image of the suffering Jesus that he presents because Lenten suffering is the way to the imagined kingdom. The way of the cross, as Romero understands it, is conjoined to a view full of hope.

The people, then, are to accept their suffering as an image of Christ's suffering only to see it as a way to the glorification they will share with Christ. Romero preaches in this Lenten sermon that

Christ set on the summit of Tabor is the most beautiful image of liberation. Thus God loves men: forced out of sin, of death, and of the inferno, living his eternal life, immortal, glorious. This is our

destiny, and to speak of this heaven is not alienation but motivation to work, with more enthusiasm, the great responsibilities of
the earth. No one works the earth and the political liberation of
the people with such enthusiasm as one who hopes that the
liberatory struggles of history shall incorporate themselves into the
great liberation of Christ. (*Su Pensamiento*, 8: 293)[7]

As they suffer pain, as they internalize the image of the Lenten Christ,
Romero asks his hearers also to look toward the image of the transfiguration, the image of Christ ablaze with the glory of God on Mount Tabor.
It is the image both of the kingdom to come and the kingdom on earth,
which mirrors that which is to come. Romero is careful to distinguish
between political liberation and the liberation that comes, finally,
through the salvific work of Christ. The two types of liberation are not
unconnected; political liberation is a representative image of the final
liberation that exists beyond history. Still, political liberation is only an
image found within history. The people who work for it know that they
work with the hope that this historical liberation, itself a light, will
become part of the final glorious transfiguration of history itself.

Earlier in the sermon Romero speaks to this point by reminding
his parishioners that Christ, transfigured on Mount Tabor, stood between Moses and Elijah, who represent "the two great Lents of Israel"
("las dos grandiosas cuaresmas de Israel") (290). Theologically, for
Romero, this image tells Christians that Christ "is the fullness of all the
history of Israel" ("es la plentitud de toda la historia de Israel") (290).
This image is crucial because it demonstrates that transfiguration manifests the hoped for and thereby imagined kingdoms to come on earth
and in heaven. Consider, for instance, the figure of Moses. He, like Jesus,
is a Lenten figure. Presumably, like Christ he is both an analogical and
synecdochal model for the people of El Salvador as they experience Lent
in their own lives. As Romero reminds his parishioners, Moses spent
"forty years wandering the desert in search of the promised land"
("Cuarenta años atravesando el desierto para llegar a la tierra pro-
metida") (290). Moses labored to deliver his people from Egypt and then
suffered with them as they were exiled to their Lenten desert, all the
time seeking to help his people live as a people of God. Moses, however,
was only allowed a vision of the promised land (Deuteronomy 34:4). He

suffered, he labored to have his community live by God's command-
ments on earth, but he never saw the realization of the promise, he never
experienced the land flowing with milk and honey. It remained, for him,
a vision beyond the pain of history.

Pain

The Lenten sermon discussed above provides a helpful introduc-
tion to some of the ways in which Romero deals with pain in the Pastoral
Letters. It invites readers of Romero to study the implications of the
Easter dating of the first Letter and the feast of the Transfiguration dating
of the second, third, and fourth; the intertextual quality of Romero's
rhetoricization of pain; the analogical and synecdochal glorification of
Lenten suffering. These aspects do not exhaust the complexity of the
Pastoral Letters but they are key indicators of the ways in which the
Letters rhetoricize pain. The Letters are concerned with three primary
dimensions of pain: (1) Salvadoran pain as historical background; (2)
the Church and the people as victims of pain; (3) pain as the final
adjudicator of all social questions. Within these categories, Romero
rhetoricizes pain with reference both to actual Salvadorans and to
characters and ideas from other texts.

That pain is the foundation of the Letters initially reminds one
that Romero, as the archbishop of San Salvador, was a liberation
theologian. That Romero had made a preferential option for the poor,
as do all liberation theologians, is well known. More interesting is the
way in which the Letters name the pain of the oppressed as that to which
Romero is committed, that from which Romero speaks. The Letters
range from simply naming the pain with only the aid of descriptive
language to intertextual allusions that force the reader of the Letters into
worlds other than that which is immediately lived.

Early in the second Letter, "The Church, the Body of Christ in
History," Romero simply refers to the pain of the Salvadoran situation.
Speaking of the hope that he and his people have for a better society,
Romero claims that this word of hope is not naive but that "It is
accompanied by the blood of its priests and campesinos" that cry out
against oppression (*Voice* 64). The only world to which these words

direct their readers is the world in which they live. This Letter, in this instance, rhetoricizes pain with nouns that obviously and immediately speak it: blood and grief. That they are linked to words common to the Salvadoran ear, priests and campesinos, only helps to locate them in the lived, historical reality of the people. The first Letter, "The Easter Church," foreshadows this simple description and provides a specific name when it refers in its opening to the execution of Rutilio Grande, S.J. (54). Grande, a longtime friend of Romero's and a leading proponent of liberation theology, was shot to death in 1977 by representatives of the Salvadoran political right (Brockman 8–13).[8] The first Letter's reference to the murder of Grande directs readers back into their own lived histories. So too the second Letter "speaks of the priests and laity who have been murdered or disappeared (*Voice* 76), and the third writes of the hunger, injury, and murder that afflicts the people (87).

This way of naming the pain of the oppressed is perhaps closer to the reality of the oppressed's lives than is allusive intertextuality. However, while it directs the oppressed back into their own world, it is still distant from the named pain. It is, finally, language about the pain and not the pain itself. This, certainly, is the foremost problem for any language that attempts to speak pain. Even if it is possible to distinguish, as it is with Romero's Letters, between an intertextual strategy and a strategy that appeals to physical reality, language tends to complicate the latter. Language always transforms the physical into language. Thus, the rhetorician can't simply study the physical reality to which Romero's seemingly simple descriptions point. Rather, the rhetorician as rhetorician must study the language about the physical reality. The physical reality is present only as the language substitutes for it. This point is most easily understood when one considers the metaphorical quality of this seemingly simple naming. The blood of the second Letter, for instance, is immediately personified by Romero into speaking subjects who call their oppressors to justice. In speaking for those pained who have no voice, Romero here attempts to return their voices to them. An integral part of their material being, blood, is given voice. It, like the blood of Abel, cries from the ground. At this point, the simple nouns used by the Letter to describe the pain of the oppressed lose their simplicity as they become part of an intertextual play. This is not to say that readers of this Letter need to involve themselves in the story of Cain and Abel in order to understand the import of the personified blood. However, the personified blood, crying out, certainly echoes the story of Cain and Abel and does so even more when one remembers, as would the original Salvadoran readers of the Letter, that the blood of the priests and the campesinos is spilled by other Salvadorans, their 'brothers.' The intertextual rhetoricization of pain, which Romero uses more directly in other places, is implicit in this seemingly simple description of the people's pain.

Two further examples of the way in which the Letters name the pain of the Salvadoran oppressed, and in so doing mark themselves as documents of liberation theology, are found in the third and fourth Letters. The third, "The Church and Popular Political Organizations," makes an explicit allusion to Cain and Abel. In an attempt to persuade apathetic Salvadorans that destructive pain and suffering are not to be accepted, that they should commit themselves preferentially to the poor and work for the alleviation of destructive pain, Romero asks: "How can we answer the question the Lord put to Cain, 'What have you done? Listen to the sound of your brother's blood, crying out to me from the ground' " (87).

Romero, here, makes the analogical link between the experience of the people and the Biblical character explicit. But, unlike the direction readers might take in response to the crying blood of the second Letter, the readers of this passage are immediately directed into another text rather than into their own lived experience. With this reference to the image of Abel, the third Letter abstracts the reader away from history into the textual world of the Bible. Abel represents the oppressed and the Letter attempts to speak to its readers at this textual level. Such an appeal, certainly, depends entirely on either the reader's knowledge and acceptance of the story of Cain and Abel as important or on the hope that if the reader doesn't know the story, the reader will be attracted enough to the claims of the Letter to learn it.

The fourth Letter, "The Church's Mission amid the National Crisis," also provides an example of this intertextuality. In an attempt to highlight the suffering of the campesinos and to call for a conversion to them, it refers to a graph, prepared by a legal aid group, which represents the rate of murder and arrest suffered by the campesinos at the hands of various segments of the Salvadoran security and military forces. Romero emphasizes that the rate has risen in six months from 307 to 406 and that not one victim was a member of the elite (120).

The class dialectic is clear: the Letter separates landowners from the peasants, marking them as opposites. But this dialectic is undergirded by pain. The separation of the landowners and the peasants is based on the association of the killers, jailers, and landowners. If the landowners aren't being killed or jailed, it suggests, then the landowners belong with the killers and jailers. Again, the veracity of this dialectic rests upon another text. It is not something that Romero knows, in terms of the exact numbers, from his own experience. He learned of it from a graph constructed by others. While this intertextual naming of oppression is similar to the analogical intertextuality that involved the image of Abel's blood in the third Letter, it differs from it significantly. The reader of the Abel analogy in the third Letter need not necessarily be literate in order to be able to move into the intertextual world to which the analogy points. The Cain and Abel story lives in an oral world beyond the Biblical text. Non- or semi-literate Roman Catholic peasants probably had and have the Cain and Abel story available to them in the oral world in which they live. To enter into the intertextual world of the graph, however, one must have access to it and the documents it represents and be able to competently read the graph and its attendant documents. If one has neither access to the material nor the ability to read it, the intertextual world is not open. The Letter points to a text to name the pain of the people, but it is, perhaps, a limited text. The graph is used by the Letter to make the point that it is the people who suffer in El Salvador, the campesinos and the urban oppressed for whom Romero, and the Church he represents, have preferentially opted. This attention to the suffering of the poor is the second of the three dimensions of pain in the Letters, emphasizing the victimage of the Church and the people. The Letters further delineate this category and suggest to those pained that they may either accept the pain as martyrs or be crushed by it, that martyrdom continues the suffering of Christ, and that martyrdom gives rise to hope.

In an extremely complex intertextual move, the second Letter, "The Church, the Body of Christ in History" also calls on the Church and the people whom it serves to be martyrs. It claims that while often the Church has perverted itself and chosen to be served rather than to serve, it has, at times, fulfilled its role as the body of Christ (73). When it has chosen to serve the world, to be the body of Christ, and by this Romero means to opt preferentially for the oppressed, the Church has been rejected and persecuted, thereby extending the legacy of Christ, of John, of Stephen, of Paul (73–74). The intertextual move is essentially a claim that the authority of the tradition, and particularly the tradition as defined by the persecution of Jesus and the earliest Christians, should be the model followed by those in El Salvador who would preferentially opt for the poor. The pain and suffering of persecution, because it arises from the body of Christ, is to be welcomed as the heritage of the Christian community. Jesus suffered, Peter and John suffered, Stephen suffered, Paul suffered; so too should the Letter's followers. The Letter doesn't, however, reveal the full nature of the heritage of martyrdom. Rather, the Letter directs its readers into both the Gospels and the fifth book of the New Testament, the Acts of the Apostles.

Stephen, for instance, as the consequence of his denunciation of the idolatrous practices of Jerusalem, was imprisoned, tried, cast from the city, and struck with stones until he died (Acts 7:54–60). Significantly, helping to stone him was one named Saul, who, as his later Christian self Paul, suffered stonings (14:19), beatings (16:23), and other kinds of torture (21:31). Beyond the obvious persecution and death that Jesus suffered and to which the Letter alludes, the authoritative models of Christian life to which the Letter points suffered as well. The acceptance of pain unto death, according to the second Letter, is the appropriate calling for the Christian living out the will of God. Those people Romero finds faithful borrow from John's Gospel and seek to die with Christ (Voice 64).

The second Letter continues this intertextual move. Referring to John 15:20, the Letter claims that persecution of the Church, when it is acting as the body of Christ, is to be expected. In fact, John reminds the Church that Christ foretold the persecution of the faithful: the servant, like the master, will suffer (79). Soon after this, however, the Letter directs its readers into the lived reality of El Salvador: "The Salvadoran people have been subject to attack. Its human rights have been trodden underfoot" (79–80). This juxtaposition demonstrates the way in which the Letters vacillate in their rhetoricization of pain between an intertextual world and the world of the people. Following upon an allusion to Christ's thoughts about persecution and martyrdom as reported by John, the Letter shifts to a claim about contemporary persecution and suffering in El Salvador. Its readers are directed away from texts to lives of Salvadorans with the metaphor "trodden underfoot."[9] While this is certainly a metaphor—not all the oppressed have been literally trodden underfoot—it is also literal; some undoubtedly were trodden underfoot. It is not difficult to believe, for instance, that of the at least fifty townspeople shot dead at Aguilares, El Salvador, in May 1977, by government troops, some were trodden underfoot during their ordeal (Brockman 31). The metaphor again reveals the dialectic involved in appeals to physical reality. On one hand, language tends to obfuscate the physical, transforming it into graphic and phonic traces. On the other hand, language can also help discriminate physical activity. There is an experienceable difference between what is called a "caress" and what is called "being trodden underfoot," and language helps humans differentiate these extralinguistic events.

The metaphorical, analogical connection that makes the Church the body of Christ not only calls upon the Church to take on persecution for the sake of God, to become a martyr, as Christ and the early Christians did. The connection runs both ways. The metaphor of the Church as the body of Christ demands that the Church should suffer because Christ suffered but that, in turn, as the Church suffers Christ suffers. While they are being trodden underfoot, Christ is in personal communion with all his people: Christ is affected by the trodding (80). The suffering of the people of Christ continues Christ's suffering. Calvary did not end with the resurrection.

Nowhere is this connection between Christ and the Church more clearly read in the Letters than in the second. It claims that "It is the church's duty in history to lend its voice to Christ so that he may speak, its feet so that he may walk today's world, its hands to build the kingdom, and to offer all its members 'to make up all that has still to be undergone by Christ' (Col. 1:24)" (7C).

The first quotation, in particular, locates the second Letter, and all the Letters, immediately in history (the Church has a duty in history); language (the Church must "lend its voice" to Christ); imagination (the building of the kingdom enabled by the metaphorical hands of Christ); pain (what Christ still must suffer). At this point, only the last of these is of primary concern. As should be clear by now, what Christ must still undergo, as he is present in the Church, his new earthly body, is persecution, pain, suffering, even death. Consider the appeal to Pauline authority. This fragment of the second Letter's ancestor, Paul's Pastoral Letter to the Church at Colossae, informs its readers that Christ's painful suffering did not end on Calvary. It continues, Paul claims, in his own flesh and in the flesh of the Church, both of which are the flesh of Christ. This fragment moves a curious reader even further into both the world of the Letter to Colossians and into the Acts of the Apostles and Paul's other Letters. One wonders what it is he suffers. The Letter to the Colossians later reveals, (4:3, 10, 18) that Paul writes from prison, in fetters. So too the fragment moves one beyond the Colossian world into other parts of the New Testament where tales of Paul's suffering abound. Immediately following the Pauline allusion, the Letter declares that should the Church forget its role as the body of Christ, Christ would remind the Church of it (70). Then, in yet another allusion, it points to Vatican II and Medellín as the marks of the true Church (70). The activities and texts of both serve as the authoritative foundations for those who would preferentially opt for the poor, for those who would argue that the Church does and must continue the suffering of Christ as it works to build the kingdom. Importantly, Romero simply invokes the names of these events in Roman Catholic history. At this point, he makes no attempt to explain them, no attempt to make the wanderings easier. If one wishes to find the connections, one must delve into the texts with only the aid of allusion.

The Christ-like experience of pain and suffering—the third dimension of pain as it is inflicted upon and accepted by the Church and the people—gives rise to hope. The Letters, especially the second, most often point to the lived history of the Salvadoran people in order to make this claim. Concerning the blood and grief of the priests and campesinos, for instance, it claims that "their blood is also an expression of a readiness for martyrdom. It is therefore the best argument for, and a testimony to, the utterly certain hope that the Church offers, as from Christ, to the world" (64). With its connective *therefore* and its use of the word *argument,* this passage invokes the world of logic that is often, if not always, based in the world of language alone.[10] One may derive the following inferential scheme from the second Letter's appeal to Paul's

Letter to the Church of Colossae, as discussed above: Paul says that the Church continues the suffering of Christ; Paul is our textual authority; therefore the Salvadoran Church, as it suffers, continues the suffering of Christ. The appeal to the blood and grief of the priests and campesinos is of a different order. Logical inference is not based on the premise of an authoritative fragment of language. Rather, it is based in the lived pain of the people. At this moment, the Letter tells its readers to look to their own pained experiences, and the pained experiences of their neighbors, in order to derive the knowledge that hope arises from persecution and martyrdom. Vacillating between intertextuality and rootedness in lived experience, this passage from the second Letter moves its readers into the blood and grief that cry from the ground (82).

Yet all is not woe. Despite the pain and suffering of their lived experiences, Salvadorans, Romero claims, will not be parted from the love of Christ and the hope that this love brings. The primary hope that the Letters find in pain is the hope of unification. This is the third element of pain with which the Letters are concerned. They propose that pain, once fully considered, can adjudicate divisions among the oppressed both within the Church and within Salvadoran society.

One of the most important facets of Romero's rhetoric and one that all liberation rhetoricians would do well to follow is that the Letters preferentially opt for the poor but they do not romanticize them. While Romero deeply identifies with his people, he does not find them faultless; he does not cringe from publicly criticizing them. Many liberation rhetoricians refuse to criticize their people out of a fear of presenting a divided front to their enemies or out of a loathing of airing dirty laundry in public. As a result, I would argue, liberation movements suffer. Israel is not served by people who are unwilling to criticize Israel's treatment of Palestinians. African Americans are not served by leaders who condone inner-city gangs or the brutality of the L.A. riots. Romero, in contrast, takes everyone to task. No healing can take place, Romero believes, until all wounds are exposed and understood. Left to fester, wounds will only continue to ruin Salvadoran society. As a result, Romero exposes all oppression, including that among the oppressed. For instance, the third Letter reports that some campesinos become corrupt and engage in oppressive activities on behalf of the government: they serve as informants, kidnappers, torturers, and even killers (92). In the fourth Letter, Romero holds that one cannot justify the sins of the oppressed simply because one has opted for them. Always, among all peoples, the failure to act lovingly must be condemned (140).

To name the pain that the oppressed inflict upon one another, pain that divides those preferred by God and the Church, the third Letter refers its readers to the lived world of the Salvadoran experience. The fourth Letter, while seeming to do the same, actually makes an inter-textual move, basing its claims upon the results of a survey which, as Brockman relates, Romero and the Church had sent to Salvadoran parishes prior to the Latin American bishops' conference held at Puebla, Mexico, and prior to the composition of the fourth Letter (187). Puebla met to confirm the direction set by Vatican II and Medellín for the Latin American Church (116), and many Latin American bishops surveyed their people prior to attending the conference in order to hear their concerns. Romero did this as well and used the survey to help him compose his fourth Letter. In this Letter, Romero condemns machismo, exploitation, the failure to serve one's family, and antagonism among the campesinos. Presumably, this list of sins was reported by campesinos themselves.[11] Usually, when the Letters direct their readers to the lived pain of the people, they do so without the aid of quantified data so common to social science, media, and advertising discourse in the United States. Typically, U.S. social scientists, newspapers, magazines, and businesses direct people outside their own words into the lived experience of the country with the aid of quantified data in the form of poll and survey results. Romero's Letters rarely use this type of evidential figuration of people's lived experience in order to discuss their pain. They usually depend on Romero's intuitive sense of the experience lived by the campesinos and their priests. The only other instance of such evidential figuration of the pain of the people's lives is the graph, to which Romero also refers in the fourth Letter, that details the number of campesino deaths and imprisonments caused by the government and its forces (120). The survey of oppressive activity that informs the fourth Letter may indicate an attempt on Romero's part, as he matured in his role as archbishop, to qualify scientifically the experiences of his people. Its effect is dialectical. It separates Romero from the people because a written text, distributed and collated by Church workers, mediates between him and the campesinos. However, it may also help Romero better to understand the campesino experience in its entirety. He no longer has to rely solely on his sense of the situation gathered only from pastoral visits.

Romero, then, holds that the oppressed must opt for each other and that they can do this only when the pain that they inflict on each other is exposed. Once exposed, it serves as the basis for unity. Just as the elite unify with the oppressed when the elite comes to understand the oppressed's suffering, so too the oppressed can use their own pain.

Not only are the poor divided and in need of unification. The Church itself is divided. Quoting from and borrowing the intertextual possibilities provided by Puebla, in the fourth Letter Romero claims that the Latin American Church is split because it has not, in its entirety, committed itself to the poor. When it does, the Church will stand as the unified body of Christ (125–26). This Letter reminds its readers of the metaphor that guides the second Letter: the Church is to be identified with Christ, which is to say that the Church is to be Christ in history. This can only be done, the Letter claims with the aid of Puebla, through a preferential option for the poor that will help the Church identify fully, as it should, with the poor of history: Christ and the oppressed of Latin America (125–26). The Church metaphorizes itself as the body of Christ, and this body can only be itself fully when it commits itself to the poor, who synecdochally represent the suffering Christ. For Romero, shared pain will heal the Church (81).

The identity and therefore the unity of the Church are based, in part, on common suffering that arises from its commitment to the lives of the oppressed. It is this commitment and unifying suffering that the Church offers to the world. The second Letter holds that the Church exists to birth into the world the love of God in Jesus Christ and that this Christ is a Christ committed to the oppressed. The second Letter also claims that as the Church represents Christ to the world, the Church will bring about, in the intertextual words of Vatican II, "the unity of the whole human race'" (66). The Church represents Christ who himself represents the poor and oppressed. Or, the Church represents the poor and oppressed who represent Christ. As sign, as sacrament, the Church offers the suffering of Christ, the poor, and itself as the way toward the unification of the human race. Just as the divided poor can be unified in their pain by their pain, just as the divided Church can be unified in a commitment to the pain of the oppressed, so too, the Letters suggest, pain can adjudicate the divisions that separate human-kind.

Imagination

The fourth Letter, "The Church's Mission amid the National Crisis," clearly identifies a, if not the, source of oppressive, destructive pain in El Salvador: idolatry. Romero condemns false imagining, the placing of things other than God into the position that God alone should hold. The fourth Letter contends that raising anything to the level of "an absolute" offends God because this false absolute often, if not always, leads to oppressive, destructive pain and suffering (*Voice* 133). All the Letters demand that the Church, as the body of Christ, denounce false images, idols formed out of distorted human customs (72). As it de-nounces false images, the Church must also uphold three true images of God: Christ, the kingdom, and Mary. This imaginative activity, im-portantly, finally leads the Letters into an area similar to the one shared by Burke and Merton: the process-oriented imagination. This is to say that the Letters' prolific object-oriented imaginative activity finally moves beyond objects into the imaginative process itself. I note and emphasize that my reading of Romero's theological rhetoric would undoubtedly violate Romero's intention, if that were discernible. As a priest and archbishop, it seems likely, for instance, that Romero would maintain that Christ is primary. Nonetheless, his Letters allow for a more complex view. They do not follow the orthodoxy of the Roman Catholic Church despite the fact that Romero served as the Church's official representative.

The first way in which the Letters move beyond imagined objects into the imaginative process itself is thematic. The seeming primacy of the image of Christ, for instance, is subverted by Romero's dedication to imagining his mother, Mary. So too the imagining of the kingdom constantly undercuts itself. Romero, like Burke and Merton, and unlike Freire, maintains a tentative view of utopia: humans imagine it and seek it but it is finally beyond human reach and understanding. The second way in which the Letters move their readers beyond imagined objects into the dimension of the imaginative process is by their use of inter-textuality. They constantly shift between texts and the images these texts propose, and thereby the Letters suggest that no one text, no one image of the kingdom, of Christ, of Mary, is fully adequate. Thus, the Letters imply that rather than focus on a specific image, the faithful should engage themselves in the intertextual imaginative process.

In his fourth Letter Romero identifies and denounces three idols that trouble Salvadoran life, three images that the Church should reveal for what they are: wealth and private property; the national security state; the popular organizations (133). The first, the idol of wealth and private property, "is at the root of structural and repressive violence" in El Salvador (134). The counterimagining, certainly, begins in this description, with an organic metaphor to describe something that brings death, not life. This idol is that on which structural and repressive violence feed, the soil in which the violence propagated by this idol finds nourishment. As it is the purpose of the fourth Letter to explicate Puebla (133), Romero refers to it, as well as to Medellín and "recent popes," in order to claim that the capitalism condemned in general by the Church finds it local representation in this idol.

The second idol, that of national security, is problematic because it allows the military elite to violently oppress the people for the good of El Salvador (134). The Letter declares, with the aid of Puebla, that this idol considers anyone not in complete compliance with the state to be an enemy and thus the just target for a variety of violent acts (134). This idol is particularly pernicious because it passes itself off as a defender of Christian civilization (134). In other words, this idol is well aware of the importance of imagining and uses imaginative construction in order to defend itself.

The fourth Letter advances an analogical counterimage by claiming that national security is in reality similar to Molech, the god satiated only by sacrifice (135). As is the case in the other Letters, this Letter presumes, in its intertextual imagining, that its readers either know the story of Molech or know how to find out about it. It refers, probably, to 2 Kings 23:10, which speaks of the reforms of King Josiah: "And he defiled To'pheth, which is in the valley of the sons of Hinnom, that no one might burn his son or his daughter as an offering to Molech." Carried to its limit, this simile implies that if Molech is the national security state's Biblical counterpart, then Romero is Josiah, the one chosen by God to reform God's people and to cleanse God's land. God, then, is YHWH, the Hebrew deity active in the political/social/religious struggles of the people who condemns "the deities that call for victims because they live on their blood as the only means to their own survival" (Sobrino, *Archbishop* 16).

The popular organizations comprise the third idol that the fourth Letter identifies. While the first two idols are wicked (*Voice* 135), this one is not. Popular organizations, to their credit, attempt to alleviate the pain of the people. However, they also tend to the evil of idolatry. The fourth Letter directs the reader back to Romero's third Letter (136), which was written to address the issue of the relationship between the Church and the popular organizations. There, in one of the most easily accessible texts in any of the Letters, Romero claims that some of these organizations have been fighting with each other (91–92) and that they often preach violence as a means of social change (98, 110). The third Letter claims that the Church is to preach nonviolence to these groups as the preferred method of social change (98, 110) and that legitimate violence is to be used only as a last resort (110).

To replace the idols of private property, national security, and popular organizations, the Letters offer three counterimages: Christ, the kingdom of God, and Mary. The end of the first Letter invokes all three:

> Like Mary, may the Church live out this happy balance of the Easter of Jesus, which ought to characterize the true salvation of men and women in Christ—namely, to feel oneself already glorified in heaven as the image and first flowering of the future life, and at the same time to be, here on earth, the light of God's pilgrim people, 'as a sign of sure hope and solace until the day the Lord come.' (62)

Mary stands as an image for the activity of Christian simile-making. She continues to exist in the life of the Church through stories and icons; Mary, it hardly need be said, is not present to the people of the Church in the material way Romero is. She is an image and is accessible to the people of the Church as an analogical partner. As Mary was to the crucifixion and resurrection of Jesus, this passage holds, her people should be to Jesus. Let them be like Mary. Let them exist in a relationship of simile with her, a relationship that would require, finally, their imaginative activity. To exist analogically with Mary is to become glorified as the image and the first flowering of the future life. As Mary's people exist analogically with her, they will themselves become an image of what is to come. Their imagining, which leads them to become the analogue to Mary and her son, leads them to become an embodied image of what is to be. The imaginative force found in the icons and stories of the Church incarnates itself in human flesh. The Letter, to describe this more fully, offers the image of a flower. But in so doing it immediately moves away from the incarnate flesh of human being. Humans become flowers linked analogically to Mary who lives in the Church as an image found in icons and stories. The Letter indicates a Marian future.

This, undoubtedly, is the kingdom of God. The Letters understand Christians to be living a double life: they live in hopes of the kingdom to come beyond the edge of space and time and also live to work at building the kingdom on earth. Hence, the end of the first Letter holds that the people, as analogues to Mary, are both flowering images of the glorification that is to come in the future life and also pilgrim lights who are the sign of the coming of the Lord. As such, these Marian analogues are to work for the alleviation of the pain of the oppressed, since Jesus, in his first coming, so dedicated himself. The Christian people are the earthly signs of God. They point to the flower of glorification beyond history and also point to the presence of Christ on earth among the oppressed.

What links the people's imaginative activity with the figure of Mary and their existence as the image of the kingdom is the figure of Christ. The people are to link with Mary because doing so allows them to "live out this happy balance of the Easter of Jesus" as Mary did. (*Voice* 62) A relationship of similitude with Mary provides one with an analogical relationship with Christ. Once one enters into that relationship, one becomes Christ's image, Christ's sign. Christ, like Mary, exists imagistically. He is not present to the people as Romero was present. This is the burden of the Christian figure of the second coming, which this passage from the end of the first Letter echoes by way of Vatican II. Christ has died, Christ has been resurrected, Christ has not come again. The Letter suggests that Christ works in the Church absently through images: Mary, icons of his life, death, and resurrection, stories, and finally, as Romero suggests, in the people themselves. The Church is the body of Christ in history, as the second Letter proclaims. As such, it represents Christ, for Christ himself is beyond history. He is that which is to come.

The Letters propose two predominant images of Jesus: he who was crucified and resurrected, and he who was transfigured. The crucified and resurrected Christ is presented by the Letters, especially the first, as the summary image of Hebrew history and the beginning image of the history of the Christian people. In this way, to reverse the normal figure, the crucified and resurrected Christ is the *omega* and the *alpha*, the end and the beginning. Romero is certainly not averse to imagining himself and the Salvadoran situation in terms of the Hebrew Bible, as the discussion concerning the god Molech demonstrates. However he, like most Christians, subsumes the images of the Hebrew Bible into Christian history. They serve only as preparatory for the final act of God in history: the birth, death, and resurrection of Christ.[12] The first Letter holds that "The event of Christian salvation, then, which we call the paschal mystery, was being prepared for by 'the wonders wrought by God among the people of the Old Testament' " (55).

The first quotation is doubly intertextual. It points to God's activity among the Old Testament people by way of a document from Vatican II and the Bible. The primary activity that the Letter specifies is Moses' liberation of the Hebrews and the passover of their firstborn sons (55). Vatican II's Jesus, as the final and most complete passover, completes and represents the passover history of Judaism. Judaism was an image of what was to come.

Yet this reality, the Letter goes on to attest, has itself become understood through images. The crucifixion and resurrection of Christ occurred once in material history but they are real to Christians only because they are carried on in images, such as those proposed by Vatican II. If the passover Christ is the *omega* of the images of the history of Jewish passover, then the passover Christ is the *alpha* of the history of the images about itself. The Letters imply that the Christian passover became absent the instant it occurred. The history of Christianity, of which these Letters are a part, is the history of the reimagining of what is absent: the crucified and resurrected Christ.

For Romero, Christ crucified and resurrected is represented in two ways: through the Eucharist and through the Church's commitment to the pained oppressed. Christ's death was the culmination of the Jewish tradition of paschal sacrifice and with the Eucharist Christ made this sacrifice available to all people at all times (56).[13] This passage, incidentally, manifests the vacillation between intertextuality and the lived experience of the people. It directs readers both to the Bible that recounts the story of the institution of the Eucharist and to the experienced act of the Mass itself, where the priest invokes the memory of the text.

A Church centered on this image of Christ represented in the Eucharist is a Eucharistic Church: it represents the death and resurrection of the lamb of God (56). Just as the Eucharist is a sign of the absent Christ for the Church, the Church is to be a sign, an image, of the absent Christ for the world. Borrowing from Medellín, the first Letter declares that the Church, as sign to the world, is to be "'truly poor, missionary and paschal'" (56). The Eucharist imagistically constitutes the Church around an absent Christ and consequently empowers it to represent Christ in the world through its commitment to the pained oppressed.

The question of how Christ should be identified by and with the Church becomes crucial in the discussion that followed the assassination of Rutilio Grande, S.J., concerning whether or not the Salvadoran Church should celebrate only one Mass in order to demonstrate the Church's resolve in the face of the murder of a priest committed to the poor. The Jesuits argued that the Church must unify the country through the act of one Mass to be held in the capital's cathedral. Romero was at first against doing so, claiming that the point of the Mass was to give glory to God: the more Masses celebrated, the more glory given. Sobrino and other Jesuits were shocked: "Here was a theology straight out of the dark ages" (*Archbishop* 15). By this they mean that Romero seemed to have thought that the people were meant to serve the Church's rituals rather than vice versa. Father Jerez, Sobrino notes, intervened and maintained with the authority of the ancient Church fathers that " 'Gloria Dei, vivens homo'—the glory of God is the living person" (15). This is to say that the Church exists only to help people better love God. The people don't exist simply to perform rites that subordinate the people to the rites. Romero was convinced, and one Mass was held.

Sobrino holds that before Romero died, he came to change Jerez's quote into " 'Gloria Dei, vivens pauper'—the glory of God is the living poor person" (16). This evolution, as reported by Sobrino, makes clear the connection between the image of Christ as represented in the Eucharist to the Church and the image of Christ represented by the Church to the world in its commitment to the poor. Christ is represented in the Mass so that the Church may become Christ to the world.

In addition to the image of Christ crucified and resurrected, the Letters offer as a model the image of Christ transfigured. The single most important representation of the image of the transfiguration appears at the end of the third Letter.

> It is striking that the five persons chosen to accompany the divine savior in that theophany on Mt. Tabor were five men of aggressive temperament and deeds. Moses, Elias,[14] Peter, James, and John. . . . Jesus channeled the aggression of their temperaments toward a rich work of construction, of building up justice and peace in the world. (*Voice* 110)

This passage both echoes and expands the sermon Romero preached during the final Lent of his life. Moses and Elijah again appear, inviting readers of the Letters to consider their images, as presented in Matthew and in the Hebrew Bible, as models for existence. Concerning Moses and Elijah, this Letter is explicitly and implicitly intertextual. Explicitly, it directs its readers to Matthew and that Gospel's representation of an image beheld by some of the disciples. The Letter's image of the transfiguration is refracted a number of times. It presents Matthew's version, which itself is a refraction of the image beheld by the chosen disciples: Peter, James, and John. Implicitly, the Letter directs its readers to the Hebrew Bible. It claims that two of the figures present in the image, Moses and Elijah, worked to build up peace and justice in the world. Romero has interpreted the lives of these two men as they are presented in the Hebrew Bible. Unless one is willing to accept Romero's interpretation, assuming his authority as author and archbishop to be decisive, one must turn to the stories of Moses and Elijah and interpret them. Certainly, a reader could accept Romero's interpretation, but this would be to defy the intertextual activity into which the Letters invite their readers.

This Letter's representation of the image of the transfiguration expands on that presented in the Lenten sermon by including Peter, James, and John as three who were also present and affected by Jesus' transfiguration. Properly speaking, they were not transfigured as was Jesus. Rather, they beheld the transfiguration of Jesus and the conversation Jesus had with Moses and Elijah. But, nonetheless, the Letter claims that they were transfigured. Their transfiguration came from Christ's. He took these aggressive men and changed them into those who worked for the kingdom of justice and peace. Romero takes this image of the transfiguration and interprets it in order to fit his vision of the Church and then presents it as a model to be contemplated by the readers of the Letter. The Letter intends its readers to become the analogues of Moses, Elijah, Peter, James, and John (110).

As the *omega* of the images of the passover tradition represented in the Hebrew Bible and as the *alpha* of the Christian images of the Eucharist, Christ stands as that upon which all human rights and duties rest (92). Christ as crucified and resurrected, as transfigured, stands as the image that unifies not only the Church but all of humanity. He is "the one and only absolute," the fourth Letter claims (136). Constituted by the representation of Christ in the Eucharist, by the image of the transfiguration that marks the second, third, and fourth Letters, the Church is to represent Christ to the world through its dedication to the pained oppressed. In so doing it works for the kingdom of God, both as it exists beyond time and space and on earth. As the third Letter says of Christ relative to the popular organizations, Christ is the God of love, not the God of conflict and death. In creating humans, he meant for them to live communally in love (92). By attending to the image of Christ represented by the Church, Romero claims, the world can be unified in love and thereby participate in the kingdom to come.

It is important to realize that for Romero the kingdom is always one that is coming: it has never fully come nor will it ever come fully to earth. God impels history but the fruition of this impulse never comes (Sobrino, *Archbishop* 178). Romero offers an imaginative vision of a world beyond the painful reality in which his people live. Finally, however, it is a realm beyond the imaginative capabilities of human beings, a realm whose images shift throughout Romero's writings, indicating the fragility of imagined objects and the dimension of the process-oriented imagination.

The second Letter, for instance, points to Isaiah 65:17 and to Revelation 21:1 in order to imagine the coming kingdom (*Voice* 69). Rather than present himself as a visionary of the kingdom, Romero turns to Biblical sources separated drastically through time and across space from the Salvadoran situation. The imagined kingdom is presented through a return to a previous world that is characterized through a look forward by looking back. Revelation 21:1 envisions the end of the current world and the appearance of a new. It tells of a beautiful and clean Jerusalem lit only by God's glory present in the Lamb, a new Jerusalem in which stands a new tree of life that bears fruit that heals the nations (cf. 21:2–22:5). Revelation 21:1 further adds nuance as it echoes Isaiah 65:17 and 66:22, the former the other vision to which Romero's second Letter points. There Isaiah speaks of a new heaven and new earth that will be the reversal of the fall. Isaiah 65:23 reads: "They shall not labor in vain, / or bear children for calamity." The imagined new heaven and new earth, then, are painless places, alternatives to the suffering of the people on the present earth.

Later in the second Letter Romero concretizes the kingdom in the experience of El Salvador. The object of Christian hope, he claims, is in part a just society that insures for all people life, homes, schooling, medical care, and the right to form organizations (*Voice* 82). Of all these characteristics of the kingdom on earth, only the right to life is present in the visions presented by Isaiah and Revelation. The remainder are specific to the Salvadoran situation, and suggest that the Biblical visions do not, finally, speak adequately to Romero's situation. While they are illuminating similes, they do not imagine, finally, what the kingdom in El Salvador may come to look like. The image must change according to situation, indicating that the kingdom upon which the images are based is not transparent to the eyes of the human imaginers. Isaiah has one sense. Revelation borrows this and changes it to fit the situation of the early Church. Romero borrows both and changes them to accord with the situation in which he finds himself.

In addition to the images of the kingdom and of the Christ, the Letters speak a new image of Mary, the mother of God. Anne Carr suggests that "Mary continues to exercise her power over the Christian imagination, especially for women but also for men in contexts like Latin America, Africa, and Asia, where she is seen as the poor one in whom God does great things" (*Transforming Grace* 193). Romero is certainly one of those in whom Mary continues to work, one of those who continues to work with Mary. This is especially true of the final Letter, which ends with glorification of the Marian image. In so doing, Romero hints at a destabilization of the image of Christ that he presents throughout the Letters. By the end of the fourth Letter Romero has begun to imagine that the authority of the image of Christ may be shared with the image of Christ's mother.

While all the Letters end with an appeal to Mary, the end of the fourth Letter is a new moment and imagistic climax in the imagining of Mary that occurs throughout the four Letters. Appealing to Puebla and Puebla's appeal to the Marian devotion of the oppressed (*Voice* 158), which again manifests the vacillation of the Letters between intertextuality and lived experience, Romero speaks sweetly of Mary's beautiful tenderness and claims that she is not simply the mother of Christ and the Church; she is also America's mother (158). The Letter offers, in a short space, four dimensions of Mary, all of which direct readers to other texts. In so doing, as I discussed above, the Letter invites its readers to participate in the imaginative process of the construction of a new image of Mary. No one text adequately imagines her. Curiously, while this intertextual strategy may distance those who cannot participate, it also invites all into the process of rhetorical theology. Thus, the Letter calls on all people to construct Mary. This is a challenge to the hierarchical Church that tends to assert its authority over matters of faith and to which Romero carefully aligns himself.

Romero borrows his first image of Mary from Pope Paul VI. Mary, Romero tells his readers, was one of the oppressed herself, "a strong woman who knew poverty and suffering, flight and exile" (158). The Letters never so identify Jesus. While Jesus sides with the oppressed, he is not presented as one of them. Mary is analogous to the pained people of the world in a way Jesus is not. Her image is their life. The second dimension is provided by Pope John Paul II. He points not to her life but to her text, the Magnificat that she delivered following the Annunciation. This pope, speaking for Romero, speaking through Romero, interprets the Magnificat as a proclamation of resistance in the face of oppression, as a declaration that God will depose the mighty if need be (159). Mary offers not only a model. Her text, the Magnificat, also serves to name a crucial dimension of the image Romero is beginning to construct. From Paul VI he borrows Mary the sufferer. From John Paul II he borrows Mary the prophet. Mary, like Jesus her son, speaks words that become influential texts for all who would follow God. She has a voice of her own and speaks the liberating message of and to the oppressed even before Christ is born.

From the bishops at Puebla Romero takes the final two dimensions of his image of the mother of Christ. She is, Puebla claims, the one who presides over Pentecost (159). Returning to the theme of the first Letter, this final image of the fourth challenges the first. There, the Pentecost was Christ's hour. Pentecost, that Letter claimed, brought about the fullness of Easter (57). The fourth Letter, however, as it constructs this quadrifid image of Mary, suggests that it is she who presides over this new Pentecost as the Church attempts to again unify the world. Pentecost may fulfill Easter, but Mary, as Christ's mother, claims this as her hour. Finally, Romero with the aid of Puebla, which in turn directs the reader to Paul VI, suggests that this Mary is common sufferer, prophet of liberation, presider, star: " 'On this journey we pray that Mary may be the 'star of a continually renewed evangelization' " (159). Mary points to Christ crucified and resurrected only because she points to that over which she presides: the preaching of the Pentecostal Christ. As presider, it is she who orchestrates the new hour. As star, it is she who illuminates what might not otherwise be seen. Christ's light, it appears, is not bright enough on its own. It needs the light of its suffering, prophetic mother.

Language, History, Liberation

The Pastoral Letters envision the dialectic of pain and imagination as taking place in the interplay of language and history. For Romero, as for Burke and Merton as postmoderns and for Freire as a fellow liberation rhetorician, language and history are crucial categories of human existence. Pain and imagination find their expression in both. Moreover, it is within the interplay of language, history, pain, and imagination that

Romero preferentially opts for the poor, marking him as a liberation rhetorician.

Imaginative language, the Letters recognize, serves both to oppress and liberate. Language is a site of contention involving the oppressors, the oppressed, and the Church. Having already noted that oppressive regimes, in the form of national security states, modify images so as to present themselves as defenders of democracy (*Voice* 134–35), the fourth Letter holds that such regimes also use their imagination in order to produce metaphors that are used to justify oppression. The fourth Letter argues that the oppressors name the oppressed as "terrorists" and "subversives" and thus justify violent attacks against them (143).

As I discussed in chapter 2, Burke focuses on the problem of the synecdochal fallacy. The fourth Letter denounces the tactic of false metaphorization. The oppressive state understands that it must justify its actions in language, and so it invents language in order to justify its actions. As the Letter suggests, the metaphors are used as part of a logical process. One is labeled a terrorist, and as a reasonable consequence, one is therefore dealt with accordingly. Romero, with his list of campesinos, laborers, slum dwellers, and others, attempts to reverse the metaphorical and logical process. Rather than subsuming these types of oppressed under reductive and harmful nouns, he attempts to name them as he feels they should be named: by their location in an oppressive society. These names retard the logical process based upon the false metaphorization. The Letter suggests that even a repressive regime cannot justify torture simply because someone is a slum dweller who seeks human rights. It must change the slum dwellers' name in order to justify its action. So, by naming the slum dweller as slum dweller, the Letter challenges the metaphorical and logical process that leads to torture.

In so doing, this passage reveals Romero's understanding of the Church's role: it must speak for the pained oppressed. Significantly, this passage does not quote any of these oppressed challenging the metaphors that lead to their pain and death. Rather, the Letter speaks for them: they are not as the state claims them to be. It does so because the Letters maintain that the oppressed are so pained that they have no voice. The figure that reoccurs throughout all the Letters is that of the pained oppressed crying: they most often can only vocalize their pain with a preverbal sound of anguish (59, 68, 74, 89). This figure reaches its zenith in the fourth Letter. Directing his readers to both Medellín and Puebla, Romero declares "that 'muted cry' of wretchedness that Medellín heard ten years ago, Puebla now describes as 'loud and clear, increasing in volume and intensity, and at times full of menace'" (119). The oppressed express their pain preverbally. The Church, as the body of Christ, must commit itself to the oppressed and in so doing both listen to the anguish and transfigure it into language. This passage is the most extensive demonstration of this transfigural process in which Romero and the Church are engaged. Hearing the cry, it is motivated to speak the pained situation of the oppressed: infant mortality, starvation wages, and the like. Interestingly, with its "so on" the Letter suggests that the list is either overwhelming or obvious. Either there are so many problems underlying the cry that they simply cannot be enumerated, or else the problems are so evident to any who hear the cry that they don't need recount.

The Letters, however, suggest that the Church should not be content only to speak for the poor. While it must transfigure their cry, it must also teach the poor to transfigure their cry for themselves. Romero admits in the third Letter that he and other members of the hierarchy are limited and consequently cannot fully express the country's situation (88). He suggests that, finally, the Letter asks all Church people to study it (88; also 92, 102). In the fourth Letter Romero expands this, suggesting that "the evangelization of the Salvadoran people cannot simply continue the tradition of preaching and encouraging en masse, or in a moralizing fashion" (140). While he doesn't fully deny the importance of this type of evangelization, Romero prefers, as does Puebla, the activity of the base ecclesial communities (153). These communities comprise a small number of people who study the gospel and use it critically to understand the world (140). They are endorsed by Puebla as groups that help the larger ecclesial institution fulfill its role as the body of Christ (155).

At this point the Letters reveal the pedagogical dimension of rhetoric to which Burke points, as I discussed in chapter 2, and to which Freire devotes much of his writing, as I discussed in chapter 4. Romero, the liberation practitioner, is not content simply to practice. Rather, his final Letter begins to envision a Church of practitioners, people who would learn to rhetoricize the dialectic of pain and imagination for themselves. I hardly need to emphasize the difference that this attitude marks between Romero and a postmodern like Richard Rorty, as I outlined Rorty's pedagogical position in chapter 1. Rorty holds that the pained oppressed cannot speak for themselves; Romero maintains that they can, that they should, and that the Church must teach them how to so speak. Romero believes that this pedagogical activity is the key to transformation.

Such transformation is aimed toward the kingdom of God both beyond space and time and within the Salvadoran context. The groups would come to engage in the imaginative linguistic wonderings and wanderings of Isaiah, Revelation, Romero, the popes, Medellín and Puebla, Jesus, and Mary. For instance Romero, while not specifying it, seems to suggest that the base communities might join in the fourth Letter's invocation of John Paul II's interpretation of Mary's Magnificat and apply this interpretation, and the Magnificat itself, to their pained existence. In turn, one must suppose, these groups would learn to read the texts through their own experience, engaging in a dialectical process in which the Letters themselves engage: text and life, language and history. The Letters look to an age beyond the one in which they are written, to an age in which Romero isn't the voice of the voiceless.

History is the location of the voice of the Church and of the pained and crying oppressed who are to be taught to speak. These voices and cries demonstrate that history, at one level, is open. Like language, history is a site of contention in which the Church and the oppressed challenge a dominant and repressive order and take responsibility for enacting the kingdom. In so entering history, the Church embodies Christ (72). His denunciations of false idols, his commitment to the oppressed, his envisionment of a new person and kingdom, his persecution, crucifixion, and resurrection took place in the specificity of a particular time and place (72). Likewise, Romero understands that as the body of Christ the Church must commit itself to history: it must speak to people in their historical location; it must work toward establishing the kingdom on earth, limited though it may be (73).

As a historical entity, the Church is neither omnipotent nor omniscient, though it does bear, unlike other historical entities, the marks of God. The third Letter, for instance, suggests that the proliferation of the popular organizations is a mark that challenges the Church to concretize itself in history. Though marked by God, the Salvadoran Church has not understood fully the dire situation of El Salvador; it has belied Christ by not leading the way to the kingdom. The popular organizations, while beset with a tendency toward idolatry, remind the Church of its historical duty, of its place in the lives of Salvadorans. They act on behalf of the oppressed and the Church must do the same (94). Their presence and activities in the lives of the people engage the Church dialectically and force it to respond, in language and acts (95–96), as the historical presence of Christ in El Salvador.

The Church offers to the world the suffering and resurrected Christ who has committed himself to the poor (95–96). This offering, following Vatican II, is claimed by the third Letter to illuminate all facets of the Church (95). Though the Church bears the light of God, it is not omniscient. All judgments that it makes necessarily depend upon the specificity of historical moments and the plurality of languages that inhabit any given time and any given space. The Church must not dictate; it must listen and guide (94, 156).

The Church offers a commitment to the pain of the oppressed and to the imagined kingdom from the vantage of the Gospels. It does not have specific political solutions given to it by Christ. Hence, in the fourth Letter Romero suggests a new form of evangelization for the Church: the "apostolate of companionship" (155–56). Such an apostolate does not offer specific political options. Rather, it serves as companion to those Roman Catholics who, led by their understanding of their lives and the gospel, have made a particular political choice that carries with it the demands of particular actions. Romero supports the pained oppressed in their attempt to find voice in history, in their attempt to challenge repressive regimes and work toward the kingdom on earth. What he does not support is the Church itself becoming explicitly and concretely politicized in history. It must be historicized, but what it makes historical is its commitment to the oppressed and the images of the kingdom, the transfiguration, the crucifixion, and the resurrection, and by the end of the fourth Letter, Mary. With this commitment to the oppressed and these images, the Church accompanies Christians who have made particular political choices. At once, Romero acknowledges the historical limitations of the Church and encourages Christians to find their voice in history so that the kingdom may come.

Though the people of El Salvador may be painfully repressed, the Church and the people as guided by the Church can voice the pain and imagine a better world in history. Finally, though, history is closed because it is ruled by God and because it ends in God beyond history. For instance, while the Church as a historical institution is open to change and limited in its understanding of both historical reality and the Word of God itself, this does not mean that Romero holds that God is limited, that the Word of God is exhausted by the limited understanding of the Church. God is always more than human understanding (150). Though the Church interprets the gospel as it lives through varying historical epochs and knows that each interpretation is limited, Romero does not suggest that God is finally relative to specific locations simply because the Church's understanding of God's Word is. God is "The Lord of history" (150), "the ultimate answer to the mystery of existence and of the history of humankind" (70). Human existence, according to the Letters, is only partially ambiguous because God is not fully revealed in history. While there are options, not all options are equal: they are limited by the parameters of pain and the imagined kingdom. And finally, the kingdom exists only in the imagination as it responds to the lived pain of the people and to the texts with which the Letters involve themselves. The Letters claim that one must work within the dialectic of pain and imagination on earth, voicing pain and building the kingdom, and look toward that kingdom beyond pain and beyond what humans can imagine: the kingdom fulfilled in eternity.

Afterword

Throughout this book I have spoken of five types of rhetoricians. As I briefly noted in the first chapter, rhetoricians are best and most fully characterized by the following pentagram within a pentagon:[1]

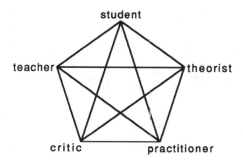

As the connecting lines indicate, none of the categories is exclusive. In fact, a rhetorician always works as more than one type. For instance, while I have categorized Burke as a theorist, he is also each of the others. His books seek to teach and he himself taught at Bennington College; to develop his theory he critiques various theories and practices; he practices rhetoric insofar as his books are structured dialectically; he is a student because he learns from others in order to develop his theory. So too Merton, Freire, and Romero work as all five types, though as some more explicitly than others. As I read them, Burke, Merton, Freire, and Romero stand as a primal group: their texts help one begin to understand how rhetoric can labor with the dialectic of pain and imagination. While their most obvious contributions may be to rhetorical theorists and practitioners, their texts speak to all types of rhetoricians.

If it is the task of theorists to ask how people can rhetoricize pain and imagination within history and language, this primal group offers a dialectic that theorists must consider. For their part, Freire and Romero challenge postmodern rhetoricians' commitment to speak pain and imagination. It is easy to make all histories ambiguous and to pluralize all languages when one lives within the comfort of U.S. elite groups. While liberation rhetoricians cannot challenge Burke's and Merton's textual commitment to the pained and the imaginative possibilities of a better world, they can challenge the postmodern's contention that all instances of pain and imagination, as they occur in language and history (and how else can they occur?), are finally unsure. From the liberation perspective, the postmodern commitment to pain and imagination may seem unrooted in the lived realities of those most in pain, of those most in need of imaginative possibilities. Burke, for instance, locates the imaginative end of human being in a mystical embrace of what is beyond the vicissitudes of human life. Though he is careful to remind his readers that the ascent to the realm of the process-oriented imagination always entails a return to the pain of earth, he never makes clear exactly what the return to earth may and should entail. Does one continue to teach one's version of mysticism at an elite New England college, or does one move to inner-city Chicago and work with nonreaders desperately trying to join a literate civilization? Romero, like Burke, suggests that there is a realm beyond human being that can be experienced and to which one must always return. Unlike Burke, however, Romero makes clear the nature of the return. What is beyond all history and language is the fullness of the kingdom of God. Once one glimpses it, however partially, one must seek to bring about the fullness of the kingdom on earth. To do this, one must preferentially opt for the oppressed and work to alleviate their pain. No doubt, were Romero able to speak to Burke he would applaud Burke's commitment to the lives of 'the people,' to use Burke's preferred figure. So too, however, Romero would castigate Burke for the seeming vacuity of his work. Burke's imaginative realm is too plural and ambiguous. It doesn't envision, for those most affected by oppressive histories and languages, a better world.

Given the dialectic between postmodern and liberation rhetorics, however, Burke and Merton offer an equally powerful criticism of their partners. Postmodern rhetoricians challenge liberation rhetoricians to pluralize all languages, even those of the oppressed, and to make all histories ambiguous, even those of the most pained. Burke and Merton rightly fear that rigid commitments to parochial languages and histories will cause further suffering and curtail imaginative possibilities. A case in point is discussed by Robert Arnove in his analysis of the Sandinista literacy campaign in postrevolutionary Nicaragua. Deeply influenced by Freire, the Nicaraguan campaign, in its first wave, respected the linguistic pluralism found in the country and chose to provide literacy instruction in both Spanish and the language used by the Miskito Indian population on the Atlantic coast. The second wave and all further education, however, was to use only Spanish. The Sandinistas, Arnove suggests, in this case came dangerously close to becoming oppressors. They chose to force their own language upon another people and consequently trafficked in pain: Miskitos who resisted the program were abused by the liberators of the country (289).

So too, relative to the theory and practice of imagination, postmodern rhetoricians would challenge Freire's theory because it finally argues that the only valid imaginative practice for the reconstruction of oppressed societies is Marxist. Burke rejects this limitation in his discussion of the relative merits of 'worker' and 'people.' Freire's imaginative practice, which claims that 'worker' is the only appropriate metaphor and synecdoche for the oppressed, denies the ambiguity of communities and thereby risks becoming irrelevant if not oppressive. Merton calls into question Freire's rejection of the validity of worldviews that precede coming to consciousness: Freire upholds *conscientização* as somehow above and beyond the limitations of human being; *Geography* demonstrates that all mind-sets are limited by language and history. Modern and premodern worldviews are kin, and premodern civilizations, no doubt marked by 'magic,' were not inferior ones. Certainly, *Geography* also debunks the notion that the oppressed can ever become pure: they will always oppress in their turn. For *Geography*, there is no egalitarian classless utopia of peace to be had.

The theorist cannot resolve this dialectic: there is no synthesis possible. At most and best—and this is no small task, no small achievement if accomplished—the theorist is to focus the dialectic between postmoderns and liberationists. What they share is deeply complex and needs much work. Despite their differences, the best of both postmoderns and liberationists are deeply concerned about pain and imagination and both seek to rhetoricize this dialectic in order to create a better world. However, their differences can be neither bracketed nor underestimated. Rather, they should be used to clarify and make more rigorous the positions of each. Merton must be challenged by Romero, Burke by Freire, Romero by Burke, Freire by Merton, and so on. In this way, the unresolvable dialectic between these pairs regarding language and history can be used to help the postmoderns and liberationists become co-workers rather than antagonists.

From the four, the theorist learns about the nature of the dialectic. The critic learns that all discursive praxes are open to study. Rhetoric is the dialectic that informs discourse, and hence all discourse is open to rhetorical criticism. This is not a new idea. It has its roots in Plato and Aristotle and finds its most recent theoretical apologies in books like Covino's *The Art of Wondering* and Terry Eagleton's ironically named *Literary Theory*. Covino, for instance, offers a revisionary reading of the history of rhetoric and includes such figures as Montaigne and Byron (47–57, 83–108). In so doing, Covino has begun to expand rhetoric as an ur-category. For him it applies not only to the likes of Cicero but also to poets and essayists. I use "ironically" to describe Eagleton's title because the point of his book is to argue that there is nothing that can be identified as "literature" and thus no "literary theory" (205–6). Eagleton claims, following Foucault, that all writing is best thought of as discursive practice and is open to rhetorical criticism. For Eagleton, like Covino, rhetoric is that which informs all and can be used to study all linguistic effort.

This book further elucidates this principle. Its subjects are four rhetoricians working in divergent areas: Burke in rhetorical theory, Merton in poetry, Freire in literacy theory, Romero in theology and ministry. Despite the differences, all four rhetoricize the dialectic of pain and imagination. However, given their differences, they are rarely read together, in any combination. This, perhaps, is because academics tend to remain within their disciplines. Romero is thus the subject of theology, Freire of literacy studies and pedagogy, Merton of poetry, Burke of literary criticism.[2] I follow the efforts of Eagleton and hope that this book serves as a model for the dispersal of disciplines in the name of rhetoric. In particular, one should range among all discursive practice, seeking the informing dialectics. If one is to engage in rhetorical criticism, one should seek to discern the movement of the primary dialectic of our epoch as it informs discourse: pain and imagination.

To practitioners of rhetoric, Burke, Merton, Freire, and Romero pose two questions: What are pain and imagination? How can you rhetoricize this dialectic? One possible answer to both questions is highlighted most by Merton and Romero. Their practices suggest that the rhetorical practitioner must become deeply involved with other texts. Both *Geography* and the Pastoral Letters reveal that one's knowledge of pain and imagination is deeply indebted to others' experiences, perceptions, and verbalizations. This is perhaps most interesting relative to Romero's practice. Unlike *Geography*, the Letters arose from the immediate situation of pain. Merton could only know of the pain of the Aztecs, for example, through other writing and his imaginative capabilities. Romero, in contrast, knew the pain of his people because he held their tortured bodies, saw their dismembered torsos. Rather than relying on this immediate experience, though, Romero chose to use other writing to help him articulate his position on pain in the Letters. This indicates that humans know in community: they depend on others to help them think. Thus, Romero may have used the articulations of the Latin American bishops at Puebla in his fourth Letter to help him gather and express his perhaps inchoate experiences and perceptions of his people's suffering.

Certainly, though, another effect of using Puebla was strategic. While it undoubtedly helped Romero formulate his position on pain, his use of it also gathered the authority of the Latin American Church into the fourth Letter. So too his appeals to the Bible, Vatican II, Paul VI, and others give his word the weight of tradition. Because much of what is the Western community perpetuates itself in the texts of philosophy, poetry, fiction, and theology, among others, any positive use of these texts enables one to claim the authority of the community.

Intertextual appeal also makes complex the situation of suffering: it hampers parochial simplification. It invites one to realize that any situation of suffering exists within a web of interpretation and meaning. One may experience one's own pain or the pain of another and think that the pain is easily understood as x. The Letters and *Geography* remind their readers, however, that the process of interpretation is not simple.

One always understands pain, as one understands anything, because one lives within a community of knowledge that tends to predetermine interpretation. Romero, for instance, challenges the oppressor Salvadoran Catholics who interpret the pain of the campesinos according to the mores of the oppressor community. He suggests, even demands, that they learn from another community of which they are a part: global Roman Catholicism as manifest in the social teachings of the Church. So too *Geography* encourages its readers to expand their interpretive capabilities. They are asked by the poem to journey as pilgrims to the other and to try to discern, with empathy, the pain that the other suffers.

Another possible answer to the questions of what are pain and imagination and how can one practice this dialectic is found in another question: For whom should one work? The answer to this question returns this discussion to the unresolvable dialectic with which the theorist must deal. The practitioner, like the theorist, must live this irresolution, forever asking questions such as the following: Can I best rhetoricize pain and imagination through a primary commitment to the language and history of an oppressed group or through a commitment to all peoples that effectively denies the supremacy of any particular group? Should I seek the relative comfort and ease of academic employment at a U.S. university? Is it possible to speak adequately of pain and imagination when one lives comfortably? Or should I forgo this life and move into the communities of the most pained, of those desperately in need of imaginative possibilities? Does this kind of commitment lead to parochial understandings of pain, to limited visions of linguistic practice and better worlds?

So too the teacher of rhetoric is challenged by Burke, Merton, Freire, and Romero to make a decision regarding community. Burke committed himself to the U.S. academic elite, Merton to the Roman Catholic Church in general with *Geography* to a literary elite in particular. Freire, even in Geneva with the World Council of Churches, understood his primary community to be that of the oppressed engaged in revolutionary struggle. Romero gave his language and life to the Salvadoran poor. The teacher must decide which community would best enable the dialectic of pain and imagination to be studied and practiced by students.

For the teacher who teaches by writing books, a decision must be made regarding audience. For all its brilliance, *Geography* is often unreadable even by the trained. It was not written for a high school dropout working on a factory farm in Nebraska. In choosing to write *Geography* as he did, Merton drastically limited its possibilities of reception. So too Burke's work is formidable. It demands that one be willing to read on for hundreds of pages, that one carefully work through its labyrinthine argumentation. Burke's work is clearly intended for the literate specialist. If one is to read his *Rhetoric of Religion,* for instance, one must know something about Heidegger in order to understand Burke's discussion of the negative (20–22).

For the rhetorician who teaches in the classroom, a decision must be made regarding the classroom itself. First, to which type of classroom should the teacher commit? Should one work in community based adult education programs outside the university system? Should one work at elite Eastern colleges? Should one commit oneself to the pedagogical practices of religious institutions? Second, even when one is able, or forced, to decide upon a classroom, one must commit oneself to a practice of teaching the dialectic. For instance, and this returns this discussion about teaching to those of theory, criticism, and practice, the teacher must decide which texts will come to constitute, within the classroom, the student's intertextual world. Following Eagleton and Covino, I would argue that the teacher must break the boundaries between discursive praxes. This book is true to this maxim: it places into play with each other two types of rhetorics (theory and practice) and four written modes (the academic essay, the long poem, dialogues, and Pastoral Letters). The rhetorician must also decide if the teaching of an intertextual world, which dominates the practice of the Western academy, is enough. There are two other options, based on the work of Burke, Merton, Freire, and Romero. Freire and Romero, in particular, suggest that in order to help students better discern the dimensions of pain and imagination, the teacher should have the students immerse themselves in the worlds of pain and imagination outside of texts. It may be worthwhile to have students visit and learn from AIDS hospices, homeless shelters, utopian communities, and the like. Perhaps this kind of non-textual study would help students better understand the problems and possibilities of rhetoricizing pain and imagination. The second option, which the life and practice of Merton suggest, is to have students explore silence as a necessary dimension of the rhetoricization of pain and imagination.[3] This could take many forms, from Christian Trappist to Quaker to Zen Buddhist practices. *Geography* arose from a hermetic life of silence and drives its readers back into the silence of what is beyond object-oriented imagination.

Finally the teacher must decide upon the practice to be taught. Currently dominating the West is the style of the academic essay, which typically offers a thesis, a body that supports the thesis, and a conclusion. In high schools across the United States, for instance, it is known as the five-paragraph theme, and is marked by what Scollon and Scollon have identified as the consciousness of Western essayist literacy (see chapter 1). While I would not suggest that the academic essay style be discarded, the works of Burke, Merton, Freire, and Romero suggest to the teacher that other forms can well explore and express the dialectic of pain and imagination. Consider Freire. His early work is obviously that of an academic trained in the Western model. By the late 1970s, however, Freire deliberately shifted to producing what he has called "talking books": dialogues. Unmarked by thesis, developing body, and conclusion, these books would perhaps be rejected by some as frivolous, unrigorous. Perhaps, however, these dialogues are rigorous in a different sense. Unlike the traditional essay, in which the author tells the reader what she is going to do, does it, and then summarizes what she has done, they require the reader to accompany the conversation's nuances and shifting perspectives. So too the writer of dialogues must learn to reveal the complexity of any issue.[4] Unlike thesis-ordered discourse, which necessarily entails exclusion of some elements of and perspectives on the issue at hand, dialogues require students to verbalize the complexity of reality. For instance, a teacher could ask students to compose a dialogue that would account for the dimensions of imagination found in Burke, Merton, Freire, and Romero. The student would create four or more characters, each of whom represents some aspect of these rhetoricians' discussions of imagination. The dialogue could explore and elucidate these discussions, insights unfolding only in relation to other insights. Such an exercise would allow the students to wander imaginatively through and delve into extremely intricate texts. My own study of these four figures, generated as it is by a thesis, limits their work. I simply have not taken into account the shifts and maneuvers each makes as they speak pain and imagination because this would have led this book dangerously close to the precipice of the incomprehensible. The ending of the chapter on Burke is closest to this precipice because it most carefully attempts, within the form of thesis-ordered writing, to write Burke's ordered disorder. Another way to have written that section would have been to write a dialogue between characters, each of whom represented a fragment of Burke, each of whom meticulously explored Burke's twisting path to the God beyond and in language.

Teachers, as Burke would argue, necessarily imply students. All teachers, practitioners, critics, and theorists remain students and thus they must constantly explore the ever fluid natures of subject, lifestyle, method, and the like. As such, in Zen terms, even these highly educated types must have "beginner's mind" (Suzuki 21). Or as Burke and Merton would say: be humble. This book, certainly, is finally the work of a student. While meant to influence theory, criticism, practice, and pedagogy, it finally reveals an autobiographical choice. I have chosen to discipline myself to the dialectic of pain and imagination and turn to Burke, Merton, Freire, and Romero as teachers. The lessons have only begun. For my own students, I suggest that you not flee from the dialectic of pain and imagination. Rather, embrace it and demand that your teachers do so as well. Perhaps then the way to proceed will become more clear.

Notes

Chapter 1. The Way to Proceed

1. This is true of the full range of human experience. Pleasure is equally difficult to represent and deserves its own rhetorical study. I am indebted to Scarry's monumental book, *The Body in Pain*, for much of my understanding of the dialectic of pain and imagination. It helped me to name what I psychosomatically "knew," but couldn't articulate. Scarry's book, without doubt, will prove to be vastly influential.

2. See Morris for a fine treatment on the interdisciplinary nature of the interpretation of pain.

3. Popular culture recognizes this sadistic temperament. The play and film *Little Shop of Horrors* presents an unfortunate stereotype but real fear: the dentist who operates out of his desire to inflict pain on his patients.

4. While this question has not been a predominant concern in the history of rhetoric, threads of it do exist. Plato's *Phaedrus*, for instance, discusses, within the context of rhetoric, the pain the lover feels for the beloved. See Kristeva's *Tales of Love* for an elucidation of this (65–66). Aristotle, for his part, placed rhetoric at the center of civic life. It mediated public relationships and thus prevented and precipitated physical combat (*Rhetoric*, 1.3). Augustine tells of his ability to mediate between warring factions and consequently stave off suffering (*On Christian Doctrine*, book 4, chapter 24). In the modern world, rhetoricians like Richards claim the point of rhetoric is to help a warring world learn to mediate conflict (*Philosophy of Rhetoric* 3).

5. I say "sociopolitical" in order to locate this discussion in the polis. Here, I am not concerned about purely organic pain (if there is such a thing), which is simply a matter of 'nature,' 'fate,' or 'god.' I would be quite willing to be convinced that there is no such thing as a 'purely organic pain,' that even say, the pain that results from bone cancer is, at least in part, caused by sociopolitical machinations. Morris, in fact, has begun to argue precisely this. Still, it seems to me that there is a significant difference between the pain caused by a welcome pregnancy and the pain caused by political torture. I am most interested in how rhetoric can and should respond to the latter although rhetoric can and should also respond to the former.

6. See the Afterword for a fuller explanation of these five faces of rhetoric.

7. I simply presume this definition to be adequate; I mean it to be a suggestive heuristic device. An argument for its validity would require a thorough explication of

the strengths and weaknesses of Valesio's equation, a study of other theories of rhetoric and dialectic that don't agree with Valesio's equation, and a comparative treatment of these other theories and Valesio's. This would be at least a booklength effort in itself.

8. Theorists of rhetoric, one of the audiences to whom I am writing, may find it odd that I've chosen Valesio as my authority for this definition of rhetoric. After all, history is replete with rhetorical icons who have developed definitions of rhetoric: in addition to Aristotle, three of the most monumental are Plato, Cicero, and Augustine. Who is Valesio? Who am I? Who are we to correct Aristotle? For one, this definition of rhetoric resonates throughout the history of the discipline. Valesio himself grounds his work in figures such as Aristotle, Heraclitus, Shakespeare, Richards, and Nietzsche (25, 145, 51, 63, respectively). I would include a host of others: Plato, Cicero, Augustine, DeQuincey, Perelman, Kristeva, to name a few. He also deliberately locates himself in the postmodern era: "the rhetorical theory for our times must be . . . post-'Marxian,' post-'Freudian,' and post-'structuralist' " (17). Valesio's definition aspires to be a globally diachronic definition. Further, to claim that I am "Valesian" is to admit myself into a scholarly consensus, thereby gathering the authoritative weight of the contemporary scholarly community about me. Valesio's definition has influenced scholars in disciplines from literary theory to ethnography. Even the most negative reception claims that it offers "brilliant formulations and impressive erudition" (Foulkes 37). The most welcoming are well represented by Deetz: "The astute critic will find here the systemic basis for a new rhetoric of public discourse which is yet to be worked out" (207). It is to this "working-out" that I hope my study will contribute.

9. This pedagogy is currently being theorized and practiced. See, for instance, *Freire for the Classroom* and Covino's *Forms of Wondering*. The former is based in a liberation perspective, the latter, a postmodern.

10. See, for instance, Hassan 91–92; Taylor 31; Lyotard, *Postmodern Condition* xxiii–iv; Wyschogrod xvi–xxii. All are concerned with language and history; they simply don't clearly say so. For instance, Hassan's traits of "indeterminacy" and "immanence" are close to Tracy's plurality and ambiguity, respectively. Taylor's "celebration of plurality" conflates Tracy's categories of language and history. Taylor's two other categories, "the need to acknowledge one's tradition" and "resistance to domination," are parts of Tracy's history category. Lyotard's loss of faith in metanarratives entails a loss of faith in grandiose claims concerning language and history. Wyschogrod's fine list of "six impulses"—differentiality, double coding, eclecticism, alterity, empowerment, materialism—all can be viewed through plurality and ambiguity. Differentiality, for instance, calls "into question" reason, "totalizing discourse," and time. All three are marked by language and history. So too alterity, her all-important category, is a function of the loss of sure language and history. One must acknowledge and turn to the other once one can no longer claim that one's language and history are superior to all others.

11. For examples of ethnographers who would support Tracy's claim, see the works of the Scollons and Street.

12. This, no doubt, is one of the points cf the debate over 'the canon.' On one side stand the defenders of the 'Western tradition;' on the other side stands a group who would open the canon to works by Western people of color and non-Westerners. In the middle are the students. The debate concerns what type of people they should become.

13. See also the work of Street. Arguing that essayist literate peoples set themselves above "non-literate" people (24), and that as a result essayist literacy dominates world-literacy education movements, Street convincingly claims that this has led to the unjust imposition of Western values in such places as Tanzania and Iran (188, 195).

14. 'Philosophical/theological' theorists have much to learn from ethnographers. Tracy's argument that a recognition of the plurality of language leads to a recognition of the ambiguity of history could only be strengthened by the work of the Scollons and Street, among others.

15. Not coincidentally, Chopp identifies Freire as a forerunner of liberation theology, thereby framing her discussion within the context of literacy and hence, rhetoric (*Praxis* 5, 7, 21–222). Also, in her most recent book, Chopp turns to Burke and posits that essential to liberation theology, especially that of women, is rhetoric. See Chopp, *Power*.

16. Morris is right to caution against a simplistic definition of pain. It is complex and always open to multiple readings. See his Culture of Pain for an elucidation of this.

17. I refer to pain that is imposed and meant to destroy. Some pain is taken on willingly as a way in which one can ultimately build oneself (the pain of fasting, for instance).

18. Similarly, Chopp argues that mass suffering has a "nonidentity" character: it is so overwhelming that symbols can't adequately contain it (*Praxis* 2).

19. Rorty includes as one of the psychic effects of pain, "humiliation." While interesting, the cross-cultural possibilities of that which brings about humiliation, pain, still need to be explored.

20. See Warnock 78–91. All treatments of Coleridge's theory are much more systematic than Coleridge's own.

21. Covino's project has definite connections to Hassan's list (see note 2). Both, I take it, emphasize imagination as linguistic technique, the ability to combine and recombine words ad infinitum.

22. Buddhism, as well, has visited the inventive site of pain. Siddhartha left behind the princely life in order to discover the end of suffering. He rejected various imaginative systems before he achieved enlightenment. Significantly, he did so while sitting in a lotus position. He metaphorized his own body into a flower, and hundreds of generations of practitioners have done likewise.

Chapter 2. Burke's Beloved Cynosure and Sinecure

1. "Malcolm" is Malcolm Cowley. "Peggy" is Cowley's first wife. "Kenneth" and "Lily" are the Burkes. Day is recounting her Greenwich Village days in the 1920s before she converted to Roman Catholicism and began, with Peter Maurin, the Catholic Worker Movement. See Day 113–14.

2. Day was not and is not alone in her attitude concerning Burke's "strange books." See Vickers 441, and Knox for anti-Burke work. See Jameson 70 and Lentricchia 54–55 for pro-Burke efforts that discuss anti-Burke attitudes.

3. Rueckert argues for the latter even though his book returns again and again to noting the primal importance of rhetoric in Burke's work. On one hand, Rueckert argues, Burke divides the study of language into four fields: grammar, rhetoric, poetics, and the ethical-personal (201) and is working toward a system (logology) that encompasses them all (227). As such, then, Rueckert's Burke views rhetoric as a subcategory, not an all-encompassing field. On the other hand, Rueckert's Burke proposes that one must study poetry both intrinsically—as poetry for its own sake—and extrinsically—as rhetoric (64). Rhetoric has at least co-primal importance in 'literary' study. Rather than one category among many, rhetoric is an ultimate category, as Burke himself might say.

4. A growing number of critics argue that Burke is, primarily, a rhetorical theorist. See Southwell 83; Covino, *Forms of Wondering* 24; Chopp, *Power* 116; and, of course, Lentricchia 114.

5. Heath argues that there is an intrinsic/extrinsic distinction between poetry and rhetoric in Burke. He claims that Burke maintains that poetry is language used for its own sake, while rhetoric is language used for an effect beyond language (76–77, 196). Heath's argument is problematic. It fails to discern the extremely porous 'boundary' between poetry and rhetoric. In one part Heath claims that for Burke the poetic motive has three ingredients, one of which is the desire to convince others to accept the poetry (81). Rhetoric, according to Heath's Burke, is internal to poetry. Poetry is intended as rhetoric. This refusal to separate poetry and rhetoric certainly calls into question Rueckert's attempt to "purify" Burke's poetics, separating it from his rhetoric theory. Rueckert seeks in Burke a poetic "chamber" (Rueckert 6) the existence of which Burke's work denies.

6. See Covino, *Art of Wondering* 122; Southwell 85–86; Nelson 165–66; Tracy 9, 72, 107, 115, 129, for examples of critics who also intimate that Burke is a postmodern.

7. At the risk of proof-texting, I offer this statement from *A Rhetoric of Motives* that seems to contradict Lentricchia's reading. Burke saw Marxism to be "but one voice among many"; for the postmodern Burke, Marxism was simply one more tradition open to analysis as ideology (199). On this matter, Southwell has two criticisms of Lentricchia (82). The second is that "it has never been possible to label Burke a Marxist." Lentricchia would agree, I think: he does not want to label Burke at all. Southwell's first criticism, that "Burke's thought is diminished by his being mustered into the partisan service of

Marxism," is less easily answered. Any writer as heterogeneous as Burke is necessarily diminished when purified in order to serve any partisan program. Unfortunately, Southwell misses the larger more interesting discussion to have with Lentricchia. Southwell asserts that Burke comprehends postmodernism and that in claiming Burke for Marxism Lentricchia reduces Burke (159-60). Lentricchia claims that Burke, read from a Marxist perspective, provides a critical theory superior to postmodernism. This is a fascinating tension and I will explore it in this chapter.

8. See Burke, *Philosophy* 139 for his own discussion of the synecdochal fallacy.

9. Though Lentricchia, as should be obvious by now, finds Burke amenable to his own project, he does claim that one can find in Burke's work a tendency away from the recognition of the ambiguity of history. Lentricchia locates this primarily in Burke's discussion of the "bureaucratization of the imaginative" and Burke's belief that the comic attitude is the appropriate one to take in the face of historical ambiguity (e.g., Lentricchia 56, 64). Rather than address this here, I will do so when I discuss the place of the imaginative in Burke's work.

10. See, for instance, "War, Contradiction, and Response" in *Philosophy of Literary Form* where Burke discusses the difficulties of interpreting war (238); "Rhetoric and Poetics" in *Language as Symbolic Action* where Burke discusses the difficulty of regionalist writing, which must maintain both its own cultural specificity and appeal to other cultures (299-301).

11. This concern with the dialectics of competing poles, and their competing pieties, is perhaps the concern of Burke's career. In *Permanence and Change*, he discusses the meaning of torture for the skeptic and the budding martyr (35). What connects the dialectical partners is the possibility of torture. The two poles, the skeptic and the martyr-to-be, have different pieties that allow them, the partners, to interpret the possible event differently. The ambiguity of history is centered, interestingly, around the question of potential pain. One member of the dialectic views it as something to be avoided, the other as something to be courted.

12. Heath argues that Burke "willingly acknowledges the problems produced by the ambiguity and pliancy of linguistic substance" (197, see also 85, 157–58). Heath's argument is similar to mine, though I deal with different materials, treat this dimension of Burke much more fully, and name this dimension "plurality."

13. This is one element of Burke that is becoming more and more understood and discussed. See Lentricchia 72–74, 80; Southwell 67; Henderson 100; Williams 205.

14. See Burke's masterful study of Genesis 1–3 in *The Rhetoric of Religion* as a further demonstration of this point. As Burke argues there, words constantly move among four levels: words about nature, about the sociopolitical, about words, about the supernatural.

15. Oravec's proposed tripartite Burkean imagination slights the generative character of Burke's theory of imagination. See especially 180–81, 185.

16. This concept is criticized by both Knox and Lentricchia: two critics who disagree on the value of Burke's work agree that this part of Burke is extremely troublesome. Knox, in his postscript, uses "bureaucratization of the imaginative" ironically to criticize Burke, asserting that Burke's system will itself lead to a bureaucratization of imaginative writing. The grounds upon which Knox bases his claim are unclear: he leaves it at the level of assertion only. Knox also claims that the "bureaucratization of the imaginative" is Burke's "bogeyman" (107).

Lentricchia offers a more sustained critique of this concept, which is central to the early Burke. I take Lentricchia's criticism to be twofold. One: the concept of the bureaucratization of the imaginative is unhelpful insofar as it denigrates "sociohistoric texture." Two: Burke's comedic response is problematic insofar as it: (1) allows Burke to transcend himself and others (he has a "privileged place" (62); (2) essentializes history by aestheticizing it. My own elucidation of Burke's concept of "bureaucratization of the imaginative" counters Lentricchia's. I find that Burke's concept takes history seriously, embeds the comedian within history, and allows for historical heterogeneity to speak. Furthermore, it involves the envisionment and technique of object-oriented imagination as Burke attempts to respond, albeit implicitly and obliquely, to the problem of pain. It is, in short, an elucidation of postmodern rhetoric.

17. Lentricchia finds "thinly veiled scorn" (61) in this description of the process. However, Lentricchia does not argue for the presence of the scorn; he only asserts it.

18. See also *A Rhetoric of Motives* 154 for a discussion of this under the title of "dissociative technique."

19. See also *A Grammar of Motives* 504, which refers one back to the discussion of incongruity in *Permanence and Change*, the companion volume to *Attitudes Toward History*.

20. Burke returns to this in *A Rhetoric of Motives* where he claims that war is a perversion of peace (20).

21. This is also true of *The Rhetoric of Religion*, which begins with a poem about the cycle of language and war (4).

22. The examples of the ways in which Burke sets *A Rhetoric of Motives* within the environment of actual and potential pain are many. See, for example: 29–30 where he links science, the Church, and the Nazi death camps; 32 where he again discusses the death camps, the church, and how post–World War II military establishments resemble the Nazis; 139 where he links the industrial revolution, Detroit car factories, and atomic warfare; 153–54 where he discusses, in the manner of *Attitudes Toward History*, linguistic techniques to counter both cold and hot wars.

23. Rueckert provides a thorough introduction to Burke's use of scapegoat theory. See 137, 147–51.

24. One should be cautious about the word *transcendence* in Burke. While it usually connotes "up," in *Attitudes Toward History* Burke defines it as "the adoption of

another point of view from which they (A & B) cease to be opposites" (336). It may go upward or downward (337) or even across as a bridge, a merger (179–80). This confusion in Burke (or maybe it is clarity considering the plurality of 'transcendence') perhaps accounts for the fact that he says that the principles/ideas are "underlying" (137). He also talks about them in terms of being at the end of a hierarchy, from which things fall (138).

25. Burke's fascination with God and his use of a Christian framework has been well discussed by Rueckert in *Kenneth Burke and the Drama of Human Relations*. Yet Rueckert has failed to notice the way in which Burke's rhetorical theory is the theory of a mystic.

26. See Heath for a summary of Burke's treatment of entelechy (176).

27. Burke's pure persuasion seems to be 'above' violence, the desire for power, and the like. In light of Kristeva's work, this is problematic. See *Revolution in Poetic Language* which details the ways in which language is "always already" full of violence. Further discussions of Burke's work must deal with this.

Chapter 3. 'Poetic Rhetoric and Baffling Illogic'

The phrase to the left of the colon comes from Carr 83. The phrase refers to Meister Eckhardt and Merton's attraction to him.

1. Lentfoehr claims that *Geography* is a demonstration of "the stunning expanse of the imaginative country of his mature mind" (52). Lentfoehr's "country" is not an ill-chosen metaphor. *Geography* should not be read as a Mertonian aberration, however, despite the fact that Lentfoehr, a Roman Catholic poet, leading critic of Merton's poetry, and dear friend of the monk, has asserted that "however highly applauded" Merton might be for *Geography*, "it is in the metaphysical-mystical lyric that he is most truly himself" (52). By "metaphysical-mystical lyric" Lentfoehr means such poetry as found in Merton's late 1950's *The Strange Island*. How she knows what is most 'truly' Merton would be an interesting question to pursue, but she makes no argument for the 'trueness' of the lyrics over and against *Geography*. Perhaps she feels that she can make such a claim because of the friendship she and Merton shared.

2. Woodcock well details the postmodern, spatial dimensions of the poem when he likens its four-part structure (South, North, East, and West) to a survey map, a mandala, and the old Aztec dance of the four directions (177).

3. Sutton suggests that this delving in the poem should be read as quest (51).

4. See Altany for a general discussion of Merton as pilgrim (3, 10).

5. Kramer argues that "the most fundamental accomplishment in *Lograire* is to imagine the coming of the white man to other cultures by describing that arrival in terms

of other people" (136); Glimm holds that *Geography* enters into "myth-dreams" of others in order to expose the world's problems (96). Both are correct, as far as they go. What they miss, however, is the precise idea that Merton, in going to the other(s) in the poem, attempts to allow the other(s) to speak across space and through time.

6. None, curiously, have attended to the place of Zen in the poem. Schmidt does claim that Merton's anti-poetry (of which *Geography* is an example, Lentfoehr holds) was influenced by his work with Zen (73). Yet she fails to argue this crucial insight, especially relative to *Geography*. Bowman also discusses Zen and Merton's poetry, but concentrates on the lyrics and *Cables to the Ace*. So too Cooper fails to see Zen as having a significant role in Merton's late poetry. While such oversight may help Cooper's thesis—that Merton was a failed mystic (166–91)—it ignores both Carr's study of Merton and Zen in the Merton texts Cooper finds to be most important. His lack of attention to Carr's book may simply be a factor of publication schedule: her book was published only three years before his. His lack of attention to the Zen in the Merton text is far stranger, however. For instance, Cooper refers to Merton's *Zen and the Birds of Appetite* in order to note Merton's allusion to Marcuse (Cooper 254), so that he, Cooper, can argue that Merton's *Cables to the Ace* is Marcusean antipoetry (260–61). Yet Cooper does nothing with Merton's reflections on Zen that surround the allusion to Marcuse. Similarly, Cooper points to Merton's work on Roland Barthes (260) but misses the important allusion to Zen found in this study.

7. Cooper tantalizingly suggests that Merton saw in the failure of modern society the possibility "for an innovative poetics: a radically experimental, postmodern anti-poetry" (259). I say "tantalizingly" because while Cooper uses "postmodern" to describe Merton's late poetry, especially *Cables to the Ace*, Cooper neither defines "postmodern" nor argues why Merton's late poetry is such. Others who have described Merton as "postmodern" include Sutton and Woodcock (177). Like Cooper, neither defines the adjective. Most notable, however, is Sutton's linking of Merton's postmodern motivation and Merton's concern for suffering. Sutton claims that Merton rejected the "idea of salvation through mystical union or divine revelation," opting instead for a solution "grounded in the existential confrontation and suffering of social reality" (56). Merton's choice, Sutton speculates with an interesting assertion, was "probably shaped by a contemporary, post-modern Catholicism" (56).

8. Sutton said it first, and perhaps best, when he wrote that "Merton's poem ends with the end of dreaming and with a sense of the failure of civilization as well as of its victims" (55). Later critics, such as Labrie (163) and Schmidt (161), simply echo Sutton's argument.

9. Merton, in his "Cargo Cults of the South Pacific," argues that all myth-dreams are inadequate; each community has only a partial expression of the whole truth (94).

10. "Niggers" is used to provide this scene with a sarcastic edge. Clearly, Merton is mimicking racist dialect.

11. Interestingly, in *Zen and the Birds of Appetite* Merton offers a Nietzschean/Burkean genealogy of 'Christianity.' In a discussion concerning comparison

of Christianity and Buddhism, Merton asks which Christianity it is one proposes to compare with Buddhism: "Christian Theology? Ethics? Mysticism? Worship? . . . The Roman Catholic Church? . . . Protestant Christianity? The Protestantism of Luther or that of Bonhoeffer? . . . The Catholicism of St. Thomas? of St. Augustine?" (41–42).

12. See Randall for a lucid and important discussion of irony in *Geography*.

13. All of canto IV of "East" explores naming, reporting the name-changing ways of both Biblical Hebrews (Jair and Nobah in stanza 1) and other European explorers.

14. This essay increasingly is becoming recognized as important to the interpretation of Merton's late poetry. Lentfoehr claims that the essay stands as Merton's philosophy of anti-poetry (97–98) and Cooper echoes this (260). Both are right and by linking Merton to Barthes have begun to link Merton to postmodernism. Yet neither discusses an extremely important dimension of this essay: the way in which Merton brings together Barthes, Zen, and a language philosophy that understands the 'sign' to be arbitrary.

15. Glimm argues it a bit differently. He claims that when *Geography* places people in other "myth-dreams" it shows how arbitrary their own are (100).

16. Glimm, for example, argues that the poem is about the violent ways Westerners have dealt with other cultures (95). Working out of their own particularity, Westerners, Glimm suggests, oppress others as they attempt to universalize their own particular histories. Certainly, much of *Geography* explores this.

17. See Randall 145–46 for a fascinating argument regarding the self-criticism to which Merton alludes in this section.

18. Kramer claims that "East" reveals the inability of the Westerner to understand the Easterner (141). This is only partially true. "East" also reveals the inability of Easterners to understand each other. They too violently universalize their own limited histories in an attempt to subsume others.

19. The entire poem provokes the same questions. For instance, see the juxtaposition of beauty-culture advertisements and Yucatan death art noted by Lentfoehr (121), Randall (195), and Schmidt (141).

20. Many critics of *Geography* discuss this in one way or another, though none explicitly address it terms of pain. Most discuss the ways the poem deals with violence. See Sutton 52; Glimm 102; Schmidt 65.

21. Schmidt argues that this sequence points to the clash of metaphorical systems (149–50). She is correct, and this only strengthens my point. Metaphors, Aristotle reminds us, are as crucial to rhetoric as they are to poetry. See *Rhetoric* 3.2; *Poetics*

22. For details on Merton's sources, see *Geography* 143–44, note 34.

23. The translation of the Spanish is my own.

24. One might relate this point to the work done by Scollon and Scollon. They argue that Athabaskan narrative technique, unlike the narrative technique of English speakers, presents itself without interpretation. The storyteller does not present a moral or a point to the audience. Rather, the audience members must interpret the story as fits their individual lives. This, Scollon and Scollon argues, reflects the Athabaskan "bush consciousness," which prizes nonintervention and autonomy (Scollon and Scollon 115–17).

25. Izutsu confirms Merton's interpretation of the course of sitting with a *Koan*. He writes: "The only authentic way to solve a Koan, in the traditional views of Rinzai Zen, is by "becoming the *Koan*" or becoming "completely one with the Koan" (168).

Chapter 4. *Zoon Phonata*

1. The effect that Freire has had on hooks is not an isolated incident. Speaking of "oppositional pedagogy" that resists the "articulations of the dominant bourgeois discourse" (261), Davis claims that it has two sources: the activities of the French left after May 1968, and "third-world attempts to reject foreign domination in education" (250). "The book," Davis asserts, "that made the case for a manifesto of oppositional pedagogy is Paulo Freire's well-known *Pedagogy of the Oppressed*" (250).

2. The place of the religious in Freire has sparked intense debate. Bowers finds in Freire a view that religion is destined to become a matter of personal belief or something to be replaced by rational thought (946–7). Zike argues that Freire is essentially a-religious (6). Rivera maintains that Freire's system is antireligious and rational and approves of this (59). Knoblauch fears that Freire's system leads to theology (135). Others approvingly identify Freire with liberation theologians (see Schipani 65–66; Giroux, "Culture, Power" 113; Elias, *Conscienctization* 62; Berthoff, "Paulo Freire" 368; Maring 33–34). In fact, Freire's work, especially *Pedagogy*, influenced the development of liberation theology and the base ecclesial communities wherein the voices of the oppressed are allowed to speak (Chopp, *Praxis* 5, 7, 21–22).

3. Collins has thus far done the most work in identifying Freire's place within the tradition of the Word. He argues that Freire has drawn upon Western philosophy (50–51), the Genesis story in which Adam names the animals as a sign of human dominion over the world (50–51), and the Christian doctrine of "Jesus as the 'Word of God' " (50–51) in his own conception of the centrality of the Word to human being. Collins' book is helpful because it begins to discern the way in which Freire belongs to the tradition of the Word. However, it is limited because it does not systematically argue its insight. Its claim about Freire's use of the Christian doctrine of the incarnate Word, for instance, does not point to specific places in Freire's writings in order to substantiate itself. Furthermore, and most important, Collins does not detail the ways in which Freire understands the Word to be informed by the dialectic of pain and imagination.

4. This is an undeveloped minority position. Berthoff (Foreword xviii) and Stanley (374) simply link Freire and rhetoric by placing his name and the word *rhetoric*

within proximity to one another. Knoblauch (126–35) goes further, offering a definition of rhetoric, a systematization of the four kinds of "rhetorical" statements, and a claim that Freire's theory is one of these kinds (dialogical). Helpful as they are, Berthoff's and Stanley's attempts to link Freire and rhetoric are limited. They simply assume that literacy theory and rhetorical theory are the same thing. Knoblauch's is the stronger position. It, however, lacks development.

5. Bugbee argues that Freire's definition of oppression is so abstract that it is empty (432). Even if Freire wishes to specify oppression in terms of class, as Bugbee rightly argues that Freire does, Bugbee claims that Freire still does not adequately characterize the class relationships that inform his theory. What may save Freire from oversimplifying historical struggle is his recognition that while class struggle is universal, it does not have a universal shape; it is different in each context (Freire and Faundez 59). Freire's foremost U.S. proponent Giroux would disagree with me. Without close textual analysis, Giroux claims that "Freire rejects the idea that there is a universalized form of oppression." For Freire, he argues, "domination cannot be reduced exclusively to a form of class domination" ("Culture, Power"108–9).

6. See Bourdieu for a fine example of class theory and analysis.

7. See Zike for a fine treatment of this. He well argues that one must understand suffering if one wants to achieve self-transcendence.

8. My understanding of the generative words is culled from a number of sources in Freire, especially *Education as the Practice* and the Appendix to this piece (41–84; see also *Pedagogy* 101–18).

9. This aspect of Freire's theory, I must note, has been strongly criticized by some commentators (Schipani 73; Elias, *Conscientizatior* 41–42; Griffith 78; Stanley 392). They are unhappy with Freire's certainty. Unlike Merton and Burke, Freire is sure that utopia is possible.

10. Bugbee rightly identifies both history and language as central to the process of *conscientização* (421). Most Freire commentators concentrate on Freire's concern with history to the detriment of his concern about language (Bowers 947; Elias, "Social Learning" 25; McLaren 224–25; Schipani 66; Ordonez 146; Zike 20; Giroux, "Culture, Power" 119–20). But a few commentators, like Bugbee, have begun to address the connection between language and history in Freire's theory. Berthoff has said it most concisely and best: "To take up Paulo Freire's slogans without his philosophy of language will be to misapprehend his philosophy of history" ('Paulo" 366–67). Berthoff reminds readers of Freire (especially Marxists) that not to attend to Freire's concentration on language or subordinate it to his concern with history is to misread Freire and to misunderstand the nature of human being ("Paulo" 366). So too Collins reminds readers of Freire that one cannot attend only to his treatment of history; for Freire history and language are co-equal and the historicization of human being is dependent upon language (45).

11. Zike alone has argued that *conscientização* is both noun and verb (62–63). As noun, it marks "a quantitative change in mental awareness": the oppressed come to exist in a way in which they haven't. As verb it marks the ways in which the oppressed participate in the "dialectic of permanence and change"; it marks the ways in which they build the world. Zike argues that given this understanding of *conscientização*, oppression for Freire is best understood as "that situation imposed by one human upon another or by a system of human beings upon others which . . . takes away from them their ability and opportunity to create history, to be human" (9). This is true, as far as it goes. What it misses, and this is surprising given Zike's insight that Freire's conscious human is Word, is that oppression also includes the denial of people as word, as *logos*. Oppression does not simply thwart the historicization of the oppressed; it thwarts as well the oppressed's birth as Word. It is only as Word that the oppressed become historicized.

12. Schipani, for instance, simply summarizes the process (12). Ordonez comes closer, noting how what Freire calls the stage of "naive transitive consciousness" marks the stage at which the oppressed are "emerging from silence" (188). Ordonez' own words alert one to realize that the process is a process of coming to language; it is a process that allows the oppressed to emerge from silence, to merge into language. However, he fails to explore his own insight. In an important mistake, Ordonez calls the final stage, which is *conscientização*, the stage of "critical consciousness" (190), rather than using Freire's phrase "critically transitive consciousness" (*Education as the Practice* 18). In dropping the word *transitive* Ordonez drops the verbal implication of Freire's discussion. So too Elias drops the word *transitive* from his discussion of this final stage, revealing that he misses the ways in which the process of *conscientização* is the coming to language, especially the coming to verb (Elias, "Social" 7–8).

13. Collins writes that "Since human consciousness is conditioned by reality as experienced and mediated through thought-language, Freire employs an analogy from grammar (transitivity) to describe states of human consciousness" (59). Collins' use of the word *analogy* tends to weaken Freire's point. Critical transitive consciousness is not 'like' a transitive verb; Freire understands it to *be* a transitive verb. Consciousness is verbal. Freire writes that "Discussing the function of thought, Nicol affirms that it should not be designated by a noun, but by a *transitive* verb" (*Extension* 137).

14. Other Freire commentators have already noted this (e.g., Schipani 17; Griffith 71–72; Elias, *Conscientization* 41–42), and the monumental amount of evidence throughout Freire's writings only validates the critical consensus (e.g., *Pedagogy* 28–30; Shor and Freire 11–12; *Politics* 17).

Chapter 5. Romero's Word of the Church in History

"Goodtidings to those who suffer" (bienaventurados a los que sufren) is a phrase from the sermon Romero delivered to mark the first anniversary of the assassination of

Father Alfonso Navarro (*Su Pensamiento* 4: 226). Unless otherwise indicated, all translations from Romero's sermons are my own. While I am responsible for the inadequacies, I thank Sarita Tamayo for her help.

1. Quéré; Sobrino, *Archbishop* 48; Levertov 15–39; Carr, *Transforming Grace* 198–99, *New Companion* 329 all testify to Romero's growing global impact.

2. For the secular American academy, Romero is perhaps an odd choice. American academics turn to poets, novelists, playwrights, and the like to develop their theories, but not preachers. Rorty argues, for instance, as I discussed in chapter 1, that people would do well to turn to novelists, ethnographers, and journalists in order to hear the voices of the pain. Rorty's idea, while not without merit, reveals what may be a bias inherent within the American postmodern movement. Many of the greatest voices of pain have been clergy; many of the best examples of pain rhetoricized are the genres of institutional religion: the sermon and the Pastoral Letter. Both are ancient genres (the Pastoral Letter, for instance, dates at least to the apostle Paul) that have been used for contemporary purposes. Consider, for instance, the sermons and letters of Dr. King. Romero, likewise, took on these genres and infused them with the concerns of El Salvador.

3. See Hennelly; Curran 88–96; and Dorr for discussions of Roman Catholic social teaching. Medellín was held in 1968, Puebla in 1979. The former convened in order to discuss how the Latin American Roman Catholic community could implement Vatican II. Puebla met in order to validate and refine Medellín. See Hennelly, Sobrino, and Brockman for more about these convocations. If liberation theology is marked by the attitude that God is found in the poorest of the poor and that those who follow Jesus as the Christ must preferentially opt for the poor (Hennelly xiii), Romero is a liberation theologian. This identity has been well established by Sobrino and Brockman.

4. There has not been, to date, any English-language academic treatment of Romero's work, including his sermons and Pastoral Letters. Sobrino's *Archbishop* covers, primarily, the sermons. Sobrino alone has begun to consider Romero's work from the vantage of rhetoric. However, his commentary leads nowhere but into a morass. Commenting on Romero's sermons, Sobrino claims that "he did employ the classic prophetic rhetorical style on occasion, as when he spoke of a rampant sexual immorality" (*Archbishop* 136). By this, since Sobrino offers no theoretical reflection on what he means by rhetoric, one can only presume that he means that Romero used hyperbolic analogy. The example provided by Sobrino quotes Romero as suggesting that God "might have rained down fire on this Sodom" (136). While Sobrino uses "rhetoric" positively here, he also uses it negatively, suggesting that rhetoric veils knowledge. He writes: "Archbishop Romero saw that the specific reason the church was persecuted was that it preached the word of truth. . . . without the slightest hint of rhetoric, but in full knowledge that the essence of the church was at stake, he repeatedly asserted of the church: 'It must be prepared not to betray the truth' " (160–61). If Sobrino's statements are taken together, his stance is obviously contradictory: Romero, the knowledgeable speaker, both used rhetoric and shunned it because it veils knowledge.

5. By "intertextual" I do not mean, to borrow Kristeva's phrase, the "banal sense of 'study of sources' " (*Revolution* 60). Nor do I mean what she calls "transposition." By this she indicates the use of one or more kinds of signifying practices by another signifying practice. For instance, Kristeva would point to a metalanguage's (e.g., literary theory's) use of narrative technique as an instance of transposition (60–61). She herself employs this category as a device to study the ways in which transposition reveals the fragility of the subjectivity of an author. She argues that poetic language, represented by the likes of Mallarmé and Joyce, manifests human beings who are "in process/on trial," which is to say that their egos are not unitary. Although it be both fruitful and fascinating to follow Kristeva's lead and approach to Romero's Pastoral Letters with attention to what they reveal about Romero's subjectivity, I deploy the notion of intertextuality as a way to examine the position in which the Letters place their readers.

6. "Oremos, hermanos, la situación de nuestro país es muy difícil pero la figura de Cristo transfigurado en plena Cuaresma no está lejos, es el camino que debemos de seguir. El camino de la transfiguración de nuestro pueblo no está lejos es el camino que nos señala la palabra de Dios este día: camino de cruz, de sacrificio, de sangre y de dolor, pero con la vista llena de esperanza puesta en la gloria de Cristo que es el Hijo elegido por el Padre para salvar al mundo. Escuchémosle!"

7. "Cristo colocado en la cumbre del Tabor es la imagen bellísima de la liberación. Así quiere Dios a los hombres: arrancados del pecado, y de la muerte, y del infierno, viviendo su vida eterne, inmortal, gloriosa. Este es nuestro destino, y hablar de ese cielo no es alienación sino motivación para trabajar con más garra, con más gusto, las grandes responsabilidades de la Tierra. Nadie trabaja la tierra y la liberación política de los pueblos con tanto entusiasmos, como aquel que espera que las luchas liberadoras de la historia se incorporarán la gran liberación de Cristo."

8. Sobrino recognizes Romero's encounter with Grande's death and his dead body as the moment at which Romero committed himself preferentially to the poor, changing from a conservative defender of the Salvadoran status quo (*Archbishop* 1–2, 9–10).

9. The verb in the Spanish text is *conculcado* (*La Voz* 85), the infinitive being *conculcar*. It can also mean "to infringe" and "to violate," among others.

10. Walsh's "therefore, the best argument for" is Romero's "por tanto, es la mejor razón" (Romero, *La Voz* 71).

11. In light of contemporary feminist concerns, it is not insignificant that Romero identifies machismo as a problem. See also his sermon "La Iglesia un servicio de liberación personal, comunitaria, trascendente" 362. It is found in *Su Pensamiento* vol. 8, 357–82. *A Martyr's Message* has translated it as "The Church: Defender of Human Dignity" 115–61. The pertinent passage is found on 123–4 in this translation. This passage also argues for the equality of women.

12. This anti-Judaism is certainly one of the least appealing parts of Romero's work. One only needs to consider the history of anti-Judaism in the West to understand the magnitude of the problem. See Ruether 65–93. I like to think that my demonstration of the fragility of Romero's images makes his discourse, and all Christian discourse, much less certain than it tends to think of itself. If the image of Mary, as I will argue below, challenges the supremacy of the image of Christ in the Letters, then perhaps there is hope for a less Christocentric, imperialistic attitude toward Judaism.

13. See Sobrino (*Archbishop* 15–31) for a discussion concerning Romero's understanding of the eucharist and the conflicts between Romero and the Salvadoran Jesuits on this issue.

14. Walsh has translated the Spanish *Elías* as the English Elias. Elias is Elijah. I will use Elijah in my discussion.

Afterword

1. Eagleton is finally the source for this model, though it would probably surprise him. He himself is a theorist and implicitly suggests, in a number of places, the other four titles (e.g., teacher and student 212, practitioner 207, critic 205, 207, 211).

2. Interdisciplinary efforts in regard to these four have been lightly tested. Though in separate books, Chopp, for instance, does indicate that she is familiar with Burke and Freire (*Power* 1, 32, 116, 129, 133 and *Praxis* 5, 7, 21–22 respectively). Presumably, the liberation concerns of both books allow for some amount of dialogue, at least in Chopp's own person, between Burke and Freire. So too Tracy refers, albeit fleetingly, to both Burke and Merton (9, 72, 94, 107). Carr, for her part, is an expert on Merton (*A Search*) and also notes the importance of Romero for many Roman Catholics and other Christians (*Transforming Grace* 198–99). Covino's *The Art of Wondering* places its revisionary efforts as Burkean (121–22, 128, 130) and *Forms of Wondering* appeals both to Freire and Burke (81–83, 8–9, 36–37, respectively).

3. See Lyotard, *The Differend*. His entire project in this book is to speak the silence between phrases.

4. See Covino, *Forms of Wondering*. The following discussion is indebted to him.

Works Cited

Adams, Daniel J. *Thomas Merton's Shared Contemplation: A Protestant Perspective.* Kalamazoo, Mich.: Cistercian, 1979.

Altany, Alan. "The Transformation of the Idea of the Sacred in the Poetry of Thomas Merton." Diss. U of Pittsburgh, 1987.

Aristotle. *Poetics.* Trans. W. Rhys Roberts. *The Rhetoric and Poetics of Aristotle.* New York: Modern, 1984.

———. *Rhetoric.* Trans. Ingram Bywater. *The Rhetoric and Poetics of Aristotle.* New York: Modern, 1984.

Arnove, Robert J. "The 1980 Nicaraguan National Literacy Campaign." In *National Literacy Campaigns.* Ed. Robert J. Arnove and Harvey J. Graff. New York: Plenum, 269–91.

Arts and Humanities Citation Index. Philadelphia: Institute for Scientific Information, 1980–90.

"Astrolabe." *The Random House College Dictionary.* Rev. ed. 1975.

Augustine. *On Christian Doctrine.* Trans. D. W. Robertson, Jr. Indianapolis: Bobbs-Merrill, 1983.

Baker, James Thomas. *Thomas Merton: Social Critic.* Lexington: U of Kentucky P, 1971.

Berthoff, Ann E. Foreword. In Freire and Macedo. xi–xxiii.

———. "Paulo Freire's Liberation Pedagogy." *Language Arts* 67.4 (1990): 362–69.

Bourdieu, Pierre. *Distinction: A Social Critique of the Judgement of Taste.* Trans. Richard Nice. Cambridge, Mass.: Harvard UP, 1984.

Bowers, C. A. "Linguistic Roots of Cultural Invasion in Paulo Freire's Pedagogy." *Teachers College Record* 84.4 (1983): 935–53.

Brockman, James, S.J. *Romero: A Life.* Maryknoll: Orbis, 1989.

Brown, Cynthia. Appendix. "Literacy in 30 Hours: Paulo Freire's Process in Northeast Brazil." In *Freire for the Classroom: A Sourcebook for Liberatory Teaching.* Ed. Ira Shor. Portsmouth, N.H.: Boynton/Cook, 1987.

Bugbee, John A. "The Freire Approach to Literacy: Review and Reflections." *Literacy Discussion* 4 (1973): 415–38.

Burke, Kenneth. *Attitudes Toward History*. 3d ed. Berkeley: U of California P, 1984.

——— . *Counter-Statement*. 3d ed. Berkeley: U of California P, 1968.

——— . *A Grammar of Motives*. Berkeley: U of California P, 1969.

——— . *Language as Symbolic Action: Essays on Life, Literature, and Method*. Berkeley: U of California P, 1966.

——— . *Permanence and Change: An Anatomy of Purpose*. 3d ed. Berkeley: U of California P, 1984.

——— . *The Philosophy of Literary Form*. 3d ed. Berkeley: U of California P, 1973.

——— . *A Rhetoric of Motives*. 3d ed. Berkeley: U of California P, 1969.

——— . *The Rhetoric of Religion: Studies in Logology*. Berkeley: U of California P, 1970.

Campos, Tomás R. "La Iglesia Y Las Organizaciones Populares En El Salvador." In *Iglesia de los Pobres y Organizaciones Populares*. San Salvador, El Salvador: UCA Editores, 1979, 147–161.

Carr, Anne E. *A Search for Wisdom and Spirit: Thomas Merton's Theology of the Self*. Notre Dame: U of Notre Dame P, 1988.

——— . *Transforming Grace: Christian Tradition and Women's Experience*. San Francisco: Harper, 1988.

Cavell, Stanley. *Disowning Knowledge: In Six Plays of Shakespeare*. Cambridge: Cambridge UP, 1987.

Chopp, Rebecca S. *The Power to Speak: Feminism, Language, God*. New York: Crossroad, 1989.

——— . *The Praxis of Suffering: An Interpretation of Liberation and Political Theologies*. Maryknoll: Orbis, 1986.

Coleridge, Samuel Taylor. *Biographia Literaria*. New York: Dutton, 1910.

Collins, Denis E., S.J. *Paulo Freire: His Life, Works and Thought*. New York: Paulist, 1977.

Cooper, David D. *Thomas Merton's Art of Denial: The Evolution of a Radical Humanist*. Athens: U of Georgia P, 1989.

Covino, William A. *The Art of Wondering: A Revisionist Return to the History of Rhetoric*. Portsmouth, NH: Boynton/Cook, 1988.

————— . *Forms of Wondering: A Dialogue on Writing, for Writers.* Portsmouth, NH: Boynton/Cook, 1990.

Curran, Charles. *Tensions in Moral Theology.* Notre Dame: U of Notre Dame P, 1988.

Davis, Robert Con. "A Manifesto for Oppositional Pedagogy: Freire, Bourdieu, Merod, and Graff." In *Reorientations: Critical Theories and Pedagogies.* Ed. Bruce Henricksen and Thais E. Morgan. Urbana: U of Illinois P, 1990.

Day, Dorothy. *The Long Loneliness.* San Francisco: Harper, 1981.

Deetz, Stanley. Rev. of *Novantiqua* by Paolo Valesio. *Philosophy and Rhetoric* 15.3 (1982): 207–11.

Derrida, Jacques. *Of Grammatology.* Trans. Gayatri Chakravorty Spivak. Baltimore: Johns Hopkins UP, 1976.

Dorr, Donald. *Option for the Poor: A Hundred Years of Vatican Social Teaching.* Dublin: Gill, 1983.

Dorris, Michael, and Louise Erdrich. *The Crown of Columbus.* New York: HarperCollins, 1991.

Eagleton, Terry. *Literary Theory.* Minneapolis: U of Minnesota P, 1983.

Elias, John. *Conscientization and Deschooling: Freire's and Illich's Proposals for Reshaping Society.* Philadelphia: Westminster, 1976.

————— . "Social Learning and Paulo Freire." *Journal of Educational Thought* 8 (1974): 5–14.

Feminism/Postmodernism. Ed. Linda J. Nicholson. New York: Routledge, 1990.

Feyerabend, Paul. *Against Method.* New York: New Left, 1975.

"Figure." *The Random House College Dictionary.* Rev. ed. 1975

Fisher, Walter. Rev. of *Novantiqua* by Paolo Valesio. *Quarterly Journal of Speech* 68.1 (1982): 91–3.

Foucault, Michel. "The Discourse on Language." Afterword. In *The Archaeology of Knowledge.* Trans. A. M. Sheridan Smith. New York: Pantheon, 1972.

Foulkes, A. P. "Critical Voices: A Survey of Recent Contributions to Literary Theory." *Journal of Literary Semantics* 11.1 (1982): 35–43.

Freire, Paulo. *Cultural Action for Freedom.* Trans. Loretta Slover. Cambridge, Mass.: Harvard Educational Review, 1988.

————— . *Education as the Practice of Freedom.* Trans. and ed. Myra Bergman Ramos. *Education for Critical Consciousness.* New York: Continuum, 1990, 1– 58.

————— . *Extension or Communication.* Trans. Louise Bigwood and Margaret Marshall. *Education for Critical Consciousness.* New York: Continuum, 1990, 91–164.

————— . Foreword. In *A Black Theology of Liberation.* By James H. Cone. Maryknoll: Orbis, 1990, vii–ix.

————— . *Pedagogy in Process: The Letters to Guinea Bissau.* Trans. Carman St. John Hunter. New York: Seabury, 1978.

————— . *Pedagogy of the Oppressed.* Trans. Myra Bergman Ramos. New York: Continuum, 1989.

————— . *The Politics of Education: Culture, Power, and Liberation.* Trans. Donaldo Macedo. South Hadley, Mass.: Bergin and Garvey, 1985.

Freire, Paulo, and Antonio Faundez. *Learning to Question: A Pedagogy of Liberation.* New York: Continuum, 1989.

Freire, Paulo, and Donaldo Macedo. *Literacy: Reading the Word and the World.* South Hadley, Mass.: Bergin and Garvey, 1987.

Freire for the Classroom: A Sourcebook for Liberatory Teaching. Ed. Ira Shor. Portsmouth, N.H.: Boynotn/Cook, 1987.

Geertz, Clifford. *The Interpretation of Cultures.* New York: Basic, 1973.

Giroux, Henry A. "Culture, Power and Transformation in the Work of Paulo Freire: Toward a Politics of Education." In *Teachers as Intellectuals: Toward a Critical Pedagogy of Learning.* Granby, Mass.: Bergin and Garvey, 1988.

————— . Introduction: Literacy and the Pedagogy of Political Empowerment. In Freire and Faundez, 1–27.

————— . *Schooling and the Struggle for Public Life.* Minneapolis: U of Minnesota P, 1988.

Glimm, James York. "Thomas Merton's Last Poem: *The Geography of Lograire.*" *Renascence* 26.2 (1974): 95–104.

Goulet, Denis. Introduction. In *Education for Critical Consciousness.* By Paulo Freire. New York: Continuum, 1990, vii–xiv.

Griffith, William S. "Paulo Freire: Utopian Perspective on Literacy Education for Revolution." In *Paulo Freire: A Revolutionary Dilemma for the Adult Educator.* Ed. Stanley M. Grabowski. Syracuse, New York: Syracuse U Publications in Continuing Education, 1972.

Gutiérrez, Gustavo. *The Power of the Poor in History*. Trans. Robert R. Barr. Maryknoll: Orbis, 1984.

Hassan, Ihab. "Postface 1982: Toward a Concept of Postmodernism." In *The Dismemberment of Orpheus: Toward a Postmodern Literature*. 2d ed. Madison: U of Wisconsin P, 1982, 259–71. Rpt. in *The Postmodern Turn: Essays in Postmodern Theory and Culture*. Columbus: Ohio State UP, 1987, 84–96.

Heath, Robert L. *Realism and Relativism: A Perspective on Kenneth Burke*. Macon, Ga.: Mercer UP, 1986.

Henderson, Greig E. *Kenneth Burke: Literature and Language as Symbolic Action*. Athens: U of Georgia P, 1988.

Hennelly, Alfred, S.J. Preface and General Introduction. In *Liberation Theology: A Documentary History*. Ed. Alfred T. Henelly, S.J. Maryknoll: Orbis, 1990.

hooks, bell, and Cornel West. *Breaking Bread: Insurgent Black Intellectual Life*. Boston: South End, 1991.

Horton, Myles, and Paulo Freire. *We Make the Road by Walking: Conversations on Education and Social Change*. Ed. Brenda Bell, John Gaventa, and John Peters. Philadelphia: Temple UP, 1990.

Izutsu, Toshihiko. *Toward a Philosophy of Zen Buddhism*. Boulder: Colorado Prajña Project, 1982.

Jameson, Frederic R. "The Symbolic Inference: or, Kenneth Burke and Ideological Analysis." In White and Brose, 68–91.

Kennedy, William J. Rev. of *Novantiqua* by Paolo Valesio. *German Quarterly* 56 (1983): 485–7.

Kilcourse, George. "Spirituality and Imagination: Thomas Merton's 'Sapiential Thinking.' " In *Toward an Integrated Humanity: Thomas Merton's Journey*. Ed. M. Basil Pennington, OCSO. Kalamazoo, Mich.: Cistercian, 1988, 114–131.

King, Martin Luther, Jr. "I Have a Dream." In *A Testament of Hope: The Essential Writings and Speeches of Martin Luther King, Jr.* Ed. James M. Washington. San Francisco: Harper, 1986, 217–220.

Knoblauch, C. H. "Rhetorical Constructions: Dialogue and Commitment." *College English*. 30.2 (1988): 125–40.

Knox, George. *Critical Moments: Kenneth Burke's Categories and Critiques*. Seattle: U of Washington P, 1957.

Kramer, Victor A. *Thomas Merton: Monk and Artist*. Kalamazoo, Mich.: Cistercian, 1984

Kristeva, Julia. *Revolution in Poetic Language*. Trans. Margaret Waller. New York: Columbia UP, 1984.

———. *Tales of Love*. Trans. Leon S. Roudiez. New York: Columbia UP, 1987.

Labrie, Ross. *The Art of Thomas Merton*. Fort Worth: Texas Christian UP, 1979.

Lentfoehr, Sister Thérèse. *Words and Silence: On the Poetry of Thomas Merton*. New York: New Directions, 1979.

Lentricchia, Frank. *Criticism and Social Change*. Chicago: U of Chicago P, 1985.

Levertov, Denise. *A Door in the Hive*. New York: New Directions, 1989.

Lyotard, Jean-François. *The Differend: Phrases in Dispute*. Trans. Georges Van Den Abbeele. Minneapolis: U of Minnesota P, 1988.

———. *The Postmodern Condition: A Report on Knowledge*. Trans. Geoff Bennington and Brian Massumi. Minneapolis: U of Minnesota P, 1984.

McLaren, Peter L. "Culture or Canon? Critical Pedagogy and the Politics of Literacy." *Harvard Educational Review* 58.2 (1988): 213–34.

"Manipulate." *The Random House College Dictionary*. Rev. ed. 1975.

Maring, G. H. "Freire's Adult Literacy Method." Literacy Work 5 (1976): 33–41.

Marsh, David. Rev. of *Novantiqua* by Paolo Valesio. *Substance* 30 (1981): 105–6.

Merton, Thomas. "Cargo Cults of the South Pacific." In *Love and Living*. Ed. Naomi Burton Stone and Brother Patrick Hart. New York: Farrar, 1978, 80–94.

———. *Contemplation in a World of Action*. New York: Doubleday, 1971.

———. *The Geography of Lograire*. New York: New Directions, 1969.

———. Introduction: Gandhi and the One-Eyed Giant. In *Gandhi on Non-Violence*. Ed. Thomas Merton. New York: New Directions, 1965, 1–20.

———. *My Argument with the Gestapo*. New York: New Directions, 1969.

———. *Mystics and Zen Masters*. New York: Farrar, 1967.

———. "Roland Barthes—Writing as Temperature." In *The Literary Essays of Thomas Merton*. Ed. Brother Patrick Hart. New York: New Directions, 1981, 140–46.

———. "War and the Crisis of Language." In *The Nonviolent Alternative*. Ed. Gordon C. Zahn. New York: Farrar, 1980, 234–47.

———. *Zen and the Birds of Appetite*. New York: New Directions, 1968.

Morris, David. *The Culture of Pain*. Berkeley: U of California P, 1993.

Mott, Michael. *The Seven Mountains of Thomas Merton*. Boston: Houghton, 1984.

Nelson, Cary. "Writing as the Accomplice of Language: Kenneth Burke and Poststructuralism." In Simons and Melia, 156–73.

Olson, David R. "From Utterance to Text: The Bias of Language in Speech and Writing." *Harvard Educational Review* 47.3 (1977): 257–81.

Oravec, Christine. "Kenneth Burke's Concept of Association." In Simons and Melia 174–95.

Ordonez, Jacinto Abel. "Paulo Freire's Concept of Freedom: A Philosophical Analysis." Diss. Loyola U of Chicago. Ann Arbor: UMI, 1982.

Perelman, Chaim. *The Realm of Rhetoric*. Trans. William Kluback. Notre Dame: U of Notre Dame P, 1982.

Plato. *Gorgias*. Trans. Walter Hamilton. New York: Penguin, 1971.

————. *Phaedrus*. Trans. Walter Hamilton. New York: Penguin, 1988.

Qúeré, France. Introduction. In *The Book of Christian Martyrs*. By Chenu, Bruno, et al. Trans. John Bowden. New York: Crossroad, 1990, vii–29.

Ramus, Peter. *Arguments in Rhetoric Against Quintillian*. Trans. Carole Newlands. Dekalb: Northern Illinois UP, 1986.

Rev. of *Novantiqua* by Paolo Valesio. *Choice* 18 (1981): 942.

Randall, Virginia. "Contrapuntal Irony and Theme in Thomas Merton's *The Geography of Lograire*." *Renascence* 28.4 (1976): 191–202.

Richards, I. A. *The Philosophy of Rhetoric*. London: Oxford UP, 1964.

Rivera, William McLeod. "The Changers: A New Breed of Adult Educator." In *Paulo Freire: A Revolutionary Dilemma for the Adult Educator*. Ed. Stanley M. Grabowski. Syracuse, New York: Syracuse U Publications in Continuing Education, 1972, 55–66.

Romero, Oscar. *A Martyr's Message of Hope: Six Homilies by Archbishop Oscar Romero*. Kansas City, Mo.: Celebration, 1981.

————. *Su Pensamiento: Homilias de Mons. Oscar Romero*. Vols. 3, 4, 6, 8. San Salvador, El Salvador: Publicaciones Pastorales del Arzobispado, 1981–89.

————. *Voice of the Voiceless: The Four Pastoral Letters and Other Statements*. Trans. Michael J. Walsh. Maryknoll: Orbis, 1990.

————. *La Voz de los sin Voz: La Palabra viva de Mons. Oscar Romero*. San Salvador, El Salvador: UCA/Editores, 1980.

Rorty, Richard. *Contingency, irony, and solidarity*. Cambridge: Cambridge UP, 1989.

Rueckert, William H. *Kenneth Burke and the Drama of Human Relations*. 2d ed. Berkeley: U of California P, 1982.

Ruether, Rosemary Radford. *Liberation Theology: Human Hope Confronts Christian History and American Power*. New York: Paulist, 1972.

Scarry, Elaine. *The Body in Pain: The Making and Unmaking of the World*. New York: Oxford UP, 1985.

Schipani, Daniel S. *Conscientization and Creativity: Paulo Freire and Christian Education*. Lanham, Mass.: UP of America, 1984.

Schmidt, Gail Ramshaw. "The Poetry of Thomas Merton: An Introduction." Diss. U of Wisconsin—Madison, 1976.

Scollon, Ron, and Suzanne Scollon. *Narrative, Literacy, and Face in Interethnic Communication*. Norwood, N.J.: Ablex, 1981.

Shor, Ira, and Paulo Freire. *A Pedagogy for Liberation: Dialogues on Transforming Education*. New York: Bergin and Garvey, 1987.

Simons, Herbert W., and Trevor Melia, eds. *The Legacy of Kenneth Burke*. Madison: U of Wisconsin P, 1989.

Sobrino, Jon, S.J. *Archbishop Romero: Memories and Reflections*. Trans. Robert R. Barr. Maryknoll: Orbis, 1990.

———— . "Presupuestos Teologicas de la Carta Pastoral." *Iglesia de los Pobres y Organizaciones Populares*. San Salvador, El Salvador: UCA Editores, 1979, 125–45.

Soelle, Dorothee. *Suffering*. Trans. Everett R. Kalin. Philadelphia: Fortress, 1975.

Southwell, Samuel B. *Kenneth Burke and Martin Heidegger: With a Note Against Deconstructionism*. Gainesville: U of Florida P, 1987.

Stanley, Manfred. "Literacy: The Crisis of a Conventional Wisdom." *School Review* 80.3 (1972): 373–408.

Steiner, George. *Language and Silence: Essays on Language, Literature, and the Inhuman*. New York: Atheneum, 1967.

Street, Brian. *Literacy in Theory and Practice*. Cambridge: Cambridge UP, 1988.

Sunim, Kusan. *The Way of Korean Zen*. Trans. Martine Fages. Ed. Stephen Batchelor. New York: Weatherhill, 1985.

Sutton, Walter. "Thomas Merton and the American Epic Tradition: The Last Poems." *Contemporary Literature* 14 (1973): 49–57.

Suzuki, Shunryu. *Zen Mind, Beginner's Mind.* New York: Weatherhill, 1977.

Swearingen, C. Jan. *Rhetoric and Irony: Western Literacy and Western Lies.* New York: Oxford UP, 1991.

Taylor, Mark Kline. *Remembering Esperanza: A Cultural-Political Challenge for North American Praxis.* Maryknoll: Orbis, 1990.

The New Companion to the Breviary with Seasonal Supplement. Indianapolis: Carmelites of Indianapolis, 1988.

The New Oxford Annotated Bible: Revised Standard Version. Ed. Herbert G. May and Bruce M. Metzger. New York: Oxford UP, 1973.

Tracy, David. *Plurality and Ambiguity.* San Francisco: Harper, 1989.

Valesio, Paolo. *Novantiqua: Rhetorics as a Contemporary Theory.* Bloomington: Indiana UP, 1980.

Vickers, Brian. *In Defense of Rhetoric.* Oxford: Clarendon, 1988.

Warnock, Mary. *Imagination.* Berkeley: U of California P, 1976.

Webb, Stephen H. *Blessed Excess: Religion and the Hyperbolic Imagination.* Albany: State U of New York P, 1993.

Weaver, Mary Jo. "Thomas Merton and Flannery O'Connor: The Urgency of Vision." In *Thomas Merton: Pilgrim in Progress.* Eds. Donald Grayston and Michael W. Higgins. Toronto: Griffin, 1983, 27–40.

White, Hayden, and Margaret Brose, eds. *Representing Kenneth Burke.* Baltimore: Johns Hopkins UP, 1982.

Wiesel, Elie. *Night.* New York: Bantam, 1982.

Williams, David Cratis. "Under the Sign of (AN)NIHILATION: Burke in the Age of Nuclear Destruction and Critical Deconstruction." In Simons and Melia, 196–223.

Woodcock, George. *Thomas Merton: Monk and Poet.* Vancouver: Douglas, 1978.

Wyschogrod, Edith. *Saints and Postmodernism: Revisioning Moral Philosophy.* Chicago: U of Chicago P, 1990.

Zike, Douglas Allen. "Transcendence: The Difference Between Secular and Christian Liberation as Seen in 'Pedagogy of the Oppressed' by Paulo Freire, and 'A Theology of Human Hope' by Ruben Alves." Diss. St. Louis U. Ann Arbor: UMI, 1983.

Index